"Chilling. Big Brother Incorporated is out to get you! A self-defence course for citizen activists, this book exposes the sneaky tactics of corporate spies and the threat they pose to democracy."—John Stauber & Sheldon Rampton, authors of *Toxic Sludge Is Good For You*

Eveline Lubbers is an investigative reporter and specialized activist living in Amsterdam. After finishing university (political science) fifteen years ago she co-founded the Jansen & Janssen Bureau, a spin-off from the powerful squatters movement of the eighties. With the Bureau she has since been monitoring police and secret services, supporting social activist groups against oppressive surveillance tactics of authorities. She has been publishing in both activist and mainstream media, on the internet, and has produced books on related subjects mainly in Dutch. For the past few years she has specialized in corporate intelligence and PR strategies of multinationals against their critics—including net-activists. Her works can be found at Evel's Writing, www.evel.nl, and the work of the bureau at www.burojansen.nl.

Battling Big Business

Countering greenwash, infiltration and other forms of corporate bullying

Edited by Eveline Lubbers

COMMON COURAGE PRESS

Monroe, Maine

First published in the USA in 2002
by Common Courage Press
1 Red Barn Road
Monroe, ME 04951
207-525-0900
info-orders@commoncouragepress.com

www.commoncouragepress.com/bbb.html

Copy editor: Laura Martz

Cover design: Rick Lawrence

Typeset at Green Books, Totnes, UK

Printed on acid-free paper
by MPG Books Ltd, Bodmin, Cornwall, UK

ISBN 1-56751-224-0 paper
ISBN 1-56751-225-9 cloth

First printing

Library of Congress Cataloging in Publication Data
is available from the publisher on request

Contents

Acknowledgements

Big hugs for

. . . my colleagues at buro Jansen & Janssen, for allowing me the necessary time and space to finish this never-ending project.

. . . the home front for putting up with me, buried in piles of paper, too often behind the computer and not always in the best of moods.

. . . my co-authors—including those whose chapters didn't make it to the final version—for their time and effort in helping to bring this book to where it is now.

. . . those people whose support kept me going: Geert Lovink, Sheila O'Donnell, Arthur Stamoulis and John Stauber, among others.

. . . and last but not least, Felipe Rodriguez and Laura Martz for their invaluable contributions towards making this book accessible for all.

Foreword

by Naomi Klein

When under attack, every entity has the right to self-defence, whether that entity is an individual, a state or a corporation. And large corporations are indeed facing mounting attacks these days, coming from a public angered by everything from sweatshop labour to genetic engineering.

They have the right to fight back. To correct critics when they are wrong. To put forward their perspective in their own words. To try to win the argument. But make no mistake: this book does not tell the story of corporations defending themselves against public concern and criticism with facts, arguments and improved practices. It tells the story of a few very powerful multinationals and their lobbyists using, in Eveline Lubbers' words, "a bag of dirty tricks" against their critics, from setting up fake activist organizations, to sending in spies to infiltrate meetings, to pressuring the state to treat legitimate activists like terrorists. Sometimes companies adopt the language of their opponents (calling gas-guzzling cars 'eco-warriors', for instance); sometimes they exhaust their critics' limited resources by tying them up in court for years (as in McDonald's infamous McLibel case). Either way, the aim is not to win an argument but to contain, intimidate and ultimately eliminate the opposition. Indeed, what becomes painfully clear in reading this important book is that it is not the substance of the criticism that so galls these massive corporations, but the very fact that they must face critics at all. Through case studies and analyses, *Battling Big Business* exposes a spirit of intolerance coursing through the corporate world: intolerance of criticism and dissent, as well as a deep aversion to public scrutiny and accountability. The great irony is that post-September 11, many of these same companies have rushed to align themselves with the 'war on terrorism', wrapping themselves in the US flag and claiming that their logos are symbols of freedom and democracy in the face of tyranny and censorship. Some business lobbyists and business-friendly politicians have even begun using the symbolism of the attack on the World Trade Center to argue that these acts of terrorism represent an extreme expression of the ideas held by peaceful and reasoned critics of corporate abuses. Italy's Silvio Berlusconi, for instance, has argued that the terrorist attacks were simply the far end of a continuum of anti-American and anti-corporate sentiment, attempting, not so subtly, to link the protesters on the streets of Genoa during the 2001 G-8 meeting with murderous religious zealots. What has become clear is that alongside the military war waged by the US government, an international propaganda war is also being waged, one attempting to 'bundle' support for pro-business policies into the war on terrorism. United States Trade Representative Robert Zoellick has even claimed that trade "promotes the values at the heart of this protracted struggle," so the US, he says, needs a new campaign to "fight terror with trade".

The message coming from the companies profiled in this book is the same: criticizing business is illegitimate and must be eliminated at all costs. Any tactic employed to achieve this end is acceptable, from wilful misrepresentation to covert operations. Any tactic, that is, except the obvious ones: honest public debate and open airings of divergent views. So in the end this book is about democracy. It is about a handful of companies that treat it with disdain, while never hesitating to use the rhetoric of democracy to accumulate higher profits. And it is about growing numbers of activists who, despite facing escalating attacks from the state and corporate world, are insisting on their right to express dissent, openly and vocally. It's worth remembering that corporate campaigning re-emerged as a dominant activist tactic precisely because our democracies were imperilled long before September 11. With governments unwilling to take on powerful corporations for fear of their countries being branded uncompetitive places to invest, environmentalists and labour activists naturally began looking for new places to exert pressure on important public policy issues. The result is that political debates over everything from global warming to labour standards are now taking place less in the halls of government than between activists and corporations—hand-to-brand. These campaigns are not reflexively anti-business, rather they are part of a swelling international movement to reclaim the most basic of our democratic rights: the right to have a direct say in how our societies are governed. When politicians willingly bow to the forces of the market, politics necessarily spills into the streets, from Seattle to New Delhi, Genoa to Buenos Aires. This trend isn't anti-democratic, as some have argued, it is the very essence of democracy.

As regular people have crashed elite gatherings by the hundreds of thousands, the response from many states has been severe: globalization activists around the world have been met with tear gas, pepper spray, mass arrests, beatings and bullets. And, as this book shows, the response from the corporate world, while harder to see at first, has been equally real. For activists, the most compelling reason to understand how corporations are responding to their campaigns is the need to stay nimble, to realize when actions are being anticipated and subverted by public relations companies, often with the help of newly hired recruits from Greenpeace and Friends of the Earth. Yet for those who don't identify as activists, but believe in the principles of open debate and free expression, this book should serve as a warning. Post-September 11, many of the strategies used to silence anti-corporate activists are being used against much broader segments of the population: university professors with unpopular views about Israel, engineers of Middle-Eastern descent who show a keen interest in politics, journalists who criticize US military strategy. All around us freedoms are being taken lightly and power is being exercised with a heavy hand. If there was ever a moment to insist on the right to vigorously challenge authority, it is now. If there was ever a book to help us do it, this is it.

Introduction

by Eveline Lubbers

Battling Big Business is not about sustainable management, corporate responsibility, or the merits of business engaging with NGOs. There are already plenty of good titles that address good intentions for real change within certain corporations.[1] Rather, my aim is to expose those companies that present themselves as born-again ethical enterprises while at the same time resorting to a bag of dirty tricks. I want to make people aware of this double agenda, and conscious that there is a strategic component in virtually every PR act, and in every contact between corporations and stakeholders.

Understanding corporate deception can help people to recognize such manipulation in order to do something about it. The best way to counter these major powers—battling big business—is to unravel their strategies and expose them to the public. Only the sharing of information can diminish the effects of such corporate deception.

For this book I invited experienced activists and investigators to expose the counter-strategies which modern oil, tobacco, fast-food and high-tech industries are using against their critics: rebranding themselves as environmentally friendly; co-opting their critics; forming front groups which masquerade as citizens' organizations; lobbying behind the scenes of governments and international agencies; suing their critics for libel; and employing private security firms to spy on, even infiltrate, the opposition.

* * *

Corporations are under more pressure from their critics these days than ever before. In a concerted effort to roll back the adverse publicity their environmental, labour and consumer records so often invite—and the attendant danger of lower share prices—many giant corporations are now resorting to counter-strategies in order to combat the activities of organized opposition.

Today, identity determines a corporation's value, over and above its actual products or services. The more companies shift toward being all about brand identity (as Naomi Klein has explained in her book *No Logo*), the more vulnerable they are to attacks on this image. At the same time, corporations are becoming as powerful as governments, and must expect to be held to account in the same way. Consumers are demanding sustainability, accountability and transparency.

Losing control in the media arena as a result of activist pressure has become a public relations nightmare for the modern multinational. The industry learned that lesson the hard way. Shell's lost battle over the Brent Spar and the human rights situation in Nigeria which haunts the oil company are now, as we will see later in this book, landmarks in the field of dealing with corporate social responsibility. Monsanto has become famous for its gross underestimation of European resistance against its introduction of genetically engineered products.

The power of spin can no longer protect big business's growing vulnerability. PR departments are not sufficiently equipped to deal with today's complicated stakeholder demands. Unless a company genuinely wants to change controversial policies, it is in desperate need of strategies to counter the effects of critical pressure.

First and foremost, a company needs to know what is coming its way. This means that nowadays business intelligence has gone beyond details about the world economy, faraway wars and news about the competition. It now must include an assessment of the risks of becoming the target of campaigners, boycotters or Net activists.

Publicly available information is not sufficient for this task. Informal data, however obtained, is worth its weight in gold. Desirable information is not limited to concrete action scenarios, but can be as broad (and vague) as long-term strategy discussions, impressions of the atmosphere inside a group, connections between organizations, networking possibilities, funding details—the list is endless. And so are the ways to get this kind of information.

The intelligence about activists, NGOs and other stakeholders, their ideas and plans thus gathered, provides the basic material for the development of corporate counter-strategies. Profiling what they do as ethical and sustainable has become common sense for modern companies, and part one of a general greenwash operation. What comes after that depends on the specific situation of the company in question and the political state of affairs at that moment.

Not every corporation will use the full scheme of deception described in this book. Some will stick to reaching out to stakeholders and beefing up their PR machines. Some, as we see in the following chapters, will engage in a complicated divide-and-rule strategy by dialoguing with 'moderate' critics and separating them from their 'radical' counterparts. And others resort to underhanded activities quite at odds with the public image they wish to portray.

When the pressure is high, some companies use several counter-strategies at once. As Shell was setting up its widely praised website, which addressed sensitive subjects like human rights and environmental damage and invited stakeholders to take part in a dialogue, it was also getting several private companies to monitor what was being said about it on the internet, as well as employing business intelligence bureaus, one of which was exposed for having one of its spies pose as an activist.

Too often in my work supporting grassroots activists, I encounter people who have got into trouble because they were unaware of these corporate reprisals. If left unchecked, corporate counter-strategies can weaken the stability of a group, drain the energy of individual activists, or dampen the success of a campaign. Whether out of denial, naïveté, arrogance, modesty, or a simple lack of time, activists often refuse to see that their campaign could become the object of manipulation. They might recognize the effects of corporate deception too late, if at all. Some security awareness could limit the damage.

Although tactics and strategies applied in European countries may differ from those in the United States or elsewhere, grassroots movements—from NGOs to NIMBY groups, concerned citizens to radical reformers—must realize they could be the next target.

The first part of this book presents a wide variety of case studies—worst-case scenarios, if you will—to explore the heretofore known limits of what can happen when a corporation shifts into high gear. The period of time these stories describe shows that the corporate front has been working on avoiding criticism for at least ten years, whereas some of the strategies even have their roots in the seventies: countering the boycott of the South African apartheid and the anti-Nestlé babyfood campaign. Each chapter focuses on a specific counter-strategy: dialogue, greenwash, censorship, monitoring or spying. Some overlap between the cases presented here is unavoidable, and this effectively links the stories. The cases here can be seen as forming a bigger picture, about which readers will, I hope, be able to draw practical conclusions of their own.

The second part explores tactical tools available to activists, journalists and other concerned citizens: exposure and beyond. Research and the publication of leaked documents are just two ways to counter corporate deception. Deconstructing the use of corporate symbols and subverting the meaning of powerful signs through simple acts of street theatre can be inspiring ways to expose them too. I hope this unravelling will inspire trust in alternatives, the power of creativity, and taking maximum advantage of new media tools. The keywords here are originality, playfulness, unexpectedness, smallness, speed, decisiveness, clarity and unstoppability.

* * *

The impact of anti-corporate campaigning grew during the making of this book, with the 'movement of movements' (often called the anti-globalization movement) in full swing. Over the past few years, the movement has been gaining in visibility, both on the streets and on the internet; attention in the mainstream media has been booming; and public opinion has been absorbing its ideas. Activists have constructively used the energy they brought back from large, sometimes global protest gatherings (also known as 'summit-hopping') to work out new ideas at the local level.

After severe police repression at the European summit and the G-8 summit in summer 2001, an increasing number of voices had been pleading for a new approach. A protester was shot down and severely injured in Gothenburg, Sweden, in June, and another was shot to death point-blank at short range in Genoa, Italy, in July. It was clear that things were going to change. But nobody could have guessed that what would change them would be something like September 11. The terrible events in New York, Washington and Pennsylvania have forced the movement to rethink its position, as Naomi Klein has pointed out in her Foreword.

Although linking campaigns to famous brands has been very useful as an eye-opener, an effective tool to help explain international affairs, it is now time to rethink this image war, but without immediately giving up the worthy anti-corporate campaigning that has fuelled the protests in the street for so long.

And the post-September 11 era has brought anti-terrorist legislation in the United States and the rest of the Western world. New bills whose contents had been on the agendas of right-wing and business groups for a long time were passed with little resistance. Civil liberties are being trampled in the rush to fight the undefined spectre of 'terrorism', the definition of which the FBI had broadened after the Battle of Seattle in 1999 to include 'anarchist groups' like Reclaim the Streets.

But the post-September 11 backlash will eventually fade. The immediate dislocating effects on anti-corporate campaigns, at least, will not last forever. Corporate social responsibility was still high on the agenda at a November 2001 global summit of public relations advisers in San Francisco.[2] And one need only look at the vast differences between the broken-off WTO talks in Seattle and the agreements reached in Qatar to understand that we owe it to our friends in the global South to continue to fight against corporate power.

Apart from the 'usual suspects'—major US and European firms—most corporations in Asia and elsewhere are hardly monitored. Enforcement of corporate responsibility is sketchy and uneven, and during hard economic times like these such policies are often cut back. Maybe now is the time to strengthen relations with our counterparts in Asia and the South and think about what we can do to address their grievances.

The Norwegian group NorWatch uses a method that could be useful elsewhere. This independent watchdog organization looks into the environmental and social track records of Norwegian multinational corporations in Asia, Africa and Latin America. NorWatch believes in getting first-hand witnesses to tell a story, so it visits the subsidiaries of the companies it investigates, inspecting the environmental situation, interviewing workers, meeting people in the community and listening to the opinions of local management.

The fact that NorWatch specifically targets Norwegian companies ensures media attention back home. This attention leads to pressure that helps the group influence the company's policies, while at the same time giving a voice to workers and communities who are in some way victims of them.

NorWatch's work has been fairly well received in Norway. It has added a concrete dimension to the globalization debate by using as examples people and companies members of the public have relationships with. This kind of campaigning could be one solution to the growing need to re-focus on locally based activities in light of both increased security and the need to re-focus on substance.[3] Another attractive strategy would be to improve investigative research to better support activist campaigns, by expanding the capacity for it and freeing more funds to safeguard the continuity of works in progress.

The origins of this book can be traced back to the third Next 5 Minutes conference, a gathering of media activists held in Amsterdam in 1999. There, I brought together a panel of specialists to reveal the range and insidious nature of some of the tactics used by corporations in their fight to control the media and consumers. Afterwards, we discussed the difficult position of activist-journalists vis-à-vis the growing need for investigative research in this field. Apart from the time and money problem and the diminishing possibilities for publishing, getting taken seriously by the mainstream media circus proved to be a matter of urgency.

This book seeks to inspire independent journalism in support of activist campaigns, both by providing a platform for investigative works and analysis and by motivating a search for new ways to get the message across.

The last chapter, The Pandora Project, is dedicated to activities beyond the book. In order to expand the reach of *Battling Big Business*, several projects are now being set up in order to create a permanent forum of experts interested in exchanging information on counterstrategies, suggesting topics for activist research, and collecting resources for anti-corporate campaigners.

This book is only a start: the battle has just begun.

Part One

Corporate
Bullying

Chapter 1

The Spread of Greenwash

Andy Rowell

*"Greenwash - (n) disinformation disseminated by an organization
so as to present an environmentally responsible public image."*
—*Concise Oxford Dictionary, 10th edition, 1999*

It's official

In the summer of 1999, nearly a decade after environmental activists first
mooted it, the term 'greenwash' finally entered the *Concise Oxford Dictionary*.
What activists had moaned about for over a decade, namely that their language
was being co-opted by big business, had finally been officially recognized.

But just as greenwashing was defined, its very nature was changing, as
business's response to environmentalism became more sophisticated. While
the preceding decade had seen some of the biggest, baddest polluters on the
planet redefine themselves as caring, green companies, these same companies
now began trying to co-opt the debate through dialogue with the opposition.
"Greenwash originally was primarily used to describe environmental advertising or environmental image-making," says Kenny Bruno, co-author of
Greenwash: The Reality Behind Corporate Environmentalism,[1] "but we have
moved into a new phase of deep greenwash which involves more comprehensive manoeuvring to co-opt the environmental movement." (See Chapter 3,
'Dialogue: Divide and Rule'.)

Bruno was the author of the original *Greenpeace Guide to Greenwashing,*
which was published in the run-up to the Earth Summit in Rio in 1992, as
companies rushed to brag about their environmental credentials. The *Guide*
used the following examples to illustrate greenwashing:

> A leader in ozone destruction takes credit for being a leader in ozone protection. A
> giant oil company professes to take a 'precautionary approach' to global warming.
> A major agrochemical manufacturer trades in a pesticide so hazardous it has been

banned in many countries, while implying it is helping [to] feed the hungry. A petrochemical firm uses the waste from one polluting process as raw material for another hazardous process, and boasts of an important recycling initiative. Another giant multinational cuts timber from virgin rainforest, replaces it with monoculture plantations and calls the project 'sustainable forest development'.[2]

Greenwashing has spawned a whole industry, as the $35 billion corporate public relations business has responded to corporate clients eager to spread a green veneer. Established PR companies such as Burson-Marsteller and Hill and Knowlton have rushed to join the bandwagon as their clients clamour to be seen as green. In essence, what they have done is to promote the language of corporate reform while helping their clients avoid making radical changes.[3] At the forefront of industry's greening efforts was American PR guru E. Bruce Harrison, who led the chemical industry's attack on Rachel Carson after her seminal work *Silent Spring* was published in 1962, heralding the birth of the modern environmental movement. The chemical companies launched an aggressive campaign to discredit both the book and Carson herself, whom they attacked for being a spinster even as she was dying of cancer.[4]

For 30 years, Harrison shaped industry's environmental PR, and by the early 1990s he was advocating the need for the "globalization of greening".[5] And greenwashing has gone global. From New Zealand to New York, South Africa to South Asia, companies have redefined their products and their activities. Aerosols have become ozone-friendly. Petrol is now green. Washing powders are phosphate-free, while most contained no phosphate in the first place. Nuclear power is suddenly the solution to climate change. And cars, the fastest-growing source of pollution, have suddenly become beneficial to the atmosphere. Indeed, the latest ads for Vauxhall cars in the UK label them "Eco Warriors".[6]

At the heart of the PR campaign has been a recent attempt to move companies into the centre of the environmental debate as institutions that can be trusted with the stewardship of the Earth and public health. New tactics have included companies' forming green-sounding front organizations, entering into partnerships with green groups and buying their way on to the boards of environmental organizations. They have also moved into environmental education. No place is safe from fake green PR.

Clouding the issue

The list of tactics and villains is practically endless, but oil companies and car companies are some of the worst offenders. As the world slowly grinds to a toxic gridlock, with motor vehicles a major contributor to climate change, the fossil fuel lobby has been at the forefront of opposition to radical action on environmental issues. Yet it continues to spin a green veneer around its polluting activities.

The world's largest carmaker, General Motors, brags of 20 years of environmental progress, while the second largest, Ford Motor Company, came under fire from Corporate Watch for working with Hill and Knowlton to greenwash its activities. Ford has produced glossy posters promoting its partnership with 'Earth's 911'—"the nation's official environmental hotline, providing community-specific information on recycling, disposing hazardous household products, composting and energy conservation."[7] The car manufacturer also bought nearly 40 percent of *Time* magazine's special Earth Day 2000 edition. Despite this, Ford's cars are the worst carbon emitters of all the major makes, according to Corporate Watch.

Some companies have even tried to completely redefine their name and purpose. Greenwashing reached a farcical level in 2000 when BP Amoco, one of the world's largest oil companies and one with a questionable human rights and environmental record, redefined itself as "bp: Beyond Petroleum". (See Chapter 2, 'bp: Beyond Petroleum?') BP and Shell, two of the world's leading oil companies, ran greenwashing ads in the run-up to the World Conference on Climate Change in The Hague in November 2000. And a Shell ad in the *Financial Times*, headed 'Cloud the Issue or Clear the Air?', read: "The issue of global warming has given rise to a heated debate. Is the burning of fossil fuels and increased concentration of carbon dioxide in the air a serious threat or just a lot of hot air?"[8] In questioning whether climate change was just 'hot air', Shell was "clouding the issue", according to Corporate Watch, which awarded Shell a special greenwashing award for the ad.[9]

The 3-D PR strategy

Many now see climate change as the most urgent yet intractable environmental issue ever faced. As over the last 40 years scientific evidence has increasingly demonstrated that manmade emissions of carbon dioxide have been causing climate change, the oil industry has set out to completely scupper the debate. Essentially, it responded with what has been called the 3-D PR strategy, which it uses to this day: *Deny* there is a problem with your product; *Delay* effective action; and *Dominate* the international agenda or negotiations about any possible solution.

A major PR and greenwashing tactic the fossil fuel industry has used is to form green-sounding front groups, which sound like environmental groups but are actually big business in varying layers of disguise. By 1988, when concern about climate change had forced the creation of the United Nations

Intergovernmental Panel on Climate Change (IPCC), the industry responded by forming the front organization the Global Climate Coalition (GCC). The GCC had a hand in delaying the UN climate negotiations with its denials that climate change existed and avoidance of effective action.[10]

The oil industry has been derisory in its dismissal of global warming. The industry press described it as "more hot poop" and "a fairy tale advanced by radical environmentalists".[11] The year after the IPCC reported its landmark finding in 1995 that "the balance of evidence suggests that there is a discernible human influence on global climate," the *Oil and Gas Journal* dismissed climate change as a "political concoction and nothing else", and the chairman of the GCC waved it off as "nothing but sound-bite politics".[12]

By 1997, as the scientific evidence for climate change was becoming overwhelming, leading oil companies, especially BP, realized their position was becoming increasingly untenable. The company, which had recently resigned from the GCC, finally admitted there was a problem. Addressing an audience at Stanford University, BP's chief executive John Browne admitted in May 1997 that "there is now an effective consensus among the world's leading scientists and serious and well-informed people outside the scientific community that there is a discernible human influence on climate." [13]

It had taken 40 years since the first alarm bells were rung for some oil companies to even admit the problem. And once they did, in the late 1990s, they focused on trying to steer international climate negotiations towards 'emissions trading', in which companies can trade emissions allowance credits rather than actually reducing pollution. This strategy allows fossil fuel companies, especially in 'gas-guzzling' America and Australia, to carry on polluting.

As part of its PR strategy, the fossil fuel lobby, led by ExxonMobil, undertook a ten year 'dirty tricks' campaign aimed at scuppering the UN's efforts to tackle climate change.[14] They got what they wanted in March 2001, when weeks after his inauguration, President Bush announced the US would not ratify the Kyoto Protocol, the international treaty to stop climate change. The Kyoto Protocol, agreed in December 1997, sets targets for cutting emissions to below 1990 levels. Bush described it as "dead", in an announcement met with dismay by countries around the world. The fossil fuel lobby was ecstatic; many pundits agreed that Bush's rejection of Kyoto was a direct payback for the oil industry's financial support for his campaign.

In July 2001 in Bonn, the international community showed that the Kyoto Protocol was still alive, despite US withdrawal, by reaching a political agreement on the rules for its implementation. Whether this will be ratified without the US remains to be seen.

Meanwhile, oil companies and their controversial brethren in the biotech and nuclear industries have added a new D to their greenwashing vocabulary:

Dialogue. Corporations have initiated image-enhancing discussions with their critics, claiming they want input from society. (See Chapter 3, 'Dialogue: Divide and Rule'.) And in another, related variant of greenwashing, companies set up working relationships with environmental organizations in a purported attempt to make up for some of the harm they cause. (See Chapter 4, 'The Sponsorship Scam'.)

A model project?

Take the case of the partnership between the world's largest conservation organization, WWF (World Wildlife Fund, known as WorldWide Fund for Nature outside the US), and the American oil company Chevron in Papua New Guinea. WWF's involvement in this partnership has embroiled it in an illegal logging scandal and drawn accusations that it helped Chevron greenwash an environmentally and culturally damaging oil development.

The problem started when Chevron found oil in the remote highlands of the country in the mid-1980s. The oilmen knew that gaining acceptance for their project would entail a public relations battle, as the country's rainforests are globally significant because of their cultural and ecological biodiversity. The oil would have to be transported by pipeline 170 miles from the 5,000-feet-high Kutubu region down the Kikori river to the Gulf of Papua, one of the last freshwater ecosystems in the Pacific. It would pass through virgin rainforest—home to over 400 species of bird, the world's second-largest butterfly and its largest moth—and through globally important mangrove wetlands. The river basin is also home to some 40,000 people from 16 different ethnic groups.[15]

With letters of protest coming in, Chevron entered into negotiations with the US arm of WWF in the early 1990s. Secret internal documents showed that Chevron wanted the WWF to "act as a buffer for the [Kutubu oil project] against environmentally damaging activities in the region, and against international environmental criticism."[16] For its part, since development was inevitably going to follow the Kutubu pipeline, WWF wanted to promote ecoforestry as an alternative to industrial logging, which was seen as the biggest environmental threat to the region. If WWF could persuade local landowners to start up ecoforestry projects, these could be an alternative to rampant deforestation. The communities would be paid for their timber, and the sustainably logged forests would be preserved.[17]

Danny Kennedy of Project Underground, a non-governmental organization that works with communities threatened by the oil and mining sectors, argues that "WWF may well have had good intentions, but they basically legitimized a dubious company at best, to introduce an insidious industrial operation into what was once a wonderful wilderness."[18]

The year after the first oil started flowing in 1992, Chevron finalized an agreement with the US WWF to develop a 'model Integrated Conservation and Development Project' (ICDP)—an ecoforestry initiative intended to promote sustainable development in the Kikori River Basin. The consortium of oil companies participating in the Chevron project would provide funding of over $1 million a year to the ICDP, initially for a six-year period.[19]

In November 1996, WWF established a for-profit umbrella company, Kikori Pacific Limited (KPL). WWF hoped the company would one day become independently financially viable, but initially it would depend on grant money channelled through WWF. KPL would mill logs from companies owned by local landowners and sell them on the domestic and international markets.[20]

But WWF insiders say its project of promoting ecoforestry in the region was almost redundant right from the start. WWF found that it could not source timber from many of the communities in the vicinity of the Chevron pipeline. Some communities had already signed agreements with industrial logging companies; others were not interested in ecoforestry because they were already receiving money and other gifts from the oil project and therefore had little incentive to work. At WWF's behest, the project sourced much of its timber from a company called Iviri Timbers. Unfortunately, Iviri cuts down mangrove forests, which is illegal under the country's Forestry Act.[21]

Despite this, WWF sought external funding for the project as a "conservation initiative of global significance" and as an ecoforestry enterprise which could be used as a model elsewhere. It got money from the MacArthur Foundation, the Department of State,[22] the World Bank-affiliated International Finance Corporation (IFC) and the Global Environmental Facility, which provided a $250,000 10-year low-interest loan. The IFC funded the Kikori project because it was "developing sustainable strategies for preserving biodiversity."[23]

WWF tried to get the Forest Stewardship Council (FSC) to accredit the Kikori timber, a central ingredient in the successful international marketing of KPL, as a model ecoforestry project. FSC, a non-governmental non-profit organization, was set up in 1993 to support environmentally sustainable forest stewardship and management, as defined by a set of guiding principles. If you buy an FSC-accredited piece of wood, you know it has been grown in a sustainable way.

According to both the IFC and internal WWF documents, by early 2000 Kikori Pacific exported its first shipment. The customer was an Australian company called the Woodage, which specializes in sustainable timber. The wood's destination was the 2000 Sydney Olympics. It was sold as "environmentally friendly", according to the US WWF's website.[24] (Despite WWF's efforts, for some reason, the timber never made it to the Games.)

Meanwhile, though, concern was growing within WWF about KPL's reliance on illegal mangrove logging. A confidential internal WWF report written in mid-2000 shows how flawed the project had become. The report stressed that the project was in "financial crisis" and said KPL had in fact been fated to fail from the start. "Since KPL's inception, a number of decisions have been made that, with the benefit of hindsight, have proven to be unwise," the report said. It noted that Iviri Timbers' mangrove logging was illegal and pointed out that "from its inception, one of the aims of KPL has been to obtain FSC certification." Because certified operations must conform to Papua New Guinea law, "in this sense, KPL was doomed to failure from the beginning."[25]

The author of the confidential report also noted that "[a] number of WWF staff [had] privately expressed concerns about the fact that the Iviri Timbers operation is illegal." The document's main conclusion: "KPL should stop logging mangroves."[26] But six months later, WWF still had not stopped the illegal logging: an investigation team from Britain's Channel 4 filmed the illegal mangroves floating down the Kikori river.[27]

After the Channel 4 report, WWF maintained that logging mangroves was legal on a small scale but announced it would phase it out anyway.

A lighter shade of green

What has WWF gained from this project? On the one hand it stands accused of greenwashing a highly damaging project; on the other it has found itself involved in a project dependent on oil money and "illegal" according to its own reports.[28] Yet for years WWF has tried to sell this timber as sustainable.

Other NGOs have criticized WWF. "They, like many environmentalists, need to rethink the strategy of collaboration with big business interests that has failed to reverse ecosystem degradation across the globe", wrote Project Underground's Danny Kennedy. "It should act as a cautionary tale to all environmental organizations and their members expecting to collude with corporate power without compromise."[29]

The Intergovernmental Panel on Climate Change, the world's leading group of climate scientists, is now saying that global warming will wreak havoc on the world's climate in a much more severe, unpredictable way than was previously thought. Meanwhile, WWF is collaborating with an oil company as it tears into virgin rainforest—something that could be construed as painting the deckchairs on the Titanic a lighter shade of green. In essence, this is what greenwashing is all about.

bp: Beyond Petroleum?

Sharon Beder

In 2000 the transnational oil giant BP Amoco rebranded itself as 'bp', with the slogan "beyond petroleum". The rebranding was part of an effort to portray BP as an energy company, not just an oil company: one that incorporated solar energy in its portfolio and was willing to move away from oil. BP replaced its logo with a vibrant green-white-and-yellow sunburst named after Helios, the ancient Greek sun god. The logo was meant to connote "commitment to the environment and solar power" and promote the new bp "as the supermajor of choice for the environmentally-aware motorist." [1] The lower-case letters were chosen "because focus groups say bp is friendlier than the old imperialistic BP", which stood for British Petroleum. [2]

Along with its new name, bp launched a new line of petrol stations in the US, UK and Australia called bp connect, intended to "reposition BP Amoco, an old-economy gas station giant, into a progressive, environmentally friendly retailer." [3] Petrol is just one of many items for sale at the high-tech stations, which are equipped with solar panels. [4]

This was not the first time BP had revamped its logo and appearance to improve its environmental image. In 1989, as British Petroleum, it underwent a similar makeover. At a cost of about £100 million, it shorted its name to BP, redesigned its logo and refurbished its petrol stations to promote a greener, more socially responsible image. David Walton, head of public relations, said BP's image was "a major commercial and political asset. Like any asset, it has to be managed and looked after." [5]

This earlier attempt at reputation management met with ridicule in some quarters. Jolyon Jenkins wrote in the *New Statesman and Society* that BP, a company responsible for clearing large areas of rainforest in Brazil, responded to a rise in environmental consciousness in the late 1980s with "a £20 million 'reimaging campaign' in which it daubed all its property in green paint and advertised its annual report under the slogan 'Now We're Greener Than Ever.'" [6] In 1990 BP had to apologize for an ad campaign that claimed that its new unleaded petrol caused no pollution. [7]

It seems the new bp still likes green paint: its petrol stations are to be painted in green, white and yellow to symbolize environmental responsibility and the sun. But BP didn't really get its green claims taken seriously until 1997, when it left the Global Climate Coalition (GCC), a group of 50 corporations and trade associations that had been claiming global warming was unproven and action to prevent it unwarranted. In several speeches that year, CEO John Browne argued it was time to act to prevent greenhouse warming rather than continue to debate whether it would occur.[8]

With this new stance on climate change, BP earned a reputation as an environmental progressive in an industry that largely refused to accept the likelihood of global warming, and Browne received praise from environmental groups including Greenpeace.

The question, though, is whether BP's move was an indicator of environmental leadership or a cynical attempt to manage its reputation—after all, it subsequently joined other groups that lobby for profit-friendly environmental policies. When BP left the GCC, it was receiving adverse publicity because of its activities in Colombia. The dramatic break with other oil companies on the issue of global warming provided a useful diversion as well as a much-needed refurbishment for a reputation under attack on human rights grounds. In 1997, amid favourable publicity about its stance on global warming, BP's share price and profit rose.

BP's dangerous bedfellows

In 1996 BP was accused of human rights violations in Colombia, leading to damaging media publicity in the UK. Its Casanare oil field has oil reserves valued at approximately $40 billion.[9] The Colombian government has a poor human rights record, and both the police and army are held responsible for serious abuses of human rights including extrajudicial killings, forced disappearances, torture and beatings. These official security forces are much feared by the people, as are the right-wing paramilitary forces, which appear to operate as death squads with government impunity, attacking local protesters, communities they suspect of being sympathetic to guerrillas, and people they deem socially undesirable, such as prostitutes and street children. Anti-government guerrillas have also made enemies among the local population. Combined violence by government forces, the paramilitary and the guerrillas resulted in between 2,000 and 3,000 deaths in 1998 and 300,000 civilians being displaced from their homes.[10]

BP's oil operations in Colombia have been a target for guerrillas who believe the oil industry should be nationalized. BP has installed several layers of preventive protection for its staff and installations. Firstly, it depends on the Colombian army, which created a special brigade of 3,000 soldiers for the purpose.[11] In 1996, BP agreed to pay the Defence Ministry between $54 million and $60 million over three years to augment the battalion with 150 officers and 500 soldiers.[12]

BP also depends on the police force, which patrols the perimeter of its facilities; the company pays £3 million a year for the service.[13] In 1992 BP hired the British firm Defence Systems Limited (DSL), which set up a subsidiary Defence Systems Colombia (DSC) for its BP operations.[14] According to research by the UK TV show *World in Action* based on the testimony of former DSL officers and the police themselves, DSC has given Colombian police "lethal military training" since 1996.[15]

But critics say this physical security has come at too high a price in human rights abuses. BP has been accused of forming its own army and of being associated with state repression. The military forces that protect its assets in Colombia are said to have connections with the right-wing paramilitary. And BP has been accused of hiring security people with past histories of human rights abuses, and even murder.[16]

The heavy security had troubling implications for local people protesting about the environmental impact of BP's operations. The company admitted to early environmental damage, as a result of what Browne calls "honest mistakes" made before local regulations had been clarified rather than "wilful and reckless mistakes".[17] BP's operations in Colombia have caused problems including deforestation, pollution of crucial water sources, landslides, earthquakes and ground contamination. *World in Action* pointed out: "The company which had gone into Colombia trumpeting the highest green standards was fined $215,000—the biggest-ever environmental fine in Colombian history."[18]

"Members of the local community involved in legitimate protest against the impact of the oil companies, including BP, have frequently been labelled subversive and subsequently been victims of human rights violations by security forces and their paramilitary allies", according to Amnesty International.[19] Daniel Bland, a researcher with Human Rights Watch, said local people have testified that if there is "any kind of organized protest against BP in any way, the leaders of those protests are singled out for persecution for harassment and for death threats." Such threats are taken very seriously: six members of one group, the El Morro Association, have been murdered since it began its campaign against damage done by BP to their road and their water supply.[20]

In March 1997 BP was cleared of human rights abuses by a Colombian government inquiry. However, according to *Blowout Magazine,* the Special Commission conducting the inquiry found the army brigade protecting BP's assets guilty of "civilian massacre, extrajudicial execution, rape, kidnap and torture."[21] Human Rights Watch also claims there have been "reports of killings, beatings and arrests committed by those forces responsible for protecting the companies' (BP's, Occidental Petroleum's, Royal Dutch/Shell's, and national oil company ECOPETROL's) installations."[22] BP denies any responsibility for military repression of anti-BP protesters, and says it has no control over the soldiers it hires to defend its Colombian sites. But Human Rights Watch argues that BP cannot avoid responsibility for human rights violations committed by government forces in defence of its own interests.[23]

Moreover, Richard Howitt, a British member of the European parliament, obtained internal Colombian government documents which stated that BP had given the Colombian military photographs, videos and other information about peasant protesters concerned about environmental damage. The information had allegedly led to intimidation, beatings, disappearances and deaths.[24] A former DSC adviser also told *World in Action* about "a controversial proposal by DSC to set up a spy network in Casanare to target anti-BP protesters."[25]

BP CEO John Browne responded: "We don't pass materials to the military . . . We have, as part of the licensing process, in order to produce evidence that we have had meetings on the environment, passed videotapes to the environmental department with the full knowledge and agreement of the community involved. That's the extent of it."[26]

But Human Rights Watch noted that when the contract between the Colombian military and BP came up for renewal in June 1999, the flow of funds was altered so that rather than paying the army directly, BP paid the state-owned ECOPETROL, which in turn paid the Defence Ministry. It continued making direct payments to the police.[27]

Old problem, new spin

bp's activities in Colombia are not unusual: it uses armed security guards in several countries. Nor are human rights criticisms new to the company. BP operated in South Africa during the apartheid regime, and was considered an enemy by the international anti-apartheid movement because it sold oil and gas to the military and co-operated with local refineries despite an international embargo. Its products were boycotted at the request of the NGO TransAfrica, which argued: "Without crude oil, the South African government would stop working. So BP is keeping the apartheid government alive."[28]

bp now features its human rights position prominently on its website (www.bp.com), and its executives have given many speeches to promote it, some to NGOs. The site says that everywhere the company operates it establishes "clear ethical standards for ourselves and our contractors, ensuring that the whole of the local communities benefit from our presence."

In countries where human rights are at issue, BP management claims it is better that it continue its operations. "Without development, and without business," a BP executive told Amnesty International, "fundamental human rights cannot be secured. Far from being in conflict, one is dependent upon the other."[29]

Another executive told a 1997 Amnesty International conference in the UK that BP was "a force for good" in Colombia: "Surely we should not deny Casanare the development which is available to others."[30] In 1998 Browne claimed BP had spent $25 million in Casanare since 1992 on the development of local businesses, social housing, infrastructure and training. This compared with $6 billion it had invested in its own business operations in Colombia.[31] Meanwhile, "a company's obligation to provide security for its staff is paramount."[32]

But the company's arguments that its activities contribute to better political and civil rights are not borne out by history. There is little evidence that its years of operating in the Nigerian Delta, South-western Iran, Kuwait, Iraq, Papua New Guinea, Algeria, Libya, Somalia, Yemen and Aden have led to such progress.[33]

Only the logo is green

Certainly BP's record of environmental protection has been no better than other oil companies'.[34] In 1991 it was cited as most polluting company in the US, based on Environmental Protection Agency (EPA) toxic release data. And in 1992 Greenpeace International named it one of Scotland's two largest polluters.[35] Nor has it become a model company since its apparent environmental conversion in 1997. In 1999, it was charged with burning polluted gases at its Ohio refinery and agreed to pay a $1.7 million fine.[36] In July 2000 BP paid a $10 million fine to the EPA and agreed to reduce air pollution coming from its US refineries by tens of thousands of tons.

bp's existing and proposed activities in Alaska have worried indigenous people and environmental groups. "Between January 1997 and March 1998, BP Amoco was responsible for 104 oil spills in America's Arctic", according to US PIRG research.[37] In 1999 BP admitted illegally dumping hazardous waste at its 'environmentally friendly' oil field in Alaska and was fined $500,000 for failing to report it. It paid $6.5 million more in civil penalties to settle claims associated with the waste's disposal.[38]

bp has invested heavily in solar power and introduced a programme to reduce its own greenhouse gas emissions. But despite its investment in solar energy, the company remains committed to ever-increasing production and usage of oil and gas. Director of Policy David Rice told the Global Public Affairs Institute in London, "We make no secret of our intention to grow our core exploration and production business and to continue our search for new sources of oil and gas."[39]

And while bp has promised to reduce its own emissions, it does not accept the need to reduce those arising from the products it sells. Browne argues that the company's contribution is relatively small: "If one adds up the emissions from all of BP's operations and from all the products we sell, it comes to around one percent of the total emissions from human activity."[40] Yet this—surely a conservative estimate—is still a huge amount for one company to be responsible for, and certainly a more important contribution than that of bp's own operations. By 1999 BP's emissions were greater than those of Central America, Canada or Britain, according to Corporate Watch.[41] And Athan Manuel of US PIRG estimates (perhaps generously) that BP's recent acquisitions mean the company is now responsible for about 3 percent of worldwide greenhouse emissions.[42]

bp continues to explore for oil, often in environmentally sensitive areas such as the Atlantic Frontier, the foothills of the Andes and Alaska. bp's Northstar project involves the first undersea pipeline in the Arctic, and the Army Corps of Engineers calculates that during its 15-year lifetime "the total probability of one or more large oil spills . . . is approximately 11 percent to 24 percent."[43]

bp is seeking government permission to explore in the Arctic National Wildlife Refuge (ANWR), one of Alaska's last remaining pristine wilderness areas,[44] through lobbying and donating to politicians and funding the lobby group Arctic Power.[45] During his election campaign, President George W. Bush pledged to open the refuge to oil drilling; Congress was to vote on the matter later in 2001. A new industry front group, the Energy Stewardship Alliance, was set up to campaign for drilling to be allowed, but it is essentially Arctic Power under a new name. Its co-ordinator, Roger Herrera, also co-ordinated Arctic Power. Herrera is a retired manager of operations for BP's Sohio Alaska Petroleum Company, and in 1997 he was a paid lobbyist for BP America.[46]

BP has emphasized its solar investments while being attacked for its Arctic exploration. In March 1999 it launched its 'Plug in the Sun' programme, based on its investment in solar energy and the installation of solar panels on petrol stations around the world. Its ads said, "We can fill you up by sunshine"—but it was still petrol that people were putting in their cars. For this programme it was awarded a Greenwash Award by Corporate Watch. In a similar satirical vein, Greenpeace USA gave CEO Browne an award for the 'Best Impression of an Environmentalist'.[47]

An investment in image

It seems bp is investing more in image than environment. Would a company spend hundreds of millions of dollars in solar investment just to enhance its reputation? Well, bp has already spent that much just on its 'beyond petroleum' rebranding. Research and preparation cost $7 million; bp said it would spend $200 million between 2000 and 2002 rebranding its facilities and changing signs and stationery and $400 million more on advertising its gasoline and pushing its new logo.[48]

In the end, despite bp's rhetoric about social responsibility, triple bottom lines and enlightened self-interest, profits seem to count most. An oil company might invest in solar energy and admit that global warming should be prevented, but it will do all it can to ensure it can go on drilling for fossil fuels and expanding its markets for them.

Chapter 3

Dialogue: Divide and Rule

Andy Rowell

Acting on the advice of external public relations consultants, companies have started to initiate dialogue with the opposition, so as to co-opt their critics and pre-empt conflict and adverse media coverage. "To get on the green," advised E. Bruce Harrison in his 1993 book *Going Green*, "be the model of openness. Initiate dialogue. I have seen openness and dialogue become magic keys for many greening executives in recent years. Openness means letting people watch what you do. And dialogue means constant conversation with everybody who has a stake in your environmental performance."[1]

The argument is fairly simple: if the workings of business can be seen to be open and transparent, then what could they have to hide? Gone are the bad old days of uncaring, secretive big business. The 'new' chief executive throws the doors open and says, "Come on in, have a look around, and let's talk." And if they're talking to everyone, they can build up trust.

Or can they? The move toward openness and dialogue is not a business strategy, but a public relations strategy—the new phase of sophisticated greenwashing. Analysts believe dialogue is the most important co-optation tactic that companies are now using to overcome opposition to their operations. It works on the principle of divide and rule. Ronald Duchin of the PR company Mongoven, Biscoe and Duchin has outlined a three-step strategy for how corporations can defeat public interest activists, whom he divides into four distinct categories: 'radicals', 'opportunists', 'idealists' and 'realists'. The goal is to isolate the radicals, 'cultivate' the idealists and 'educate' them into becoming realists, then co-opt the realists into agreeing with industry.[2] On the advice of the PR advisers, dialogue became a key corporate strategy in the 1990s.

The Brent Spar and the Ogoni: two PR crises

1995 was a pivotal year for interaction between the business community and the environmental movement. First, Shell and Greenpeace became embroiled in the Brent Spar fiasco. Greenpeace succeeded in its campaign to prevent Shell from dumping the Brent Spar, a redundant oil platform, into the Atlantic. But although Shell took a dramatic U-turn with its decision to abandon the dump, Greenpeace's victory proved hollow when it was forced to apologize for muddling its figures on the amount of oil left on the abandoned platform. The fact that both sides had suffered public humiliation would forever change the rules of the environmental debate on both sides of the Atlantic.

Of equal importance was a tragedy being played out in Nigeria, where the military murdered Ken Saro-Wiwa and eight other Ogoni activists for protesting against the oil industry in the Niger Delta, and Shell in particular. The brutal hanging of Saro-Wiwa provoked global outrage and further tarnished Shell's already battered image. This time, in many people's eyes, the company had blood on its hands. For the company, the Ogoni had gone from a small irrelevant nation in a part of Africa nobody had ever heard of to a major public relations disaster that threatened to undermine the very core of the company.

The Brent Spar and Ogoni controversies changed the face of environmental PR, with companies realizing that it was not just the business community they had to woo. They now had to win over society at large, including people who belonged to the new corporate buzzword group, 'stakeholders'. Most importantly, external consultants were advising Shell that it had to count among these stakeholders its critics from both the environmental and human rights movements.

Just a year later, in 1996, Greenpeace held a conference entitled 'Brent Spar . . . and after' for the business community in London. John Elkington, head of the environmental consultancy SustainAbility and someone who has done much to further the use of dialogue, addressed the audience. He outlined a new paradigm for business: 'broader industry/social alliances'. He stressed the need for companies to go beyond compliance, to be seen to be totally transparent and to strive for global consistency and harmonization of standards. Elkington concluded: "I would recommend strongly that any company considering a stakeholder dialogue process try and involve Greenpeace from the outset."[3]

The oil industry was hearing the same message of the need for dialogue, global standards and something more than compliance from other quarters, too. As the oil industry moved further into frontier areas—areas which are inherently culturally and ecologically sensitive—the growth around the world of indigenous protests like the Ogoni's prompted many companies to start seeking advice from business security companies (see Chapter 13, 'Corporate Intelligence') as well as more traditional PR professionals.

In autumn 1997 John Bray, head of research at the London security firm Control Risks, advised the oil industry on how to counter pressure groups in a lecture entitled 'Political Risk and the New Frontier'. It was no longer acceptable practice to operate purely according to national environmental and social laws, he said. Rather, companies must operate and be seen to be operating at a uniform set of international standards worldwide. With many local groups linked to international pressure groups in the US and Europe, companies needed to try to undermine those links by increasing dialogue with stakeholders.

The bottom line, said Bray, is that if you engage in dialogue, you win. But if you meet a group that will not compromise, then you have a problem.[4]

So the business security consultants, environmental consultants and PR executives were all on the same message: what was needed was more dialogue and transparency in decision-making.

As Shell began to revamp its global PR operations, its executives saw another potentially explosive PR problem on the horizon. They decided to overcome it through their new secret weapon: stakeholder dialogue.

Shell's solution: stakeholder dialogues

Shell had found a huge gas reservoir in a remote area of the Peruvian rainforest which it was looking to exploit. The area was extremely culturally and ecologically sensitive. While conducting preliminary exploration in the mid-'80s, Shell encountered the Nahua Indians, a tribe with no communication links to the outside world. Contacts with outsiders who entered the newly opened area touched off a whooping cough and influenza epidemic that killed off an estimated 50 percent of the Nahua population.[5]

Shell adopted a new public approach to the resumption of its Peruvian operations at Camisea, where its 40-year, $2.7 billion project was set to be one of the largest gas operations in South America. In a pre-emptive strike against its critics, the company promised "openness, transparency and consultations".[6] These consultations were held in 1997 and 1998, when Shell pioneered a sophisticated stakeholder process it hoped would become an industry blueprint. The company held a series of workshops in London, Lima and Washington to which some 90 interested parties were invited. The workshops in Washington and London were facilitated by the Business and Environment Consultancy, a subsidiary of the Environment Council, an environmental charity in England.[7]

Crucially, not up for discussion was whether the gas project should go ahead, but *how* it should go ahead. The process divided the NGO community on whether to take part, with more radical groups such as Project Underground, Rainforest Action and Amazon Watch becoming marginalized because they were unwilling to participate in a Shell-sponsored process. "Shell's international consultation process appears to be aimed in part at neutralizing the most critical opinions," said Steve Kretzmann of Project

Underground, "by offering a 'reasonable' process of open dialogue where any-thing is discussed but very little, in overall terms, is really on the table."[8]

Wolfgang Mai from the German NGO Brot für die Welt (Bread for the World), who attended the London workshop, said its mandate was "obscure" and "the negative points have clearly outweighed the positive."[9] Nick Mayhew of Oikos, a UK-based charity that works on sustainable issues, added, "Time was very limited, the processes inadequate, and at no point was the company willing seriously to consider the view that it should not be there at all."[10]

The Shell project even generated its own website for a while, until Shell and Mobil—another participant in the Camisea project consortium—decided to pull out, citing unresolved issues.[11] But though the project fell through, the dialogue had worked well. According to Peter Sandman, a PR guru on whose advice the Camisea stakeholder project had been set up, some environmental organizations had ended up lobbying the Peruvian govern-ment on Shell's behalf to push for the project to go ahead.[12]

Profits and principles—do we have a choice?

But Shell's stakeholder dialogue initiative was just one part of a massive cam-paign by the company to redefine itself from corporate arch-villain to good corporate citizen. Moreover, Shell's spin doctors went even further, attempt-ing to try to reposition it as a company working not just for profit but for the common good. In 1998, the company launched a booklet called *Profits and Principles—Does There Have To Be a Choice?* The title has become the catch phrase for Shell's ongoing media and advertising campaign.

The inside cover of *Profits and Principles* reflected the two key themes dreamed up by the PR flacks, openness and dialogue. In friendly handwrit-ing, the message read: "We care about what you think of us. We want you to know more about how we strive to live up to our principles. This report is part of a dialogue, and we will continue to seek your views."[13]

Although Shell maintained the booklet was a genuine report on its envi-ronmental and ethical performance, in fact it was greenwashing at its best. The report was written by Peter Knight of Associates in Advertising, a human resources consultancy. It was published in Shell's three main shareholder/employee countries: the Netherlands, the UK and the US.

One need not look far to find questionable statements in the booklet, in which Shell addresses two contentious issues, climate change and Nigeria. For example, the company said it "did not seek to influence" Saro-Wiwa's trial, but the two chief prosecution witnesses said in signed affidavits Shell had bribed them to testify against Saro-Wiwa.[14]

Regarding climate change, on the one hand Shell attempted to justify its continuing membership in the Global Climate Coalition (it would later pull out) that had done so much to scupper and delay the UN climate negotiations. On the other hand, the company said "prudent precautionary measures are called for" and "the world needs to take action now."[15] In 1998 Shell spent some $6.5 billion on exploration and production of oil and gas[16]—hardly a precautionary measure.

1999 saw the publication of Shell's next greenwashing report, *People, Planet & Profits—An Act of Commitment,* which encouraged people to air their views on Shell either through reply cards included with the report or online at www.shell.com (see Chapter 12, 'Cyber-surveillance').

Shell published its third report in the greenwashing series, *People, Planet & Profits—How Do We Stand?* in 2000. It was totally integrated into the website and updated during the year. Dialogue had become the key to Shell's online strategy. One part of the site now talks of 'Listening and Responding: Establishing a Dialogue': "A year ago we launched Shell's first co-ordinated global communications program. Openness, transparency and accountability are central to good relations with our stakeholders. . . . And we have listened—and changed as a business. Dialogue is not something which can be turned on and off like a tap. We are committed to continuing the process of discussion."[17]

But has Shell changed? November 2000 saw the fifth anniversary of the execution of Ken Saro-Wiwa. As part of its ongoing Profits and Principles campaign, Shell ran an ad in which a beautiful black face stared out at the reader. The caption read: "None of Our Business? Or the Heart of Our Business? Human Rights. It's not the usual business priority. At Shell, we are committed to supporting fundamental human rights."[18]

Five years after Saro-Wiwa's death, not much had changed in Nigeria. Millions of people face a daily struggle to gain access to basic necessities such as clean water, health care and education. "Ogoni people still languish in poverty, deprivation, marginalization and environmental devastation", says a spokesperson for MOSOP, the Movement for Survival of the Ogoni People.[19]

"When Shell says that it respects human rights, I do not believe them," responds Ike Okonta of Nigeria's Environmental Rights Action. "You cannot devolve the environmental well-being of a people from the general conception of human rights. Right now in the Delta, everything Shell does by way of oil exploration leads to devastation of the environment. Shell still works with the Nigerian government to make sure that the local people, who are trying to restore their farmlands, don't stand up and protest."

"Shell has refused to learn from what happened in November 1995. If you take from November [2000], you will see that Shell has spent so much on spin since then. Instead of taking simple steps and entering into partnership with us, Shell is spending money on lies. You cannot whitewash lies, however skilled you are. Somewhere along the line the facts will come out in the sun."[20]

Dialogues proliferate

By the late 1990s, other companies with equally contentious environmental records began to follow Shell's example and use dialogue forums set up by the Environment Council. In 1998 British Nuclear Fuels, which runs the controversial Sellafield site in Cumbria, England, started an ongoing discussion forum with NGOs facilitated by the Environment Council. Representatives from such environmental groups as Greenpeace, Friends of the Earth and Cumbrians Opposed to a Radioactive Environment (CORE) took part, along with representatives from the company, the nuclear industry, the local council, the national government, and independent inspectors and regulators.[21] Once again the process was controversial, and by November 2000 many of the environmental groups, such as Greenpeace, CORE and WANA (Welsh Anti-Nuclear Alliance), had withdrawn.[22] Greenpeace pulled out of the dialogue process, saying it believed that "little can be gained by our continuation in the current process."[23]

In 1998, the controversial British mining company Rio Tinto held two forums with NGOs to discuss its code of business practices. The Green Alliance, an environmental NGO in the UK that sees its role as 'bringing together relevant interest groups and individuals to debate environmental problems and explore solutions', chaired the meetings. More radical groups like the World Development Movement, Friends of the Earth and Minewatch again stayed away, while 28 more moderate groups including Oxfam, Amnesty International and Save the Children participated. The main issues up for discussion were: What social and environmental standards do you expect a company like Rio Tinto to meet? What measures might it take to meet these goals? And: How should Rio Tinto report on its activities?[24]

PARTiZANS (People Against RTZ and Subsidiaries), Rio Tinto's leading NGO critic, was not allowed to attend. PARTiZANS urged a boycott of the second meeting, stating, "It is, we believe, highly dangerous for any independent NGO to be going into meetings purportedly to help the company determine its policies . . . when these agendas have not been exposed to considered debate by all affected by them. Surely it is a betrayal of the many communities fighting the company in 'the South' for such meetings to occur without their knowledge, participation, carefully considered input—or [even] soliciting their opinion as to whether they should take place at all."[25] PARTiZANS saw the whole process as a divide-and-rule strategy to pit those wanting a constructive dialogue against those considered by Rio Tinto to be 'beyond the pale'.[26]

In 1999, the year after the Rio Tinto discussions, Monsanto approached the Environment Council to see if it would facilitate roundtable discussions between the company and the UK's NGO community.[27] Monsanto had seen a haemorrhaging of support for biotech crops, as its high-profile public relations campaign backfired spectacularly, with the Advertising Standards Authority ruling it was inaccurate and misleading. Monsanto now wanted to try a different tactic: the 'National Stakeholder Dialogue on GMOs'. By November 1999, the Environment Council announced it had Monsanto's "commitment" and "indications that other biotechnology companies would participate in a dialogue should it proceed". The UK Government had signalled its support and indicated it would take an active role, the council said.[28]

The move angered anti-GM campaigners from GenetiX Snowball. Monsanto had served an injunction on some of them and was trying to prevent them from challenging it in court. "On one hand Monsanto wants to prevent a court trial which would explore the dangers of genetic engineering, yet on the other it says it wants to enter into dialogue with environmental groups about the issues," argued Kathryn Tulip of GenetiX Snowball. "It seems very much like a cynical PR exercise, an attempt to divide and conquer the opponents of genetic engineering."[29]

Monsanto, like Shell, had suddenly found a new commitment to talking to its critics. Indeed, Bob Shapiro, then head of Monsanto, addressed the Greenpeace Business Conference in London in 1999. "We are now publicly committed to dialogue with people and groups who have a stake in this issue," said Shapiro, arguing that dialogue is a "search for answers, a search for constructive solutions that work for a wide range of people." Shapiro finished his speech by saying, "We are committed to engage openly, honestly and non-defensively in the kind of discussion that can produce good answers for all of us."[30]

But by the start of 2000, the whole dialogue process was in trouble. Before full negotiations could even take place, the majority of prominent environmental groups, including leading GM critics such as GenetiX Snowball, Greenpeace, Friends of the Earth and GeneWatch UK, had withdrawn. Many said no serious dialogue was possible while the introduction of GM crops continued apace. "Monsanto's behaviour has been so appalling to date with the introduction of GMOs, that without a moratorium on GMOs I doubt there is any sincerity in their offer," said Andrew Wood of GenetiX Snowball.[31]

Other campaigners agreed. "Everyone is suspicious it's just a PR ploy," said Dr Sue Mayer of GeneWatch UK. "Until you have got a moratorium on commercial use and patenting, you cannot really have any confidence in this process, because it doesn't really mean anything. It's the wrong discussion. People want to talk about food and sustainable agriculture, not GMOs."

Charlie Kronick of Greenpeace added, "The only way you could have sensible dialogue is if they stop releasing GMOs into the environment."[32]

Monsanto, however, kept pushing for the process to continue. "There is a great desire for there to be a dialogue. There is no point, in Monsanto's view, in groups sitting either side of the fence and the whole debate about GM crops being polarized," argued press spokesperson Alex Woolfall. "All the groups do want some sort of discussion about genetic engineering and agriculture and whether it's right or wrong."[33]

By July, the Environment Council admitted to 'difficult' problems in convening further meetings and a 'protracted' process.[34] But most observers felt the process was all but dead. "If there are NGOs that are not involved, it could be that it becomes a non-viable dialogue," says Mhairi Dunlop, from the Environment Council. "If the big players are not there, it becomes non-viable."[35]

One of the key players in the process had been Clare Devereux, co-ordinator of the Five Year Freeze Coalition, made up of over 100 national trade union, religious, environmental, consumer and development groups, 500 local authorities and 100 companies. In total, the coalition represents some 3 million members.

"The Five Year Freeze participated in the recent stakeholder dialogue on GM with the mandate of Freeze supporters, many of whom had been invited to participate individually but felt they would rather be represented by the Freeze," says Devereux. "The process of preliminary steps to dialogue took five months—during which time the debate had changed considerably as a result of the swiftly moving external situation—and it was felt that such a long, drawn-out process was allowing both government and industry to stall for time and use the process as a public relations exercise."[36]

The Environment Council dialogue was used not only for classic greenwashing purposes but also to divide and rule. Devereux said the Freeze's participation "resulted in an industry participant attempting to discredit and divide the Freeze alliance—not a situation which inspired confidence in such a process." During the stalled dialogue process, Martin Livermore of DuPont approached four central Freeze organizations—UNISON, Townswomen's Guilds, the Local Government Association and the National Federation of Women's Institutes— questioning whether their rank and file actually supported the Freeze and asking the groups to join an alternative coalition instead.[37]

The final question is whether participants see any signs of real change in companies' behaviour as a result of these dialogues. The answer seems to be that most have come away fairly skeptical of the intentions of the companies they were supposedly 'negotiating' with. "Very rarely do you ever have the impression that companies engaging in discussion are interested in changing their strategy," says Dr Sue Mayer of GeneWatch UK, who has undertaken negotiations with the biotech industry. "Monsanto told me that despite their PR campaign about wanting discussion about biotechnology, they had invested too much money in their Roundup Ready soybeans for there ever to be a real debate. People were going to have to eat them whether they liked it or not."[38]

The pitfalls of dialogue

The non-profit community is being offered a 'done deal'. Just as proponents of globalization say 'There Is No Alternative' (or 'TINA'), so the proponents of dialogue say the process is inevitable. "That NGOs will have to interact with companies is not in doubt; how they will interact is the question," writes Simon Heap of Intrac in his book *NGOs Engaging with Business: A World of Difference and a Difference to the World.*[39]

Heap admits that "one outcome of the shift towards solution-seeking by some NGOs has been greater polarization of the NGO sector" and that "the risks of becoming, or being perceived as being, co-opted or compromised" still weigh heavily on NGOs' minds when they consider collaboration with companies. Indeed, Heap says that "before engagement with companies, it is crucial for NGOs to consider the impact of the engagement on corporate accountability and the balance of power between companies and the general public. If the engagement will help to shift that balance in favour of the company, the NGO should not engage."

But Heap concludes his two-year study into NGO-business co-operation by stating that: "The potential for NGO-private partnerships is not a short-term phenomenon likely to be blown off course when the next economic recession bites. . . . There is a need for both the NGO and the private sector to play the long game on this."

This kind of thinking led to a conference called 'Finding Common Ground—Industry and NGOs in Dialogue and Partnership' in summer 2000. One leading delegate, Andre Driessen of the Dutch Employers Association, said the real advantage in sitting down at the table with NGOs is that it removes the public from the debate, so the NGOs are no longer playing to an audience. Geoffrey Chandler of Amnesty International's UK Business Group, an ex-Shell executive who has done much to foster co-operation between the business community and Amnesty, agreed with this analysis.[40]

Indeed, many of the current stakeholder dialogues are fundamentally undemocratic. Deals are being struck with no public involvement whatsoever, and whether these partnerships are operating for the common good is often open to question. The Monsanto dialogue process in the UK was labelled a 'National Stakeholder Dialogue' even though it was nothing of the sort. The process was not open to members of the public, only to interested NGOs. It is precisely this kind of undemocratic campaigning by large NGOs that has led to the growth in grassroots campaigns and action, as the bigger groups are increasingly seen as part of the problem and not the solution.

Mark Dowie, the former editor of *Mother Jones* magazine, wrote about this subject in a book called *Losing Ground*, a major criticism of the mainstream American environmental movement. He criticized what he called "third-wave environmentalism", in which environmentalists worked closely and did deals with their former adversaries. "The essence of third-wave environmentalism is the shift of the battle for the environment from the courtroom to the board-room," wrote Dowie. "In fact, third-wave environmentalism represents nothing so much as the institutionalization of compromise."[41]

Dowie went so far as to say that "the closer mainstream environmentalists get to corporations and regulators the more difficult it becomes to maintain their independence and identity as adversaries. . . . they can do a lot of damage by helping corporate polluters create the public impression that they are a lot greener than they really are."[42]

Indeed, *Mother Jones* itself, once seen as a bastion of radicalism, became the centre of controversy when its website, www.motherjones.com, started running Shell ads. *Mother Jones* received a torrent of objections from outraged readers. "I'm shocked and dumbfounded. The organization I have looked to for over 25 years for information not totally dominated by multinational cor-porations has now sold its soul to Shell and its misleading greenwash ads," said one reader. "Shell today, Exxon tomorrow, Pepsi next month. Eventually, the risk for *Mother Jones* to become co-opted increases," lamented another.[43]

"Our decision to run the ad campaign does not constitute an endorsement of its content nor a confirmation of its validity," retorted Brooke Shelby Biggs, the producer of *Mother Jones'* website. "While we reserve the right to reject advertising that we believe is false, libelous or hateful, we respect and value the right of free expression. . . . Shell's website includes a forum area where users are invited to discuss the company's record and policies. We encourage MoJo Wire readers to participate and to give feedback on Shell's campaign."[44]

So even *Mother Jones* had fallen into the greenwashing trap, which raises the question: have others been fooled too?

A defining battle

Many see the conflict between corporations and democracy as one of the defining battles of the 21st century, made all the more urgent by issues such as genetic engineering and climate change. What we are witnessing is the continuation and intensification of a process aptly summarized by Australian scholar Alex Carey:

> The twentieth century has been characterized by three developments of great political importance, the growth of democracy, the growth of corporate power and the growth of corporate propaganda as a means of protecting corporate power against democracy. [45]

An increasing segment of society believes the environmental issues facing us are so urgent that compromise with corporations is no longer an option. They see dialogue and greenwashing as delaying tactics at a point when there is no time left for delay.

Others argue that compromise with companies is the only way forward. It is time to have this important debate. Perhaps those who continue to sit down and negotiate with companies, apparently safely insulated by an arrogant belief that they know what is best, should stop and answer one simple question: who actually benefits from the relationship?

Chapter 4

The Sponsorship Scam

Jessica Wilson

"I have decided to rent out my five-year-old daughter's favourite soft panda toy to developers and polluters, to give them a more cuddly and acceptable 'greenwashed' image," read one letter to the editor of New Zealand's national newspaper, the *Sunday Star Times*.[1] The writer was responding to front-page revelations about oil giant Shell's sponsorship relationship with World Wide Fund for Nature-New Zealand (WWF-NZ).

The edition of 8 October 2000 featured a story headed "WWF and Shell strengthen their relationship."[2] More reports in the paper that week brought to light details including plans to give Shell a seat on WWF-NZ's board of trustees in return for sponsorship of WWF-NZ's education programme.[3] A fortnight later, the paper printed extracts from internal WWF-NZ documents describing a scheme to reward people buying Shell gas with membership in the environmental group. The plan never got off the ground; a *Sunday Star Times* reporter called the very idea "bizarre".[4]

For readers, the story brought sharply into focus the issue of corporate sponsorship and the possible motivations of companies seeking to associate themselves with environmentally friendly images. More often than not, sponsorship is merely a convenient public relations tool, enabling corporations to manufacture a green veneer while continuing business as usual.

Over the last decade, New Zealand has seen more companies try to associate their brands with 'clean, green' images. Visitors to the Auckland Zoo can walk through the McDonald's Rainforest. Students can attend a Youth Environment Summit sponsored by BP. Schools are invited to enter an environmental art competition sponsored by a major food manufacturer called Mother Earth. Spending money to link a company and its products to environmental issues has become increasingly common around the world. Forging relationships with groups like WWF is one way to go about it.

Winning young hearts and minds

Meanwhile, the targeting of sponsorship at the youth market is gaining in popularity. By some estimates, kids in the United States annually spend $24 billion of their own money and influence $488 billion worth of purchases.[5] As young consumers have become more important to marketers, companies have turned their attention to getting their 'clean, green' messages to children.

A sponsorship mix containing components of greenness and youth holds obvious attractions. Corporations are beginning to realize that kids are concerned about the environment. As companies try to influence consumers at an impressionable age, they can cash in by promoting themselves and their brands as 'environmentally friendly'. Get them while they're young, and you've got them for life.

Thus, seeming green has become part of the battle for the hearts and minds of young consumers and future voters. Evidence can be seen in escalating corporate sponsorship of environmental education resources. Companies with a clean, green tale to tell are producing everything from poster packs and fact sheets to CD-ROMs and videos, mostly distributed free to schools.

In a 1995 study investigating commercial pressures on kids in school, the US watchdog group Consumers Union uncovered a resource kit produced by the American Coal Foundation promoting coal as the fuel of choice; a pack produced by the Polystyrene Packaging Council teaching kids that plastics are great; a kit called 'Planet Patrol' put out by Procter & Gamble claiming disposable diapers are environmentally sound; and a McDonald's kit called 'The Rain Forest Imperative' designed to quell suspicions that the company uses rainforest beef.[6]

Five years later, little had changed. Teacher John Borowski reported in *PR Watch* that at the April 2000 National Science Teachers Convention he had seen coal-industry-produced videos and teachers' guides on display that dismissed global warming as a fallacy. A video entitled 'The Dynamic Forest', put out by forestry interests, promoted the benefits of logging. Also in attendance was the American Farm Bureau, whose materials invited teachers "to reconsider the dangers of chemical biocides".[7] "Multinational corporations now view our children's schools as convenient locations for the dissemination of propaganda debunking environmental concerns, and as the tip of an unimaginably profitable marketing iceberg," Borowski wrote.[8]

At the release of a report on advertising trends in schools, Alex Molnar, head of the University of Milwaukee's Center for the Analysis of Commercialism in Education (CACE), echoed Borowski's views. Corporate sponsorship, Molnar said, has become so pervasive that "commercial activities now shape the structure of the school day, influence the content of the school curriculum and determine whether children have access to a variety of technologies."[9]

"At a time when many children are literally made sick by the air they breathe, they are being told that some of the nation's biggest polluters are their friends," Molnar says.[10]

He might be describing the situation in New Zealand. Here, too, industries likely to have the greatest impact on the environment have taken the most active interest in getting their message into the classrooms.

Witness the educational efforts of the mining industry. All through the school year, the Waihi Gold Mining Company, a subsidiary of international giant Normandy Mining, runs guided tours of its mine site for school groups. It has recently constructed an 'Education Center' which, according to a half-page ad in teachers' magazine *Starters & Strategies*, "has classroom space where students can participate in a circuit of activities relating to mining. . . . staff can discuss curriculum requirements with teachers with a view to planning activities that will complement and enhance classroom programmes and help to gain the maximum benefit from a visit to the [mine]."[11]

Waihi Gold also sends schools a free information kit containing a video describing the company's stringent environmental controls. Sunlit shots of the mine are accompanied by a voice-over explaining the company's "quick, clean and easy" modern mining methods. Also inside is a bumper sticker with the slogan "Everything is either grown or mined—Support Mining—Support Farming."

The New Zealand Minerals Industry Association (NZMIA) has sent every school in the country a free set of booklets on the benefits of mining. A range of "resources" for teachers and students is available on its website.[12] "Busy teachers" are invited to keep up with news through the association's email list. One school resource packet on coal-mining informs students coal is "very important" for electricity generation, leaving aside any discussion of the contribution burning coal makes to global warming.

Environmental researcher Barry Weeber of green group Forest and Bird says the materials are designed "to give kids the impression mining is an environmentally benign activity and that the industry is doing all the things it should do to make sure it doesn't have any impact on the environment."[13] In Weeber's view, this carefully manufactured image is not unrelated to the industry's desire to free up access to minerals and see new mining ventures established within protected areas.

Other New Zealand industries have shown similar enthusiasm for getting their clean, green messages into the classroom. A school resource kit sponsored by the Plastics Environmental Advisory Council tells kids plastic shopping bags are better than their paper equivalent: not only do they weigh less, they also use a quarter of the energy to produce and take up a third of the landfill space. Contrary to claims by some environmental groups, plastic "compares very favourably with alternative products", the kit says.

Also keen to promote the benefits of plastic is Coca-Cola, which has sponsored a resource on the many uses of plastic soda bottles, like making watering cans or sand timers. PET (polyethylene terephthalate) bottles, the resource says, were "specially designed for easy disposal after use". When you run out of uses for empties, you should crush them and place them "in a refuse receptacle, or in a household incinerator where [they] will burn clean and safe."

The fishing industry also delivers its own green messages to New Zealand classrooms. A range of school resources informs students of its sustainable practices.[14] Any discussion of issues that could lead kids to question the industry's environmental claims, such as the incidence of marine mammal by-catch associated with fisheries, is avoided. One resource sponsored by the New Zealand Mussel Industry Council even goes so far as to tell students mussel farming presents "no environmental problems".[15]

Oil company BP has also got in on the sponsorship act. Its website boasts that its high-profile sponsorship programme has "a deliberate focus on young people."[16] In addition to sponsoring events like the Youth Environment Summit, the company produces school booklets on subjects like air and water pollution. BP's environmental material also studiously avoids serious discussion of the contribution burning fossil fuels makes to global warming.

Inside the Shell Classroom

Not to be outdone, BP's competitor Shell is dabbling in green education in a different way. As a sponsor of WWF-NZ's education programme, Shell funds positions for two WWF-NZ teachers who cater for visiting school groups. Shell gets naming rights to WWF-NZ's classroom, and WWF-NZ must ensure Shell's support is recognized in signage at the 'Shell Classroom' and in all publications relating to the programme.[17] WWF-NZ's teachers are even given Shell-logo clothing to wear during class. The company can thus promote itself as environmentally concerned without any discernible changes to its practices.

Shell's relationship with WWF-NZ provides an enlightening case study of the motivations of a company seeking to buff its reputation through sponsorship. It also shows how sponsorship can foist compromises on recipient organizations.

Since the early 1990s, Shell has been a major WWF-NZ sponsor. While Shell's financial support has varied over the years, it is doubtful, to say the least, that it has ever matched the company's claims about its commitment to the environment. The amount of money Shell donates to WWF-NZ is minuscule when considered in a broad context. In 1999-2000, Shell New Zealand's after-tax operating profit was NZ$177.4 million.[18] That year it gave WWF-NZ approximately NZ$100,000.

Yet the company has consistently used the relationship to convey the impression that that commitment is substantial. Shell promotional material on display in the Shell Classroom claims, "By investing in environmental education, particularly at school level, we believe we are on the right track to preserving the environment and its millions of species for future generations." A similar statement appears in Shell's 1999/2000 annual report.[19]

Corporate communications adviser Aimee Driscoll offered a somewhat different explanation for Shell's relationship with WWF-NZ. Asked how she would respond to criticisms that the company is using WWF-NZ to green its image, Driscoll replied, "We are trying to green our image. I'll be absolutely honest [about] that."[20]

Driscoll volunteered the opinion that Shell has one of "the worst reputations" in an industry she happily conceded is seen as "non-environmentally friendly". Shell wants to associate its brand with "warm, caring, friendly, youth" images, "all those sorts of things", she explained. By working with WWF, "we're trying to improve our reputation and show that the environment is important to us."

In October 2000 the company launched a major ad campaign promoting its sponsorship of WWF-NZ. Quarter-page colour advertisements in major daily newspapers featured a photo of schoolchildren in Shell caps. "Shell NZ has long supported WWF and its aims," the ad intoned. "We're proud sponsors of WWF's environmental education initiatives in New Zealand and are operating our business in accordance with the principles of sustainable development—balancing economic growth with environmental care and social responsibility." The ad included a WWF-NZ membership coupon.

It was this campaign that sparked the *Sunday Star Times* investigation, which uncovered discussions about giving Shell a seat on WWF-NZ's board of trustees. Documents obtained by the newspaper showed chairperson Paul Bowe had raised the matter at a WWF-NZ board meeting.[21] When a reporter approached WWF's head office in Switzerland for comment, international programme director Chris Hails responded that he would be astonished if board positions at WWF anywhere were linked to contributions.[22] But as the *Sunday Star Times* coverage showed, putting corporate sponsors on the board was far from an unknown practice for WWF-NZ. The former general manager of sponsor Air New Zealand chairs the board. Another of its nine members is the managing director of Toyota New Zealand, which provides WWF-NZ with two staff cars. The former corporate relations manager for Brierley Investments Ltd, a sponsor until 2000, also holds a seat.

The reporter Guyon Espiner also uncovered documents in which the WWF-NZ chair applauded Shell's PR manager, Antonius Papaspiropoulos, for his promotion of the link between the organizations. Papaspiropoulos asked the WWF chair to provide comment for an internal performance review in 1999. Bowe appeared happy to do so, writing that "Shell has increased its public and customer image due to Antonius being very proactive in using WWF branding. There is potential for more." [23] Commenting in the same review on the benefits of the relationship for both organizations, Bowe wrote, "WWF satisfaction with Shell Oil New Zealand Ltd via Antonius is of the highest level. There must be two winners in any sponsorship potential. Shell has a huge opportunity to further enhance its image and profits."

Bowe's comments illustrate the extremely close link between Shell and WWF-NZ. More than that, however, they raise serious questions about the appropriateness of an environmental group helping to boost the sales of an oil company.

WWF-NZ was aware the public might not see the relationship with Shell favourably. Prior to the launch of the October 2000 ad campaign, WWF-NZ chief executive Jo Breese wrote to Shell's communications manager warning of "the possibility of some adverse reaction to the association having an increased profile." Breese wrote: "From both our perspectives we would want to ensure any adverse reaction was minimized and we had plans in place to deal with it." [24] It's unknown whether any plan was ever drawn up, but when the prediction of adverse publicity proved right, the ads disappeared from the papers.

But that was not the end of the matter. As other media outlets picked up the story following the *Sunday Star Times* investigation, more disquieting details of the organizations' relationship came to light. During an interview on New Zealand's National Radio, WWF-NZ's Bowe and Shell's Papaspiropoulos were presented with a copy of a 1998 joint press release that began with the claim that "thanks to Shell, New Zealand's rare Southern Right Whale has been saved from extinction." [25]

As the interviewer explained to listeners, the southern right whale had been protected within the Southern Ocean Whale Sanctuary since 1994. Shell's claim that it was responsible for the species' survival was based on the fact that it had funded an expedition for researchers to study the whale's behaviour and collect population data. Shell had channelled the money through WWF-NZ, enabling the group to take an administration fee and allowing Shell to link its brand publicly with WWF-NZ.

When asked by the interviewer to explain Shell's claim, Papaspiropoulos said it was sometimes necessary to "accentuate the truth" to gain media attention. This novel turn of phrase drew an astonished response from the interviewer. "You have to accentuate the truth in order to get some reportage of something that . . . didn't in fact happen?" she asked. "Yeah, absolutely," he replied.

Was WWF-NZ happy with the press release? the interviewer asked. Yes, Bowe said. Without Shell's sponsorship, valuable information collected on the expedition would never have been obtained. Within WWF-NZ, however, his evaluation was not universally shared. Reviewing a report by the researchers, the chair of organization's Scientific Advisory Committee wrote, "I feel as though WWF-NZ is not getting very much out of the reports from this project so far. We can say we helped to find out how many whales [there are]. . . and that we have helped take samples for DNA analysis, but we cannot say what we have done to help the conservation of the whales." [26]

Before the interview drew to a close, the reporter asked Bowe: "For the benefit of the public, who I think would probably like to know that there was some kind of rigorous study done of sponsors as opposed to their bank balances, who wouldn't you accept sponsorship from?" A long pause followed while he pondered the answer. Prompted by the interviewer, he was eventually able to say that WWF did have a protocol on accepting funding from certain companies, but he didn't have it with him and wasn't quite sure which companies they were.

Sleeping with the enemy

Internationally, WWF has frequently come under attack for its corporate sponsorships. In Australia, it recently drew criticism for a highly controversial $1.2 million deal with mining giant Rio Tinto funding the jointly developed 'Frogs!' programme, which appears largely designed to meet the sponsor's needs. Interviewed in *Mining Monitor*, WWF Australia Conservation Director Ray Nias explained how Rio Tinto had approached the group seeking a project to fund that would "involve the community, have a scientific background and could be linked in with [the company's] remote area presence." [27]

Other environmental groups have also come under attack for accepting corporate sponsorship. As the *Sunday Star Times* probed the Shell-WWF relationship, Britain's *Independent* newspaper was asking similar questions about alliances between Greenpeace and the advertising industry. Under the headline 'Greenpeace gets in bed with its foes', the paper reported details of a controversial deal between the group and advertising firm HHCL—part of the Chime Communications group, whose clients include Monsanto and British Nuclear Fuels.[28] Was Greenpeace being used to legitimize companies that were only paying lip service to green issues? asked *The Independent*.

No, said Greenpeace campaign director John Sauven. "We worked with bp, but still felt free to criticize its exploration for oil in the Arctic." Friends of the

Earth, however, warned in the same article of the dangers of such associations. Where oil companies are concerned, policy and campaigns director Tony Juniper cautioned: "The challenge is not so much talking about giving renewable oil cans or the company recycling, but to get out of fossil fuels. . . . That's the scale of the challenge they have to face up to and they are not going to face up to it by giving themselves a gloss by aligning themselves with green organizations."

For its part, WWF has responded to criticisms with the assertion that engaging with industry can help it promote good environmental practice. Other environmental groups ignore business and "snipe from the side", says international programme director Chris Hails.[29]

But critics take a different view of the effects such relationships bring. In a letter to WWF on its alliance with Rio Tinto, John Maitland, general secretary of Australia's Construction, Forestry, Mining and Energy Union, wrote, "Those of us who are fighting for our rights, and in some cases our very existence, against Rio Tinto will now be confronted with [its] PR machine. . . smoothly asserting how wonderful the company is because it has a relationship with WWF. The partnership will be used to counterbalance an overwhelming volume of negative activity by the company elsewhere."[30]

In the same letter, Maitland dismissed as a pittance the AUS$1.2 million the company provided to the group. "This is equivalent to about one or two days' revenue from one major coal mine in Australia. It is less than the cost of a single truck, of which the company has many hundreds," he wrote.

New Zealand environmentalist Cath Wallace echoes Maitland's sentiments. Corporations like Shell are essentially buying a green reputation with sponsorship dollars, she says.[31] They're seldom motivated by genuine environmental concern: behind the green veneer, more often than not it's business as usual.[32] Wallace is equally critical of groups that put their 'brands' up for sale. Speaking about WWF-NZ's relationship with Shell, she says, "Linking an environmental group's name to a product that is known to be behind one of the major causes of climate destabilization is just irresponsible."[33]

Another common defence used by organizations receiving corporate cash is that it supports programmes that would otherwise not get funded. But the reality is that the sponsor often determines the nature and content of the work undertaken. In most cases, sponsorship is directed towards projects that maximize benefits for the sponsor, not for the environment. Witness Shell's funding of whale research or Rio Tinto's funding for frogs. Donor-driven projects like these may contribute to conservation research in some way, but they can also distract the recipient organization from higher-priority issues.

Perhaps the most pernicious aspect of corporate sponsorship is its potential to compromise the environmental movement's ability to raise concerns about a sponsor's activities. When recipient groups censor their criticisms for fear of jeopardizing existing or future relationships, the ability of the move-ment as a whole to highlight issues or bring about change is diluted. For the sponsors, this is great news. Not only can their dollars buy environmental respectability, they can purchase the silence of potential critics, or at least temper their responses.

A case in point: WWF-NZ has always maintained that it reserves the right to criticize sponsors' activities and that it does not hesitate to do so when nec-essary. But correspondence between WWF-NZ and Shell about the latter's activities in Nigeria suggests WWF-NZ has been less than vigorous in exercis-ing that right.

In 1995, Shell was the subject of intense media publicity for its controver-sial role in Nigeria. The company's oil fields had created major environmental and social problems in oil-rich Ogoniland, damaging scarce agricultural land and fisheries and causing major pollution problems. On 5 December of that year, Shell wrote WWF-NZ a thank-you letter. "We very much appreciate your balanced and considered view on this issue," the letter read. "We believe WWF is making a significant contribution to the future well-being of the envi-ronment by fostering cooperative, rather than confrontational, approaches to these issues. . . . As you can imagine your approach is very welcome to us at the moment."[34] Less than a month before the date on the letter, Nigerian authorities had executed Ogoni opposition leader Ken Saro-Wiwa, who had led a campaign against Shell's operations in Nigeria.

Despite WWF's vocal public support for corporate sponsorship, some people within the organization are prepared to acknowledge its dangers, at least privately. In an internal email circulated in May 2000, a senior WWF staff member urged reconsideration of a potential sponsorship deal between WWF-Philippines and Shell, warning, "It is clear from our discussions with Shell that the strength of our negotiating position resides in our reluctance to take [the company's] funds."[35]

Chapter 5

The Greens Get Eaten

George Monbiot

Environmentalism as an argument has been comprehensively won. As a practice it is all but extinct. Just as people in Britain have united around the demand for effective public transport, car sales have broken all records. In January 2002 the superstore chain Sainsbury's announced a six percent increase in sales: the number of its customers is now matched only by the number of people professing to deplore its impact on national life. *The Guardian*'s environmental reporting is fuller than that of any other British newspaper, but on Saturday it was offering readers two transatlantic tickets for the price of one.

The planet, in other words, will not be saved by wishful thinking. Without the effective regulation of both citizens and corporations, we will, between us, destroy the conditions which make life worth living. This is why some of us still bother to go to the polling booths: in the hope that governments will prevent the rich from hoarding all their wealth, stop our neighbours from murdering us and prevent us, collectively, from wrecking our surroundings.

Because regulation works, companies will do whatever they can to prevent it. They will threaten governments with disinvestment, and the loss of thousands of jobs. They will use media campaigns to recruit public opinion to their cause. But one of their simplest and most successful strategies is to buy their critics. By this means, they not only divide their opponents and acquire inside information about how they operate; but they also benefit from what public relations companies call 'image transfer': absorbing other people's credibility.

Over the past 20 years, the majority of Britain's most prominent greens have been hired by companies whose practices they once contested. Jonathon Porritt, David Bellamy, Sara Parkin, Tom Burke, Des Wilson and scores of others are taking money from some of the world's most destructive corporations, while boosting the companies' green credentials. Now they have been joined by a man who was, until very recently, rightly admired for his courage and integrity: the former director of Greenpeace UK, Lord Melchett. In January 2002 he started work at the PR firm Burson-Marsteller. Burson-Marsteller's core business is defending companies which destroy the environment and threaten human rights from public opinion and pressure groups like Greenpeace.

So what are we to make of these defections? Do they demonstrate only the moral frailty of the defectors, or are they indicative of a much deeper problem, afflicting the movement as a whole? I believe environmentalism is in serious trouble, and that the prominent people who have crossed the line are not the only ones who have lost their sense of direction.

There are plenty of personal reasons for apostasy. Rich and powerful greens must perpetually contest their class interest. Environmentalism, just as much as socialism, involves the restraint of wealth and power. Peter Melchett, like Tolstoy, Kropotkin, Engels, Orwell and Tony Benn, was engaged in counter-identity politics, which require a great deal of purpose and self-confidence to sustain. In Tolstoy's novel *Resurrection*, Prince Nekhlyudov recalls that when he blew his money on hunting and gambling and seduced another man's mistress, his friends and even his mother congratulated him, but when he talked about the redistribution of wealth and gave some of his land to his peasants they were dismayed. "At last Nekhlyudov gave in: that is, he left off believing in his ideals and began to believe in those of other people."

Lord Melchett was also poorly rewarded. There is an inverse relationship between the public utility of your work and the amount you get paid. He won't disclose how much Burson-Marsteller will be giving him, but I suspect the world's biggest PR company has rather more to spend on its prize catch than Greenpeace.

But, while all popular movements have lost people to the opposition, green politics has fewer inbuilt restraints than most. Environmentalism is perhaps the most ideologically diverse political movement in world history, which is both its greatest strength and its greatest weakness. There is a long-standing split, growing wider by the day, between people who believe that the principal solutions lie in enhanced democracy and those who believe they lie in enhanced technology (leaving existing social structures intact while improving production processes and conserving resources). And, while the movement still attracts radicals, some are beginning to complain that it is being captured by professional campaigners whose organizations are increasingly corporate and remote. They exhort their members to send money and sign petitions, but discourage active participation in their campaigns. Members of Greenpeace, in particular, are beginning to feel fed up with funding other people's heroics.

As the movement becomes professionalized and bureaucratized (and there are serviceable reasons why some parts of it should) it has also fallen prey to ruthless careerism. The big money today is in something called 'corporate social responsibility', or CSR. At the heart of CSR is the notion that companies can regulate their own behaviour. By hiring green specialists to advise them on better management practices, they hope to persuade governments and the public that there is no need for compulsory measures. The great thing about voluntary restraint is that you can opt into or out of it as you please. There are no mandatory inspections, there is no sustained pressure for implementation. As soon as it becomes burdensome, the commitment can be dropped.

In 2000, for example, Tony Blair, prompted by corporate lobbyists, publicly asked Britain's major companies to publish environmental reports by the end of 2001. The request, which remained voluntary, managed to defuse some of the mounting public pressure for government action. But by January 1st 2002, only 54 of the biggest 200 companies had done so. Because the voluntary measure was a substitute for regulation, the public now has no means of assessing the performance of the firms which have failed to report.

So the environmentalists taking the corporate buck in the name of cleaning up companies' performance are, in truth, helping them to stay dirty by bypassing democratic constraints. But because corporations have invested so heavily in avoiding democracy, CSR has become big business for greens.

In this social climate, it's not hard to see why Peter Melchett imagined that he could move to Burson-Marsteller without betraying his ideals. It was a staggeringly naïve and stupid decision, which has destroyed his credibility and seriously damaged Greenpeace's (as well, paradoxically, as reducing his market value for Burson-Marsteller), but it is consistent with the thinking prevalent in some of the bigger organizations.

Environmentalism, like almost everything else, is in danger of being swallowed by the corporate leviathan. If this happens, it will disappear without trace. No one threatens its survival as much as the greens who have taken the company shilling.

Published in The Guardian *15th January 2002*

Chapter 6

Krafting a Smokescreen

Kathryn Mulvey

In May 1998, Philip Morris and other major US tobacco corporations agreed to settle a lawsuit filed by the state of Minnesota over alleged violations of consumer protection, antitrust and commercial laws. Under the terms of the settlement, the corporations were forced to turn over millions of internal documents dating roughly from the 1950s onward.[1] This wealth of previously secret information provides a rare glimpse into the inner workings of a transnational corporation and the seriousness with which it has viewed a well-organized, strategic grassroots campaign and boycott.

The documents, which can be viewed on the internet[2] and at documentation centres in Minneapolis and Guildford, England, provide hard evidence of what the tobacco companies knew about the dangers and addictiveness of their products, when they knew it, and how they aimed advertising and promotion at children.

The corporate accountability organization Infact launched its tobacco industry campaign in May 1993. In April 1994, it publicly challenged the industry to stop tobacco marketing and promotion that appeals to children and young people; stop spreading tobacco addiction internationally; stop influence over and interference in public policy on issues of tobacco and health; stop deceiving people about the dangers of tobacco; and pay the high costs of health care associated with the tobacco epidemic.

This chapter examines the impact of Infact's campaign, and the responses it elicited from Philip Morris, as revealed in once-secret meeting notes, executive memos, corporate reports and more which were made public under the lawsuit settlement.

First, it looks at how Philip Morris uses its Kraft Foods division to support its tobacco business and shows why the Kraft boycott has been such a threat to the parent corporation. A Philip Morris spokesperson said in a memo that Infact's anti-tobacco-marketing campaign had the potential to touch other divisions of the company, "namely food and beer products". He went on to acknowledge that food and beer were "one area where the Philip Morris corporate name has kept many people away from our other companies' products."[3] Second, it reviews some of the ways Philip Morris has tried to counteract the campaign, from intelligence-gathering to public relations. Finally, it examines the toll Infact's campaign has taken on one of the largest and most powerful corporations in the world—despite the company's best efforts to neutralize it.

Kraft: Philip Morris's secret weapon

Working with allies around the world, Infact has pressured Philip Morris—the world's largest and most profitable tobacco transnational—to stop addicting new customers and manipulating public policy in the interest of profits. A key strategy in the campaign has been a widespread boycott of Philip Morris's Kraft Foods. Infact activists and allies have confronted Philip Morris through letter-writing campaigns, petition drives, call-in days, in-person deliveries to corporate offices, visibility actions, leafleting blitzes, counter-recruitment protests, shareholder meeting demonstrations and direct dialogue with corporate decision-makers.

In a show of moving into the food business, Philip Morris acquired General Foods in 1985, Kraft in 1988 and Nabisco in 2000.[4] These acquisitions made it look better to the public (by hinting at a move toward phasing out tobacco) and the policymakers (by vastly increasing the company's size and political muscle). As author Larry White put it in his book *Merchants of Death: The American Tobacco Industry*, the food businesses "contribute their image, legitimacy and constituency to bolster cigarettes against the unsympathetic (to cigarettes) outside world."[5] Meanwhile, Philip Morris continued to grow its tobacco business tremendously: its international tobacco profits grew by 274 percent between 1990 and 2000.[6]

Kraft has served as a 'back door' through which tobacco money can reach political candidates who want to avoid obvious ties to the tobacco industry in the current public climate.[7] Outside the US, too, Philip Morris has tried to use its food companies to influence tobacco policy, according to a July 2000 report by a committee of experts to the World Health Organization (WHO), led by Swiss public health official Dr Thomas Zeltner.[8] For example, current Philip Morris CEO Geoffrey Bible noted in 1988, when president of the company's international tobacco division, that WHO "has extraordinary influence on government and consumers". In trying to find a way to "reorient" WHO's activities on this front, Bible proposed the company "think through how we could use our food companies, size, technology, and capability with governments by helping them with their food problems."[9]

Going on the defensive

Philip Morris took Infact very seriously from the beginning. Within weeks after Infact announced its campaign, internal memos were flying between Philip Morris's top executives. A handwritten note across the top of one bears the initials of then-CEO Michael A. Miles and reads, "This group could be real trouble. We are gearing up to defend."[10] A 1993 company memo notes, "We should keep a close intelligence watch and when they get down to a boycott tactic (it will most probably not be a tobacco product), then we will have to fight with everything we have."[11]

The degree of concern generated by Infact's campaign is evident in the extent to which Philip Morris monitored Infact activists: "They [Infact] began with a postcard writing campaign & apparently have gotten a hold of our 800 number. What next???"[12] One internal memo noted, "A box of Post's 'Banana Nut Crunch' cereal was found at Larry's Market, in Portland, Oregon bearing a sticker on the front of the box: Stop Marketing Tobacco to Children—Boycott Philip Morris."[13] Nearly every postcard, phone call, news release and letter from activists was tracked, counted, and used to develop a coordinated response.[14]

After Philip Morris executives learned Infact was targeting their company, they immediately consulted with General Electric (GE).[15] Infact's campaign against GE as the driving force behind nuclear weapons production and promotion had just reached a successful conclusion that saw GE moving out of the business in early 1993. Infact was executive producer of the documentary *Deadly Deception: General Electric, Nuclear Weapons and Our Environment*, which won a 1991 Academy Award and helped push GE out of the nuclear weapons business.

Philip Morris showed its fear of comparable publicity in an internal training manual on Infact's campaign, which warned that "Risk always exists that the group [Infact] will use innovative tactics e.g. documentaries that could involve and activate a larger segment, particularly outside the US."[16] (Infact was to live up to that fear with the 2000 release of *Making a Killing: Philip Morris, Kraft and Global Tobacco Addiction*.[17] Within a few months, activists and allies had shown the film to thousands of people in more than 30 countries.)

After its consultation with GE, it hired Burson-Marsteller, one of the public relations firms used by Nestlé (the target of Infact's Infant Formula Campaign) for help in learning more about Infact.[18] Burston-Marsteller advised Philip Morris to reassure managers at Kraft and its other subsidiaries, as well as retailers and shareholders "that the effort against PM will have little, if any, impact financially and the best policy—at least for now—is to 'wait it out'."[19]

In fact, Philip Morris never really thought "waiting it out" was a viable option. One early internal document reveals that the company was very aware of the campaigners' endurance. Infact "has demonstrated that it is willing to wage long-term campaigns against its target companies and will devote all its energy and resources into 'fighting the abuses of transnational corporations'." [20]

A complex and costly corporate strategy

Far from waiting out a negligible impact, the company was busy developing a complex strategy during the campaign's early stages, as this memo to key people in Philip Morris's and Kraft's international divisions indicates:

"In order to ensure that all of Philip Morris's operating companies are prepared to respond, if need be, to any actions taken by the 'consumer activist organization Infact', I am setting up informational sessions with each operating unit. Senior executives who you think should be informed will be briefed by Barry Holt and Burson-Marsteller. . . . This briefing could be followed by a crisis preparedness plan or intra-company communication plan." [21]

The company outlined a training programme for upper- and mid-level managers that detailed scenarios and responses. For instance, if activists or demonstrators approached grocery store managers asking them to support the boycott, company representatives were to "assure customers [retailers] that everything is under control." If Infact "enlists the help of influential health and religious groups," representatives should "assure suppliers that [the] campaign will not impact sales." [22]

A false declaration of independence
In an attempt to counter support for the boycott, Philip Morris tried to convince the public that its food and tobacco businesses were separate. As the boycott launch approached, Burson-Marsteller advised Philip Morris that "(t)o highlight the independence of the companies, each should consider drafting its own statement to be used in response to press inquiries about the boycott." The PR firm also recommended Philip Morris have "fully briefed and trained spokespeople at each of the targets of the boycott". [23]

By August 1994, four months after the boycott's launch, the tobacco giant had developed its overall message: "PM operating companies are independent and actions taken against one or more of them have no effect on the others." [24] Until very recently, the company consistently emphasized this declaration of the independence of its divisions in statements to the media and in other public forums.

Feigning ignorance
What Philip Morris said—or more importantly, didn't say—publicly about the impact of consumer pressure sharply contrasted with the flurry of inter-

nal activity in response to it.

With the aid of Burson-Marsteller, Philip Morris had adopted a set of strategic recommendations including the development of "a communications network to report on signs that the boycott may be spreading", coupled with a plan to "not respond to or acknowledge the boycott directly, as this will give the boycott credibility."[25] Internal documents included regular reports from managers around the country about communication from boycotters. Some of these reports went all the way to the CEO.

The fault line between Philip Morris's internal and external postures became evident in the fall of 1994, when the Interfaith Center on Corporate Responsibility filed a shareholder resolution calling on the company to spin off its tobacco operations from Kraft, specifically citing Infact's boycott as one financial reason for the separation.[26] By this time, Philip Morris had held detailed strategy sessions regarding the boycott[27] and was on record in the media calling it "unfair" and "unwarranted".[28] Yet the company attempted to block the shareholder resolution by telling the Securities and Exchange Commission (which oversees proposals presented to shareholders) that there was no boycott,[29] demonstrating how desperate it was to keep shareholders from becoming aware of the action.

"Krafting" a corporate image

Following Infact's boycott launch in 1994, Philip Morris increased image advertising associated with the targeted brands. Ads for Kraft products substantially jumped in 1994. In 1996 and 1997, the company began airing prime-time TV ads promoting philanthropic good works under the Post and Maxwell House brand names.[30] The ad blitz was an indication that the corporation knew its image was at risk, according to marketing expert Jim Post, a professor of management policy at Boston University School of Management.[31]

From 1998 to 2000, as Infact stepped up the pressure, Philip Morris increased its spending on corporate advertising in the US by a staggering 1,712 percent.[32] In the fall of 1998, as Infact focused its boycott on Kraft Macaroni & Cheese, the corporation began a $50 million image ad campaign touting Kraft's "family values". Kraft Macaroni & Cheese is one of Philip Morris's most valuable and heavily advertised products.[33]

The lavish spending continued in 2000, with more than $300 million spent on ads designed to polish the company's image with the public and policymakers.[34] Central to this spending spree was the October 1999 introduction of an ad campaign with the theme 'Working to Make a Difference: The People of Philip Morris', which highlights the corporation's ownership of Kraft. In this departure from its longtime strategy, the corporation began to risk Kraft's image to boost Philip Morris's. Internal documents include polls showing that linking the corporate names would benefit Philip Morris but harm Kraft.[35] It seemed clear that the power brokers would go to great lengths to protect tobacco profits.

It looked like this new approach of trying to turn its enemy's strategy to its own advantage might be backfiring, though. A Harris Interactive poll released in February 2001 found that an astounding 16 percent of respondents familiar with Philip Morris had boycotted its products in the past year.[36] Boycotts can achieve their objectives if just a small proportion of consumers actively participate: 5 percent, according to the late Cesar Chavez, leader of the United Farm Workers. And the Kraft boycott is becoming more visible at the time of writing. The December 2000 issue of *Harper's* included a half-page ad sponsored by Infact and Adbusters that asked, "Why are you buying your food from a tobacco company?" and urged readers to join the boycott.[37]

Effects of campaign pressure

Boycotts are proven to be effective. Grassroots consumer campaigns like Infact's alter the cost/benefit ratio for corporations to continue engaging in the practices targeted. Prior to a boycott, these benefits are generally high and the costs low or non-existent. As boycott pressure cuts into sales, corporations become concerned not only about current losses but also about the potential future impact on expansion plans or critical business segments.

In fact, lost sales are only a small fraction of the overall financial impact of a strategic consumer boycott campaign. Other boycott-attributable costs include management time spent dealing with the boycott and its impact (which could have been spent on acquiring new sales and increasing shareholder value); public relations, advertising, and corporate giving to maintain public goodwill; reduced stock value (as Burson-Marsteller points out, "Boycott announcements have an immediate and pronounced effect on target firms' stock prices"[38]), harm to the company name, reputation, and image (among any corporation's most valuable assets); and internal friction created when one business segment drags down another. All these factors affect the cost/benefit ratio for a corporation, giving it an incentive to change its behaviour.

Kraft also lost in the form of brain drain as its image as a 'hot' employer started to show nicotine stains. A November 1999 *Business Week* cover story on Philip Morris revealed "What It's Like to Work at America's Most Reviled Company". Robert Eckert, then President and CEO of Kraft, admitted the food business was feeling the "notoriety" of the tobacco business. The article noted that that year, "activists at the University of North Carolina at Chapel Hill and the University of Wisconsin staged protests when Kraft tried to recruit on those campuses." A *Fortune* magazine ranking of MBA fantasy jobs subsequently listed Kraft Foods as "no longer so hot" an employer—down to 62nd from 32nd.[39]

Philip Morris clearly recognized the threat to employee morale posed by public exposure and pressure. In the proxy statement distributed to shareholders for the 2000 annual meeting, management cited "increased employee retention and motivational issues" and the impact of "the current litigation and regulatory environment . . . on all company executives (including those executives in non-tobacco areas of the business)" as part of its rationale for granting special bonuses to thousands of employees.[40]

Despite the payoff—and speculation that he was a potential successor to Philip Morris Chair and CEO Geoffrey Bible—in May 2000 Eckert unexpectedly resigned to take over at toymaker Mattel.[41] At least two of his top deputies followed him out the door. Less than a month before his resignation, Eckert had received an open letter organized by Infact and signed by 58 religious leaders from around the US, urging him to use his influence to stop Philip Morris's abusive practices or to separate Kraft from the tobacco giant.

According to food industry analyst Erika Gritman Long, "it's absolutely essential (to retain employees) because this is an incredibly execution-sensitive business." Long says losing talent is a "tremendous" earnings risk.[42]

A look toward the future

The experience of Infact and other organizations has long proven that concerted grassroots campaigning can and does change corporate behaviour.

Clearly, Infact's tobacco industry campaign and Kraft boycott have forced Philip Morris to respond in numerous and costly ways—and contributed to life-saving gains. Since May 1993, tobacco corporations have been forced to admit to their product's addictive and deadly effects; they have begun to pay some of the enormous health care costs associated with it; their once-powerful lobbying arm, the Tobacco Institute, has been shut down; and they have given up some of their most outrageous promotional tactics in the US. People around the world are beginning to hold these corporations accountable for the harm they cause.

Yet Philip Morris continues aggressively promoting tobacco using devices like the Marlboro Man. The continuing prevalence of this image—arguably the world's leading source of youth tobacco addiction—underscores the lack of authority on the part of independent governments to regulate the tobacco giants. The world's largest and most profitable tobacco corporation uses the cowboy, linked to the myth of American freedom, to expand the global market for its addictive and deadly product. Meanwhile, it employs increasingly expensive and sophisticated public relations to cover its tracks, even going so far as to stake out a 'reasonable' position in favour of 'sensible' regulations.

As Infact makes it harder for Philip Morris to go on with business as usual, it is also working with the Network for Accountability of Tobacco Transnationals (NATT) to secure public policy advances to protect the health and lives of future generations. The WHO-initiated Framework Convention on Tobacco Control has the potential to prevent the further spread of tobacco addiction, limit the political power of tobacco transnationals, and set global standards affecting other industries whose policies, practices or products endanger health or the environment.

Our long-term success will depend on the ongoing refinement of campaign tactics based on direct and indirect responses from Philip Morris and its allies. By providing an unprecedented view inside a transnational corporation, Philip Morris's documents enhance our planning and analysis, maximizing the impact of our campaigning.

| Chapter 7 |

Joining Forces: Big Business Rallies after Seattle

Olivier Hoedeman and Ann Doherty

The spectacular failure of the World Trade Organization (WTO) Summit in Seattle at the end of 1999 was a major victory for critics of neoliberal global- ization, but this official debacle also marked the start of a large-scale counter- offensive. Corporate leaders had seen the backlash against corporate-led globalization coming for a couple of years, foreshadowed as it was by the derailment of negotiations for a Multilateral Agreement on Investment (MAI) by activists around the world in 1998.[1] A year before Seattle, the president of a US business lobby group had warned that "the enemies of an open market system have marshaled a serious counterattack on further liberalization of trade and investment and on multinational companies as the main agents of globalization."[2] Although in the period before Seattle examples can be found of corporate campaigning against citizens' movements critical of the neolib- eral trade agenda, the unexpected outcome of the WTO Summit served as a rousing wake-up call for business to intensify its counter-offensive.

In the post-Seattle period, attempts to stop the rise of what business calls 'globophobia' have intensified dramatically. Organized in a diverse web of lobby groups and indispensably assisted by the PR industry, business in North America and Europe is scrambling to regain the upper hand. In this reinvig- orated offensive, corporate lobby groups are determined to divide their critics and strip away their legitimacy.

Ironically, in doing so, business is borrowing heavily from NGO tactics that have proven successful in the backlash against economic globalization. As corporations and their lobby groups have ventured into a cyberwar over the world economy in recent years, industry-run websites propagating the bless- ings of trade liberalization have mushroomed. Assisted by the PR industry, lobby groups have also become increasingly successful at mimicking grass- roots campaigning. Such 'astroturf' exercises intended to give the impression of popular support for the corporate trade agenda play a significant role in post-Seattle trade battles, particularly in the United States.

While US business has carried out multimillion-dollar campaigns—including high-profile PR activities—in its effort to regain control over the trade debate, European corporations have generally avoided open confrontation. Worried that a public counter-campaign might backfire and strengthen the position of WTO critics, European business has preferred to step up its behind-the-scenes lobbying efforts. The most aggressive global corporate player, the International Chamber of Commerce (the self-proclaimed "world business organization" made up of corporations from both sides of the Atlantic) is unabashedly "making the case for the global economy" in fora including the United Nations.

The Seattle PR disaster

Business had high hopes for the Third Ministerial Conference of the WTO in Seattle, scheduled from November 29 to December 3, 1999. At this gathering of trade ministers from around the world, a highly anticipated new round of negotiations on further world trade liberalization was to be kick-started. The 'Millennium Round', which business had promoted for several years, was not only to cover negotiations on all areas of trade but also expand the WTO's mandate to include new areas such as investment. The Millennium Round was viewed as the most efficient way to ensure that the wave of economic deregulation that had swept the world throughout the 1990s, facilitating the unprecedented economic expansion of transnational corporations, would continue. What unravelled, however, proved a nasty surprise for the corporate sector.

The WTO negotiators received a warm welcome on the opening day of the Seattle Summit in the form of the largest demonstrations witnessed in the US since the Vietnam War. Massive street protests continued throughout the event, assembling an estimated 20,000 to 50,000 people a day. These demonstrations united trade unions, NGOs and activist groups sharing a deep frustration with the WTO's neglect of social and environmental concerns. Protesters identified the WTO as the prime symbol of a model of corporate-led globalization that was increasing social gaps and environmental devastation in many places around the world.[3]

This public outrage directly contributed to a subsequent impasse in the negotiations. The summit closed without results and, significantly, without launching the anticipated new round of negotiations. The entire first day of talks was cancelled after demonstrators 'shut down the WTO' by blocking access to the conference centre, curtailing the remaining negotiating time. But most importantly, the massive presence of WTO critics deepened the divide between governments, in particular in empowering southern negotiators to speak out against the undemocratic negotiating process that was being entirely dominated by the US, the EU and other industrialized countries.

The corporate world's first reaction to the activists' dramatic victory in the Battle of Seattle was one of disappointment and disbelief. "The business reaction [to the summit failure] is that we had a PR disaster here," said Harry L. Freeman of the Coalition of Service Industries, an influential US business lobby group.[4] *PR Week* agreed, and concluded that "guerrilla PR completely seized the initiative in Seattle."[5] For many corporations, Seattle was the first clear indication that the backlash against economic globalization should be seen as a serious threat. A week after the failed summit, Adnan Kassar, president of the powerful International Chamber of Commerce, beseeched "the world business community" to respond to the threat coming from "highly organized and sophisticated groups that, for many different reasons, are hostile to trade." Kassar warned in *Business Line* magazine: "They know how to exploit the internet to co-ordinate their lobbying and are adept at winning media attention." He concluded that "these non-governmental organizations have become a powerful force on the world political scene."[6]

Picking up the pieces in Davos

The corporate elite had its next major international tête-à-tête just weeks later, at the annual meeting of the World Economic Forum (WEF) in Davos, at the end of January 2000. Outside the conference centre, a miniature Seattle unfolded, as demonstrators from Switzerland and neighbouring countries surged through the ski resort's narrow streets in defiance of this gathering of some 2,000 self-proclaimed 'global leaders' from the business, finance and political sectors. The ghost of Seattle haunted the official proceedings as well. "What this conference is about is that nobody knows how to respond to Seattle," a WEF participant confided to the *Observer* newspaper.[7]

The event's organizers, in previous years uncompromising in their pursuit of global neoliberal transformation, had opted for a more conciliatory tone in light of the recent fiasco. "If we fail to draw the right lessons from Seattle, the backlash will gather momentum," said WEF co-ordinator Claus Smadja, who called for an urgent departure from what he termed "globalization machismo".[8] From the Davos podia, one business leader after another defended economic globalization while arguing for reforms and more inclusive forms of "global governance" in collaboration with the more "responsible" NGOs. But despite this carefully orchestrated exercise in front of the media, the corporate participants' confusion was apparent. Many voices argued for a confrontational approach to dealing with protesters. Lewis B. Campbell, CEO of US-based Textron, for example, called upon "supporters of free trade" to build an international coalition to push the cause of globalization in order not to lose "the propaganda war". "The international business community must take the lead," said Campbell, with reference to NAFTA, which survived grassroots opposition thanks to a massive mobilization by the business sector.[9]

The US: a full-steam counter-offensive

Since Seattle, US business has engaged in a multifaceted, multimillion-dollar counter-campaign involving individual corporations, lobby groups like the Business Roundtable and the US Chamber of Commerce, corporate-sponsored think tanks, and of course the ever-faithful PR industry. Even before Seattle, powerful neoliberal think tanks like the Council on Foreign Relations and the Institute for International Economics had already started to develop a strategic response to the backlash against their political agenda.[10] Afterwards, a new one was founded "to educate the public about the rapid changes associated with globalization". Among the first activities hosted by the Washington, DC-based Cordell Hull Institute[11] was a seminar entitled 'After Seattle: Restoring Momentum in the WTO'. The title concealed the underlying motive of the strategy session, which was how opposition to the WTO could most effectively be undermined. Among the questions discussed by the participants was "How can we delegitimize NGOs?" One tactic proposed was to approach charitable foundations and ask them to cut off funding for organizations critical of the WTO.[12]

The PR industry was quick to jump to assistance after the WTO debacle, undoubtedly sniffing out major new market opportunities. Just a few months later, the Washington, DC-based PR company Black, Kelly, Scruggs & Healy sent its corporate clients a 'Guide to the Seattle Meltdown: A Compendium of Activists at the WTO Ministerial.'[13] In an accompanying letter, the PR firm's managing director warned against the "potential ability of the emerging coalition of these groups to seriously impact broader, longer-term corporate interests". He ended his introduction to the report, which describes 48 WTO-critical groups, by advertising his company's willingness "to defend clients against attacks" from these groups.[14] In fact, the compendium reveals very limited insight into the dynamics of grassroots organizing and gives the impression of being the meagre result of a fairly random tour around NGO websites.

Painting a grim picture of the future of corporate interests was a common feature of the PR industry's first analyses of Seattle. Take, for instance, the conclusions of an essay by Wes Pedersen of the Public Affairs Council on how activist groups used the internet to mobilize. "Countering the growing influence of these cyber-powered anti-American, anti-corporate international organizations," wrote Pedersen, "is one of the greatest challenges US corporate and government Public Affairs practitioners will face in this new millennium."[15] Control Risk Group, the 'international business risk consultancy', also joined the choir of scaremongers. "Seattle should serve as a wake-up call for what is likely to be an escalation of various types of direct-action campaigns against a wide range of large, multinational corporations in the coming year," the company wrote in its newsletter *Trendline*.[16] The hawks at Control Risk concluded that "governments have been too soft on crimes involving direct political action" and singled out Bill Clinton, who "rewarded the window-kicking hooligans in Seattle by declaring that their message needed to be heard."[17]

The PR industry eventually moved beyond this heavy-handed rhetoric, refining its analysis and developing effective new counter-strategies, many of which are deeply problematic from a democratic point of view. In an analysis of the lessons the industry should learn from Seattle, Public Relations Management (PRM) asked itself how "a ragtag band of non-elected, supposedly poorly funded NGOs . . . pulled off this successful public relations coup?"[18] The answer: loose and flexible network structures and a fast-flowing exchange of information through the internet, which enables net-warriors to operate like swarms of bees and defeat much more powerful opponents. In these 'net wars', hierarchically organized corporations and business groupings are at a serious disadvantage, PRM wrote. It concluded that "as Seattle demonstrated, the battle can move to the streets."[19] PR giant Edelman came to a similar conclusion: "Corporations need to change to win," and to do so "they need to adopt strategies and tactics that are similar to NGOs."[20] One important lesson is "to communicate in human terms rather than economic or scientific terms as well as incorporate grassroots efforts."[21] Such strategic advice has by no means fallen on deaf ears.

A battle fought on astroturf

The biggest post-Seattle trade battle in the US took place around the Clinton administration's proposal to grant Permanent Normal Trade Relations (PNTR) status to China. The proposed law would eliminate the annual parliamentary review of US-China trade relations and give goods produced in China unlimited access to the US market. All this was claimed necessary to ease China's entry into the WTO.[22] For US corporations, the main appeal was not so much to ensure a foothold in the Chinese consumer market but rather to guarantee unconditional access to US markets for goods they produce in China under commercially ideal, but often socially and environmentally deplorable, conditions. No less important was the need to achieve a symbolic victory for the corporate globalization agenda. Shortly after Seattle, neoliberal guru Fred Bergsten issued a warning outlining the disastrous consequences that would result from losing the PNTR debate. "If Seattle 'victors' are permitted to carry the day on China, the global liberalization program of the past half century will be at serious risk," wrote Bergsten, who heads the powerful corporate-sponsored think tank the Institute for International Economics.[23]

Bergsten's warning clearly reflected the mood among US corporate interests: the China PNTR bill was a must-win. Convincing Congress to support the legislation was no easy task, and a serious obstacle was the fact that the trade unions and NGOs that overwhelmingly opposed the bill had the public on their side. An April 2000 poll showed that 79 percent of US voters opposed PNTR with China.[24] In the six months after Seattle, the business lobby carried out what was likely the most expensive corporate political campaign in history. More than US$113 million was spent on lobbying, political donations, advertising and astroturf activities to persuade Congress to vote for the bill.[25]

Phenomenal lobbying machinery was put into place. During the first half of 2000, the US Chamber of Commerce, the Business Roundtable, the American Farm Bureau Federation and other prominent members of the pro-PNTR coalition paid lobbyists more than $30 million to massage the minds of Congress members. Motorola and Boeing, with major commercial interests in China, spent more than $7 million between them. The effectiveness of these efforts was boosted by "a seamless interplay between the White House and corporate PNTR lobbying efforts", according to Public Citizen, one of the many NGOs campaigning against permanent trade status with China.[26] In order to manoeuvre the bill through Congress, President Clinton staffed a 'China War Room' with 150 people who worked in tandem with the corporate campaigners. Another tool to create political support for the bill was a staggering $68 million in 'donations' given to members of Congress and their parties during the run-up to the vote. One member reported he was offered $200,000 to vote in favour of PNTR. No more subtly, members of Congress were threatened that if they failed to support the bill they would lose future funding.

Aside from this direct pressure, business invested in a tremendously costly effort to manufacture the impression that the China bill enjoyed widespread public support. Advertisements on national and local television, on the radio and in newspapers functioned to simulate public support and thereby influence members of Congress. Two major corporate lobby groups, the Business Roundtable and the US Chamber of Commerce, spent more than $12 million on such exercises. And individual corporations like Motorola, Exxon-Mobil and Microsoft spent millions on their own ads in favour of the bill. A typical television spot featured a US worker confirming that: "I work in America, and trade with China works for me." These misleading advertisements were part of the corporate strategy to gloss over the inconvenient fact that US trade unions overwhelmingly opposed PNTR.

In addition to advertising, a massive astroturf operation designed by specialized PR firms was launched.[27] Corporate lobby groups recruited and trained managers and employees and then flew them to Washington to perform as PNTR supporters. These phony grassroots teams also visited members of Congress in their home states, armed with glossy 'local' propaganda that had in fact been produced by Washington PR firms. Retired staff members from pro-PNTR corporations were sent CD-ROMs and computer disks with sample letters they were urged to send to congressional leaders and local newspapers. Hundreds of college kids were hired for pro-PNTR 'rallies', and free 10-minute telephone calling cards with pro-PNTR slogans were handed out in front of subway stations by temporary workers in the guise of 'activists'. The Business Roundtable employed no less than 80 full-time field organizers for its PNTR campaign, in an impressive indication of the magnitude of these local astroturf efforts.[28]

In May 2000, after months of political battle at record high costs, the House of Representatives approved the PNTR bill. The vote was 237 for and 197 against, in stark contrast to public opinion, which remained hostile.[29] Part of the explanation for the success of the corporate campaign was simply the overwhelming financial resources that had been thrown into the battle, dwarfing the campaign budgets of labour and environment groups. But no less remarkable was the degree to which the corporate lobby implemented the advice of the PR industry and adopted strategies that had brought success to NGOs in the past.

The post-Seattle cyberwar

After Seattle, one of the PR industry's most urgent recommendations was that business seek equal footing in cyberspace discussions over the global economy by establishing a solid presence on the internet. This recommendation has eagerly been embraced. During the PNTR battle, the corporate lobby group Business Roundtable launched a flashy 'educational' website full of pro-free-trade material.[30] A burgeoning number of industry websites take a far more confrontational approach. www.truthabouttrade.com is primarily aimed at demonizing critics of economic globalization. According to this site, run by US agribusiness, "the environmental radicals who rioted in Seattle were using misstatements of fact, flawed science, outright lies, and brute force to impose an anti-trade, anti-growth agenda that threatens the very livelihood of American farmers and farm economy." The site further warns: "They got away with it once, but we will not let them do it again." Along with far-from-accurate information on "anti-trade" and "anti-agriculture" groups, it listed "*huge* East Coast foundations" said to fund WTO-critical organizations and displayed a complex diagram linking activist groups and funders.[31]

www.truthabouttrade.com mirrors the broader trend of websites aggressively lashing out at opponents of the corporate agenda, whether fair-trade groups or environment or consumer protection organizations. www.NoMoreScares.com attacks "those who profit from fear" by publicizing what it calls "irresponsible and groundless health scares".[32] Among those lambasted and ridiculed are activists who oppose bovine growth hormone, hormone-disrupting chemicals and genetically modified food. The very similar www.earthfiends.org is a spoof site attacking Friends of the Earth (FoE), a leading activist group that campaigns against the WTO and genetically modified food. Designed to mirror the Friends of the Earth site, it lampoons FoE with statements like "We continue to fight for our jobs and for the causes of paranoid maniacs the world over" and "Changing the World Because We Scare".[33]

Europe: business backs away from the fire

"NGOs have been very successful in depicting business as 'nasty multinationals'. This has affected business support for free trade. Instead of actively lobbying for a new round and taking a clear trade policy stance, business has in many cases decided to withdraw from the debate."—European Trade Commissioner Pascal Lamy[34]

Although no less frustrated about the growing backlash against globalization, European business has opted for a far mellower public profile than its US counterpart. While the US corporate world has engaged in an all-out confrontational counter-offensive, EU-based transnationals have generally tried to steer clear of direct confrontation with their critics. Says a *Financial Times* journalist, "Companies are reluctant to speak about trade as they fear public attacks by NGOs."[35] And for those that do, European political realities make open counter-campaigning a far less compelling choice than it might be in the US.

As far as EU politics is concerned, the corporate trade agenda faces less of an immediate threat. While there are strong WTO-critical NGOs and grass-roots campaigns in numerous European countries, the established political system still stubbornly backs continued global deregulation. Moreover, European business continues to enjoy extremely cosy working relations with the Brussels-based European Commission, as well as with many EU member governments. In particular, connections with Trade Commissioner Pascal Lamy, a tireless crusader for the WTO Millennium Round who sticks closely to the corporate trade agenda, have been mutually satisfying. Under these circumstances, business undoubtedly believes a more confrontational approach would only risk strengthening the position of the critics. Corporate lobby groups like the European Roundtable of Industrialists (ERT), the European Services Forum (ESF) and the European employers' organization UNICE have intensified their behind-the-scenes lobbying and left the public counter-campaigning to Lamy.

At the national level too, business has made the most of its privileged political access. In the UK, for instance, the LOTIS Committee, a financial services lobby group, worked closely with government officials on a counter-offensive against growing opposition in civil society to the WTO's GATS services negotiations. Within the LOTIS Committee, high-level officials from the Department of Trade and Industry strategized with corporate leaders from investment banks, consultancy corporations and other financial services firms including Goldman Sachs International, Morgan Stanley, Merrill Lynch and PricewaterhouseCoopers.[36]

European business has also at times engaged in open campaigning to counter the growing critique of corporate globalization. The Swedish employers' organization Svenskt Nringsliv, for instance, in autumn 2001 launched an information campaign on globalization targeting Swedish high school students. And the Association of German Industries (BDI) has recently developed plans for an NGO-style campaign to win public support for business-friendly international trade and investment policies. A leaked strategy paper from the Association of German Industries showed that industry is gathering information about critical NGOs and drafting counter-strategies to "take the wind out of the sails of the opponents."[37]

As in the US, pro-business think tanks have stepped in to play a crucial role in post-Seattle corporate politics in Europe. Brussels-based institutes like the European Policy Centre (EPC) and the Centre for European Policy Studies (CEPS) have been essential in helping to redefine corporate strategy. While trying hard to position themselves as broad-based fora for debate and objective sources of analysis on EU policy developments, the EPC and CEPS are overwhelmingly industry-dominated in origin, membership and funding.[38] At several EPC meetings, corporate members evaluated the happenings in Seattle and made plans to counter the backlash. Worried about the "growing power of anti-trade NGOs and the encouragement given to them by the failure of the Seattle talks", the EPC's Stanley Crossick recommended that businesses focus on "improving their communications" and fine-tuning lobbying. Crossick, known as the godfather of Brussels lobbying, urged industry to "take more proactive positions in dealing with the new breed of NGOs", but he called for a cautious approach, as "companies must be seen to wish only to curb the activities of the extremist NGOs." He suggested emphasizing that "NGOs must be accountable; they need rules to balance their rights."[39]

Ironically, demands for 'accountability' and 'rules' to control NGO behaviour have become a standard feature of the corporate reaction to the backlash against globalization. Only a few weeks after Seattle, two European business lobbies "invited" NGOs to "adopt a code of conduct". The two groups, Eurocommerce and the Free Trade Association, claimed this would help NGOs "strengthen their position in the expanding dialogue with inter-national institutions" such as the WTO. They insisted that NGOs respect the "democratic legitimacy of governments within the WTO" and guarantee "absolute transparency" concerning their membership and finances.[40] The proposed code never got off the ground—maybe because it was to cover "all NGOs, including the business community". Most business lobby groups would never accept that kind of full disclosure.

The demand for a code of conduct for NGOs resurfaced repeatedly, for example in the report 'NGO Rights and Responsibilities—A New Deal for Global Governance'. released in June 2000 by the UK-based Foreign Policy Centre (FPC), a think tank linked to the New Labour party. Referring to recent demonstrations in both Seattle and London, the FPC argues for an NGO code of conduct to "make the protesters accountable."[41] Under this "new deal", NGOs would agree to "minimum standards of accountability" and in return "be rewarded with a place at the negotiating table".[42] The pro-posal included "independent verification" of NGO behaviour by a new "reg-ulatory body." Each NGO would be judged worthy of certification based on "transparency, accountability, internal democracy and 'helpful knowledge', a measure of its expertise". Despite the carefully chosen wording, the intention was clear: to marginalize grassroots activist groups that do not work with tra-ditional hierarchical organizational structures.

A strange bird in the flock of European corporate think tanks is the London-based International Policy Network (IPN), which has close links to right-wing US think tanks like the Competitive Enterprise Institute and the Cato Institute.[43] Like its North American counterparts, the IPN mixes a zealous defence of unregulated markets with fierce anti-environmentalism and has gone on the offensive against WTO protesters. Major newspapers have run op-ed pieces by the IPN with titles like 'Riots Inc.—the business of protesting global-ization', in which the organization denounces the anti-globalization movement as "a foundation-, union- and government-funded coalition of convenience."[44]

"If you are a European taxpayer or union member," wrote Ms. Okonski of the IPN in the *The Wall Street Journal*, "chances are you are also a passive

investor in the ventures that wrecked Goteborg, Genoa, Seattle, and the rest."
The IPN articles include a detailed, but factually incorrect, overview of the
funding sources for activist groups and movements. (For instance, Ms. Okonski
claims European trade unions provide millions of dollars of support to "anti-
globalization groups", while in reality most European trade unions have taken
a very reformist stance in the debate over economic globalization and have sys-
tematically kept more radical critics of neoliberalism at arm's length.)

Dialogue and co-optation in Europe's PR industry

Seattle also opened up lucrative new opportunities for the booming Brussels-
based PR industry. Burson-Marsteller, Hill & Knowlton and dozens of other
firms and consultancies that specialize in intelligence-gathering, lobbying,
media strategizing and other 'communication' services are helping big business handle the crisis in its trade policy agenda. A look inside *European Voice*,
a magazine widely read in the Brussels corridors of power, reveals several pages
of advertisements for consulting firms, many of which explicitly stress their
services on WTO issues and NGO relations. Edelman Europe, for example,
advertises "direct communications for corporations and associations on WTO
public affairs", and boasts: "We work on the highest profile EU and international trade issues for multinational companies and trade associations." The
identities of the clients and the specific issues are, unfortunately, covered by
the usual veil of secrecy.

One of the most novel services offered by the PR industry is "NGO dialogue". As the Edelman firm puts it, "governments and corporations will only
succeed by establishing working relationships with NGOs that are not adver-
sarial." [45] As many corporations have discovered, luring NGOs into dialogue is
often a volatile proposition. Yet in the case of post-Seattle trade policies, corporate lobby groups in the EU have had such discussions served to them on a
silver platter. By the run-up to Seattle, the European Commission (EC) had set
up a controversial process of "dialogues with civil society", [46] inviting interested
"NGOs"—defined as both business lobby groups and non-profit groups—the
chance to discuss trade policy with Brussels civil servants. On the premise of
taking into account the concerns of civil society, the EC would present its position, listen to the supportive comments of the business lobbyists and the fierce
critiques of the campaigners . . . and keep its WTO policies unchanged.

For business, it was a win-win situation. The fundamental nature of the
EU's international trade agenda was not up for discussion, and groups like
UNICE and the European Services Forum (ESF) were already engaged in
parallel processes of co-operation with the EC. But the meetings were a
golden opportunity for business to identify globalization critics and set up an

'early warning system' to analyze new developments. Listening to campaigners from around Europe explaining their positions to EC staff was an ideal form of intelligence-gathering for lobbyists, enabling them to assess the strong and weak points of their opponents' arguments and fine-tune their own lobbying strategy and public rhetoric.

The NGOs had been offered a channel through which to voice their opinions, but the dialogues turned out to be a virtual political black hole. Campaigners ended up wasting a lot of scarce time and energy speaking into the deaf ears of neoliberal trade officials in Brussels instead of reaching the public. Many activist groups quickly concluded the 'dialogues' were mere window dressing, and the number of participating NGOs plummeted. These dialogues are a prime example of how to absent a controversial issue from public debate.

Moreover, the EC and business have consciously used the process to divide WTO critics into the categories of more and less radical, to the extent that some moderate environmental groups are now engaging in partnerships with the EC and business and have abandoned their opposition to the Millennium Round. No wonder Andre Driessen of the Dutch Employers' Federation suggested at a PR industry conference that "NGO-industry dialogue is a powerful tool to further the cause of international trade and economic development." [47]

The "world business organization's" counter-campaign

The Paris-based International Chamber of Commerce (ICC), the self-proclaimed "world business organization", has taken the international lead in the defence of trade liberalization. This corporate lobby group is keen to pull the rug from underneath WTO critics by dispelling public fears. As ICC President Adnan Kassar explains, "Growing globophobia and rising criticism of multinational business pose a special challenge to ICC as the only organization that speaks for business everywhere." [48] According to ICC Secretary-General Maria Livanos Cattaui, who leads the group's communication offensive, "Business must overcome the 'communications deficit' that is partly responsible for the growing backlash against globalization." [49]

A month before Seattle, the ICC launched a new section of its website "to present the case for the global economy." [50] Since then it has gradually expanded its use of the internet. The site prominently features a section on one of the strongest weapons in the ICC's arsenal against globalization critics: the Global Compact with the United Nations. [51] In this non-binding agreement launched in July 2000, ICC member corporations promise to become "global corporate citizens" and embrace UN social, environmental and human rights principles in their mission statements and practices. The ICC has stridently promoted its membership in the Global Compact in order to improve the image of its corporations while at the same time fiercely resisting suggestions that the principles become binding.

The ICC exploits every opportunity to spread its message, and it is clear that this eagerness is partly based on the fear that the neoliberal agenda is losing its grip due to recent threats by civil society. At the ICC's 33rd World Congress in May 2000, the proceedings were pervaded by this anxiety about the perceived backlash to the corporate agenda.[52] Nearly every session, regardless of the issue on the agenda, metamorphosed into a discussion about how to deal with the critics of globalization.

These debates, once again, revealed a great deal of divisiveness within corporate ranks. Some, including Shell's Phil Watts, called on business to be more proactive and directly engage in dialogue with other "stakeholders", particularly NGOs, as a way to pre-empt future action against industry. Watts' recommendations, however, provoked heated reactions from other heavyweights, like BP Amoco/Goldman Sachs chairman Peter Sutherland and former ICC President Helmut Maucher, who were overtly hostile to the idea of including NGOs in such dialogues. Maucher, who has an appalling record of NGO-bashing as the CEO of Nestlé, continues to aggressively question the legitimacy and influence of NGOs. In a post-Seattle interview with a German business newspaper, an angry Maucher stated, "This is something which the politicians should deal with: the question is in which ways NGOs should be allowed to operate."[53] Maucher and the ICC have repeatedly demanded that NGOs behave in accordance with binding rules. When the ICC met with Tony Blair in May 1998 to present its message to the G-8, it suggested a "weeding out" of certain NGOs. The ICC statement proposes that it would "be useful for the UN and other intergovernmental bodies to establish rules to clarify the legitimacy and accountability of many new non-governmental organizations engaged in the public policy dialogue."

The ICC's outspoken counter-campaigning stands in contrast to the strategizing of more secretive international business groupings. The Transatlantic Policy Network (TPN) has held quarterly closed meetings on the future of the WTO agenda since Seattle, bringing together businesspeople and neoliberal parliamentarians from the EU and the US. The crisis in the WTO's liberalization crusade and the anti-globalization backlash were also at the top of the agenda at the annual meetings of both the Trilateral Commission and the Bilderberg group in 2000. Both of these are highly secretive international bodies for elite consensus building, with Bilderberg covering Europe and North America and the Trilateral Commission also including representatives from Japanese business, academia and politics. At the Trilateral Commission's annual meeting in April 2000, countering the backlash against globalization was identified as "the critical issue of multilateral management for the future". A proposal was made to "begin devising a multi-part program to start turning the tide".[54]

The ICC has also used the 11 September 2001 attacks on the US to hit out at critics of neoliberal globalization, manipulatively grouping the anti-neoliberal activist movement with the terrorists. Cattaui, for instance, claimed on the International Chamber of Commerce website that if the November 2001 WTO Ministerial in Qatar failed to launch a new WTO round, it would be "a setback that would be acclaimed by all enemies of freer world trade and investment, including those behind the attacks at the World Trade Center and the Pentagon."[55] Dean R. O'Hare, the chair of US ICC affiliate USCIB, made a similar argument, saying "we must overcome the forces of terror and anti-globalization to continue to expand trade and investment."[56]

On the defensive

As movements questioning the social and environmental impacts of globalization continue to swell, the corporate counter-offensive will no doubt also gain in intensity. Addressing an audience of CEOs from North America, Europe and Japan, Dean O'Hare of the US Coalition of Service Industries called upon business to step up the propaganda war: "Private sector leaders must make this message a part of everything they do. It must be part of our business strategies and marketing efforts. We must constantly advance the arguments in support of trade liberalization in all our communications with our customers, our employees, and with our government representatives."[57]

Statements like these, however intimidating they may sound, should serve as an inspiration to NGOs and grassroots movements. They can be seen as an indication of the extent to which anti-trade campaigning has put business on the defensive. Indeed, the aggressive force-feeding approach adopted by industry may very well backfire, and bombardments of propaganda will likely only strengthen public mistrust of the corporate agenda. Despite massive lobbying budgets and campaigns designed by the world's leading PR firms, business is still facing the unsolved—and maybe unsolvable—challenge of convincing the public that its agenda of global economic deregulation is good for everyone.

Thanks to Lori Wallach, Greg Muttitt and our colleagues at the Corporate Europe Observatory (CEO), Belen Balanya, Adam Ma'anit and Erik Wesselius, for help with this article.

Chapter 8

Using Libel Laws to Silence Critics

Franny Armstrong and Will Ross

The McDonald's Corporation sells cheap hamburgers made from cheap ingredients. The people who make them work long hours for low wages and cannot join unions. It's junk food: high in fat, sugar and salt, and low in fibre and minerals. The animals whose bodies go into it often live and die in cruel conditions. The company's advertising misleads adults, and it manipulates children into pestering their parents to take them to McDonald's.

It is thanks to two remarkable Londoners that we can safely print these remarks. All of them have been examined and judged to be true in the course of the longest and most unlikely libel trial in English history.[1] All of them appeared in gleeful press coverage on the day after the verdict, as newspapers and TV stations fought to outdo one another's righteous indignation. All of them are common knowledge among those who stop to consider where their food comes from.

The McLibel trial is commonly told as a David and Goliath story, a fairy tale in which the little people, armed only with quick mind and noble countenance, outwit and finally defeat the sluggish giant. It's a good yarn, but it's just the latest chapter of a much longer, more complicated story.

SLAPPing critics with libel suits

Despite all that's wrong with McDonald's, as far as the British press is concerned all we see is happy clowns and smiling children. McDonald's calls its foods "nutritious",[2] its jobs "challenging and rewarding"[3] and itself an "environmental leader".[4] It spends a total of $3 billion a year creating and reinforcing an association with health, sport, ecology and enjoyment.[5] The press does not examine the corporation's methods and rarely questions its advertising. How has the UK's notoriously invasive, unruly, sensation-seeking media managed to sustain such a gigantic blind spot?

Two reasons: the advertising carrot and the legal stick. The former is obvious: no media organization will hurry to bite a hand that feeds it so much advertising revenue. The latter requires a bit more explanation.

An article is printed, somewhere public. The article alleges that a certain corporation produces food which is, say, not very nutritious after all. The corporation feels, with some justification, that this has a negative impact on its reputation. Since it is possible that the allegations are a malicious fabrication, there is a legal mechanism that allows the corporation to defend itself: a libel trial. The corporation is the claimant, and if it is vindicated, it can expect a public apology, compensation for its legal costs and a considerable amount of money in damages.

You might think that it would have to produce a convincing argument that its food is nutritious. But no. A peculiar quirk of UK libel law puts the burden of proof on the defendant. The person or organization producing the allegations must demonstrate that they are true, using primary sources. They must bring an eminent nutritionist to court to hold forth about the importance of fibre and vitamins, or locate an abattoir worker who has witnessed animal suffering, or fly a cattleman from Brazil to produce paperwork that points to the claimant. All the claimant has to do is start the case, then sit back while its critics pay vast sums to libel lawyers in pursuit of watertight proof.

This makes the British libel trial a powerful cousin to the American SLAPP, or 'strategic lawsuit against public participation'. It can be used to defend oneself against an unprincipled attack, but it is also a way to intimidate and silence a critic. Like a SLAPP, it favours the wealthy and powerful and functions most effectively as a deterrent.[6]

Mounting a libel defence is staggeringly, ruinously expensive. If the defence succeeds—the criticisms levelled at the claimant are found to be correct—then the claimant has to pay everybody's legal expenses. It might sound risky, but to get to that point the defendant may well have gambled hundreds of thousands of pounds on proving beyond question the truth of what it has alleged. When defendants lose, they are often ruined: a research organization called the Transnationals Information Center was forced to close after being sued by McDonald's over one of its pamphlets.[7]

In the case of the McLibel trial, the alleged defamation occurred in a leaflet produced by a tiny activist group called London Greenpeace (no relation to Greenpeace International) which was photocopied and handed out to a few hundred people. The leaflet described McDonald's activities in a detailed and very uncomplimentary way, and the corporation sued. The five people identified in the writ as the supposed authors of the leaflet were offered a choice: prove in court that each of its many criticisms was true, or eat their words in public.

It was McDonald's standard warning shot: apologize conspicuously or start saving up for libel lawyers. That letter, or a variation, has been sent to almost every significant media organization in the UK at some time or other, and to some amazingly obscure ones too.[8] It costs McDonald's next to nothing to send.

Recipients of letters like that, with intimidating letterhead and impenetrable jargon, always react the same way. They grovel. The BBC, *The Daily Telegraph*, *The Guardian*, *The Sun*, Channel 4: almost every self-appointed guardian of the public interest has at some point capitulated to McDonald's, along with several trade unions and campaigning groups, a children's theatre club and a tea shop.

Bluffing the media into backing down

The apology or withdrawal of criticism is not the end of the story, however embarrassing: it also provides ammunition for the next round. Prince Philip— president of the WWF, and famously given to undiplomatic outbursts—once allegedly greeted a McDonald's executive with the words "So you are the people who are tearing down the Brazilian rainforests and breeding cattle."[9] The corporation took offence and denied the allegation. A royal retraction and failure to recollect were quickly forthcoming, on WWF stationery.[10]

A year later, a BBC wildlife programme about rainforest destruction included the phrase, "It doesn't seem that anyone can be blamed except you and me, the consumers," followed by a montage of shots of various hamburger outlets, including McDonald's. The corporation disliked the association and sent a letter. This time it also included the prince's retraction and the WWF's climbdown. "It is clear from the attached copy letter from the Duke of Edinburgh . . . that the World Wildlife Fund were satisfied that our clients were exonerated from any implication in the destruction of the rainforests," the company wrote.[11]

McDonald's key argument was that each national subsidiary used only local beef. This was later shown to be untrue: the McLibel defendants proved that McDonald's UK had been secretly importing beef from Brazil that very year.[12]

Yet by the time this second letter went out, it had the full weight of royal approval behind it. The BBC broadcast an apology to the effect that it "may have given the impression that McDonald's hamburgers are made with beef originating from (ranches built on former rainforests). McDonald's have informed us that they do not use such beef. We accept this, and apologize to McDonald's for any embarrassment our programme may have caused them."[13]

The year after that a third letter went out, this time to Friends of the Earth.[14] This one referred to both the prince's and the BBC's apologies and concluded: ". . . this statement should clear up any misunderstandings your organization may have, and further statements regarding Brazilian rainforests should, therefore, exclude any reference to McDonald's."

A chance remark by Prince Philip had been turned around and parlayed into a series of apparently highly credible testaments to McDonald's innocence, all without a single point being debated in court or held up for public appraisal. The truth or falsehood of the allegation, and of McDonald's counter-arguments, were never independently examined. The whole episode would still be hidden from view if not for the McLibel defendants and their extraordinary tenacity.

It is possible to imagine that the writers of these letters spoke in good faith. Perhaps they were very senior and saw only the broad policy, not the specific purchase order. Another case, however, forces us to doubt the sincerity of McDonald's indignation.

In October 1989 a local UK newspaper, the *Bournemouth Advertiser*, printed an article that referred to the "captive-bolt" method used to slaughter cattle for McDonald's burgers.[15] The corporation demanded an apology, and the newspaper printed it: "McDonald's have asked us to point out that they do not approve of the captive-bolt method."

Not true. During the McLibel trial, McDonald's executives accepted that the captive-bolt method was standard practice throughout the industry and the method their suppliers used to slaughter cattle. The McLibel judge was not impressed: "This letter was clearly written on a false basis, and the solicitors must have been misled by whoever gave them instructions."[16]

The letter to the newspaper was deceptive, but it worked: the apology was printed, and the subject was closed. Even if the whole thing had gone to court, McDonald's deception carried no risk: the newspaper article would have been on trial, not the letter. The corporation had nothing to lose and everything to gain by misleading its solicitors and misrepresenting the facts.

Intimidation tactics backfire

In retrospect, it seems clear that the last thing the corporation wanted was to take a case to trial. Its tactics were designed to intimidate critics and deter the media from straying near potentially expensive subjects.

It's not just the stories that were withdrawn and disowned—we will never know how many potential articles were not printed, leads not pursued and issues ignored. It's easy to see how it works: a bright-eyed new journalist draws up an article that describes working conditions in McDonald's. Perhaps she even gets a job there to find out what it's really like. Her editor loves the story but remembers the humiliation of printing an apology three years ago, on another paper, after an article about the unscrupulous targeting of advertising at children. The stinging reprimand from his publisher is fresh in his mind, and the story is quietly spiked.

We can't tell whether McDonald's strategy was a deliberate one or just inspired muddling through, but the result was a climate of fear and self-censorship that spread throughout the British media and made the corporation effectively immune from criticism.

We ran into this barrier repeatedly during the McLibel trial. TV stations and newspapers withdrew stories at the last minute. Chat-show producers said we couldn't mention "the issues" or the offending part of the show would be cut. It's hard to talk about the fight against a burger company without being able to say why anyone is fighting.

McDonald's tactics were spectacularly successful. It had come to dominate the UK fast food industry. Then Ronald McDonald stubbed his toe on Helen Steel and Dave Morris. After McDonald's served writs on five London Greenpeace activists, three apologized and withdrew, but Steel and Morris refused, and the corporation found itself in court.

The McLibel trial was an agonizing ordeal: two anarchists and a ragtag band of volunteers spent three years using the British legal system as a stage on which to rummage through McDonald's dirty laundry and hold up the best bits for the world to see.

They produced expert witnesses to explain that no, a high-fat low-fibre diet could not be called nutritious, and that future Chicken McNuggets sometimes had their throats cut while still fully conscious. Academics flew in, documents were unearthed from ancient archives, and senior executives were cross-examined, all in a public forum and under the spotlights of a timid but delighted press.[17] While much of the coverage revolved around Dave's jumpers and Helen's haircut, the occasional story about one of the issues in the trial did appear. No wonder McDonald's tried to buy its way out and issued frantic orders to try to contain the damage.[18]

Helen and Dave succeeded in making a case on several of the most damaging issues. In a strictly legal sense, McDonald's won the case. In every other way, it lost. Even on points Helen and Dave failed to prove, the trial exposed the inner workings of McDonald's to the public: exactly the damaging sort of transparency from which its censorship strategy had so far protected it.

In short, McDonald's was engaged in a gigantic bluff. The corporation's tactics were designed to prevent scrutiny, bully critics into silence and intimidate the press into covering something else.

Fighting the fear

We spent the McLibel years making a film about the case.[19] Right from the start it had all the qualities of a great prime-time documentary, but this was 1995, and we walked straight into the middle of the blind spot. Both Channel 4 and the BBC had already had embarrassing legal run-ins with the corporation. ITV was out of the question because of its reliance on McDonald's advertising, and Channel 5 hadn't yet been invented.

Several of the UK's top documentary names were also trying to persuade broadcasters to fund their own McLibel films. Every single one was turned down. Even Channel 4 confined itself to verbatim re-enactments of parts of the trial.

We made the film anyway, with no money, little experience, borrowed equipment, a spare room in a flat and a volunteer crew that turned out to include Ken Loach. Funding came from selling our footage to news stations around the world and from generous people who thought the story should be told. Most of the film was financed by the sale of a single shot of Helen and Dave having a legal meeting on a busy underground train.

As the trial dragged on, the big media organizations began to smell blood in the water. Demand for bits of footage picked up, and news people and TV documentary commissioners starting sniffing around, terrified that they might have missed something big. Then, shortly before the verdict was issued, the BBC suddenly offered to buy our film for a prime-time slot directly after the verdict. "No time to waste; we'll do the paperwork later; we have to ring the listings magazines right away." A fee and a broadcast slot were agreed upon. All were delighted. "Just have to run it past the legal department."

During the previous three years, of which we had spent every waking minute thinking about libel, free speech and corporate intimidation, it had occurred to us to consider what we could and couldn't safely say on film. We were pragmatic: our aim was to get the film on television, and to do that we needed to make it as safe to broadcast as it possibly could be. Ken Loach came to the rescue, lending us a top-notch media lawyer. We had the best possible advice for free throughout the production, and we followed it scrupulously. In the opinion of our lawyer, the film was accurate, was fair comment and, given the subject matter, carried minimal risk of libel litigation.

The BBC lawyer disagreed and suggested various changes to the film. The editorial board had reservations about a secretly taped meeting in which senior US McDonald's executives tried to buy Helen and Dave off. The commissioning editor watched her story being snipped to bits and finally got cold feet. The BBC dropped the film at the last minute, leaving us at the climax of the story with an all-but-finished film, a huge potential audience and no outlet.

Some good news, though: we found a big-name distributor prepared to sell the film to international TV as soon as it was ready. Better still, Channel 4 got in touch. They watched the rough cut. They were keen. "Just have to check with the lawyers. Oh, wait." The Channel 4 lawyer was more alarmed than the BBC's: "McDonald's would almost certainly sue Channel 4, and would almost certainly win." Channel 4 dropped us like a styrofoam cup of boiling coffee, and our distributor quickly followed suit.

There were other nibbles, but nobody was prepared to take on even the debilitated remnant of McDonald's legal machine. The film had become a victim of exactly the frightened self-censorship it portrayed.

So we printed leaflets and sent out VHS tapes one by one. We courted baffled receptionists at Portuguese TV stations, entered festivals, gave indignant interviews and filmed Helen and Dave handing out the same leaflets all over again outside the High Court the day after the verdict. We booked a cinema and showed the film to a full house. The papers loved it. Free Speech TV pushed us through public services channels to 9 million American homes. A network grew by word of mouth and email list, and McLibel supporters around the world adopted us.

Then, at last, an unlikely Australian in a Hawaiian shirt and flip-flops— Gil Scrine of Gil Scrine Films—did the impossible and sold the film to a national broadcaster. SBS, the Australian equivalent of Channel 4, put us in its prime-time documentary series. Things exploded from there: the film played three times a day for six weeks in a 400-seat cinema in Sydney, and we were on the front covers of magazines and the sofas of talk shows. The film was picked up by an international distributor, Journeyman Pictures, and since then has been broadcast in four European countries. As we write, it has just been picked up by Greek television.

McDonald's hasn't sued us, or any of the broadcasters who have shown the film, or the distributor, which is based in the UK and just as vulnerable as our craven TV networks. Nor has it sued Macmillan, which published a book about the trial,[20] or McSpotlight, a website about the trial and other McDonald's-related issues (somewhat to its disappointment). Nor has it sued anyone else.

The lesson: Don't back down

With any luck, this is the final chapter of the longer story. Since the start of the McLibel trial, as far as we know, McDonald's has not issued a single writ. Nobody has been asked to withdraw criticism, apologize on the air or print a retraction. The injunction against Helen and Dave has not been taken up, and the damages have been written off.

The broader business world has taken note, and 'doing a McLibel' has entered the corporate vocabulary. All it took was a supportive press release from the McLibel Support Campaign to make retailer John Lewis drop its libel suit against a National Anti-Hunt Campaign over a leaflet about pheasant shooting.

The credit for that belongs to Helen Steel and Dave Morris—and to all those others who defied threats of legal intimidation by continuing to leaflet, write, film and code—but the lesson is for everyone the corporate world order tries to silence. The preparation and sale of products for the global consumer require secrecy, so the buyer can be told a happy story as the sweatshops and abattoirs function behind a screen of posturing and spin. We can't afford to miss any opportunity to yank that screen aside and show people what they're really buying. When a corporation puffs up its legal department and struts around, it's not indignation. It's fear.

Chapter 9

McSpying

Eveline Lubbers

As soon as the weekly London Greenpeace meeting finished, Brian Bishop headed back to his office to file a report. The private investigator was on assignment to infiltrate a tiny activist group in north London. The bureau he worked for had been hired by burger giant McDonald's. His notes of May 1990 included a detailed description of a newcomer at the meeting:

> "She was about 5 ft. 6 in. tall and aged around 19-22 years. She had full, light brown hair. She was of medium build and had a fresh complexion, devoid of makeup. She was attractive in both face and figure."

He felt there was something suspicious about this new woman. Her gray stonewashed jeans "did not appear to be at all old", and the rips in the knees looked like they'd been "administered rather than worn in place".

Bishop's suspicions were well-founded, but little could he have guessed why. He had not been told that McDonald's had in fact hired two different detective agencies to infiltrate the environmentalist group. This new woman (real name: Michelle Hooker) was one of several spies sent to London Greenpeace. But the former policewoman's investigation methods went much further than Bishop's. Posing as "Shelley", she had a six-month love affair with Charlie Brooke, one of London Greenpeace's genuine campaigners.

The McLibel case

McDonald's hired at least seven detectives to find out who was behind the London Greenpeace leaflet 'What's Wrong With McDonald's?'. After it identified and sued five London Greenpeace campaigners for libel, two went to court to defend the leaflet in what is now known as the McLibel trial. Under cross-examination, the company was forced to provide full details of its three-year cloak-and-dagger operation. The court transcripts reveal the astonishing lengths McDonald's went to in procuring information about this small activist group and provide one of the few documented examples of how companies under siege use intelligence methods to fight activist groups. Even when the 'siege' is a handful of scruffy activists handing out a few hundred leaflets in north London.

London Greenpeace had been campaigning on a variety of environmental and social justice issues since the early 1970s. (The group was formed several years before the more famous Greenpeace International, and is entirely unrelated to it.) In the mid-eighties it began a campaign against McDonald's as a high-profile organization symbolizing everything it considered wrong with the prevailing corporate mentality. In 1985 it launched the International Day of Action Against McDonald's, which has been held on October 16 ever since. And in 1986 London Greenpeace produced its magnum opus: the six-page leaflet 'What's Wrong with McDonald's?: Everything they don't want you to know', which attacked almost every aspect of the corporation's business. It accused the burger giant of seducing children through advertising, promoting an unhealthy diet, exploiting its staff and contributing to environmental damage and the mistreatment of animals.

In 1989, as the campaign was growing in strength and being taken up by other groups around the world, McDonald's produced its own "McFact cards" detailing its position on many of the accusations made in the leaflet. Then, after having ignored London Greenpeace for many years, McDonald's decided to take action.[1] It sued for libel.

If McDonald's wanted to file suit to stop the campaign, it would have to do so against named individuals. In order to find out who was responsible for the production and distribution of the leaflet, its agents infiltrated London Greenpeace for varying lengths of time between October 1989 and spring 1991. Seven company spies were identified as such, but there may have been more. Some of them even remained in the group after libel writs were served to five London Greenpeace members in September 1990. Hooker stayed until May 1991, when her relationship with Brooke cooled.

McDonald's claimed the leaflet was a pack of lies. Its libel writ offered the five campaigners a stark choice: either retract the allegations made in the leaflet and apologize, or go to court.

Faced with the prospect of fighting the mega-rich international conglomerate, and with no legal aid available for libel cases, three of the campaigners reluctantly apologized. But Helen Steel and Dave Morris—now nicknamed the McLibel Two—accepted the challenge. The McLibel trial started in June 1994 and concluded in December 1996 after a marathon 314 days in court. The Guinness Book of World Records updated its entry for the longest trial in English history.

McSpying: High in fat, low in substance

"I wanted at least two teams to work independently of one another, and unknown to one another, with a view to obtaining our objective, which was to stop the distribution of the leaflet," Sid Nicholson, McDonald's UK vice-president for security, explained to the court.[2] So he employed both Bishops Investigation Bureau (part of Westhall Services, one of the oldest security firms in Britain) and Kings Investigation Bureau. Despite such reinforcements, he failed to achieve his objective of stopping the leaflet.

The agencies asked their spies to report everything the campaigners said or did that related to McDonald's. The agents were given the impression that London Greenpeace was set up specifically to campaign against the hamburger chain. But the spies' notes prove the opposite—they are scattered with remarks such as "Nothing else of relevance was discussed" and "No mention was made of Client company, either in the meeting or afterwards in the pub. Nor was any mention made of any other subject relevant to this case."

The spies' notes feature such comments from beginning to end. And where McDonald's was discussed, it was usually in the context of letters referring to the company written by members of the public, rather than the planning of activities other than the annual International Day of Action Against McDonald's. The group had even stopped reprinting the leaflet.

Although nothing of real relevance was ever found, McDonald's continued to send new spies into the group. Until at least six months after the libel writs were served, agents kept going to the meetings and reporting on London Greenpeace's reactions.

Watching me watching you

During the crucial period, attendance at London Greenpeace meetings averaged fewer than ten. With at least seven spies infiltrating the group, it is more than feasible that some meetings were made up of as many spies as campaigners. In fact, one investigator's notes showed that at one meeting in 1990, the four people who attended included one spy from each bureau and two campaigners. And since McDonald's hadn't told the agencies about each other, the spies were busily spying on each other. The court heard, for instance, how one spy had noted the behaviour of another as "suspicious". Apart from the tension this may have caused, the quorum of spies could easily have made decisions or changed the focus of the meeting back to McDonald's—if only to please their employers or fight their own boredom.

Confronted in court with these facts, Sid Nicholson stubbornly denied that the number of agents monitoring the group and attending meetings had affected the organization. But with the number of spies equal to the number of campaigners, how could it not have?

The Hamburglars

The spies acted like true detectives: tailing, breaking, entering and stealing were all part of their repertoire. For example, Roy Pocklington revealed how he sometimes arranged to leave meetings talking to certain individuals so other members of his bureau could follow them home. One night, he asked Dave Morris for his home address, saying he wanted to drop off a parcel of baby clothes for Morris's newborn son.

After his first meeting Brian Bishop wrote a report containing a curiously detailed description of London Greenpeace's offices. He noted that one window "had no security locks on the frame and opened out to the outside", adding that the office next door was occupied 24 hours a day. Questioned as to the relevance of such information, Bishop denied it was intended to advise anyone who might wish to break into the office.

Allan Clare admitted gaining entry to the group's office accompanied by a manager from his firm. He denied it was a break-in, despite admitting he had used a phone card to jimmy the lock. He told the court "the door lock on the office to London Greenpeace was basically not very strong and it was decided by me and my principals that entry to it would not be a problem." He took a number of photographs, which were later used during the trial. Elsewhere in his report, Clare wrote: "Went through the letters. Good letter re: McDs. Managed to obtain it/borrow it."

Sid Nicholson claimed he had not approved the theft of letters. He insisted he had instructed the agencies to do "nothing illegal and nothing improper" but failed to be specific. He claimed to be concerned about the reliability of people employed on his behalf but added, "People do make mistakes." He said he had never taken any action to ensure the return of the letters.

It is feasible that the agents worked with the consent of their supervisors, as Allan Clare testified in court. And McDonald's didn't seem to worry about staying within the rules. Neither the detective agencies nor the company expressed much problem with the use of unlawfully collected evidence.

One can only guess why an agent would come back with a detailed description of the office. Breaking into the premises could, for example, enable the planting of evidence, bugs or cameras. London Greenpeace cannot even now be completely sure that its office is not bugged. And no one will ever know what other plans McDonald's may have had when it first called in the detectives.

Partners in crime

Four of the agents were called to give evidence for McDonald's and questioned in detail about their involvement in the group.[3] All of them stated in one way or other that they believed it would be beneficial to appear willing and help out where they could. Subsequently they all ended up distributing the challenged leaflet.

The first witness, Brian Bishop, had attended more then 12 meetings in less than five months through 1990. He admitted to having staffed a booth where the anti-McDonald's leaflet was available to the public, some of the time on his own, at a well-attended public event. The second spy, Allan Clare, had attended at least 19 meetings and volunteered to help answer letters. The third, Roy Pocklington, had also answered letters. He told the court that on one occasion he had spent eight hours in the Greenpeace office writing replies, many of which were sent out accompanied by the leaflet at the centre of the trial. He felt he had to participate in this as "it would have looked rather odd if I had refused." But he denied having been involved in distributing the leaflet. Pocklington attended at least 26 London Greenpeace meetings and events between October 1989 and June 1990. And Michelle Hooker (who was not called as a witness) had been caught on video distributing anti-McDonald's leaflets in the street.

The McLibel Two formally argued that all this amounted to McDonald's "consenting" to the publication of the leaflet. The corporation was suing Steel and Morris for distributing the leaflet, yet its own private investigators admitted doing just that. So the McLibel Two applied to include three of the spies in the action as "third parties", effectively making them co-defendants and thus liable to contribute to any damages awarded. The judge ruled that the appropriate time for such action would be after he issued his verdict. Since after the trial McDonald's abandoned all legal action, including pursuit of damages, the McLibel Two decided to take no further steps.

Defecting to the other side

McDonald's refused to disclose the identity of any private investigators beyond the four it had called as witnesses (Bishop, Clare, Pocklington and Russell). With good reason, for the more spies it called, the more it portrayed itself as a heavy-handed multinational. It was also not keen on having the spies' notes disclosed to the defendants and hence the court and the public. Even those notes that were disclosed, after repeated requests by the defendants, often had pages missing or sections blacked out. Unsurprisingly, McDonald's decided not to call Michelle Hooker to give evidence. It didn't want to give the defendants the opportunity to cross-examine her on her relationship with Charlie Brooke or the video evidence of her distributing the leaflet.

It also decided not to call another of its spies, Frances Tiller. Back in the 1980s, Tiller had been a secretary at the Kings Investigation Bureau. When the McDonald's job came up, the small firm was experiencing a shortage of investigators and called Tiller to active duty. Years later, while studying nutritional medicine in college, she became interested in environmental issues and the arguments against fast food. In the pub one night after class, she told a student friend about the secretive job from her past. The friend happened to be the sister of Franny Armstrong, who was directing the documentary *McLibel: Two Worlds Collide.*

Tiller agreed to appear in the documentary. She also took to the witness box to give evidence for Steel and Morris, which must have come as a nasty shock to the McDonald's crew.

"I came away after every meeting with a chronic headache," Tiller said in an interview recorded for the documentary. "I was concentrating so much trying to remember everything that was said, by whom, and how many shelves were behind me and what leaflets they had on the shelves. At the same time you're trying to be very natural, talk to people and not blow your cover. It was very trying."[4] Afterwards she would immediately make out her reports for the agency.

Tiller found the activists to be friendly, ordinary people. "I'd been told they were all vegans and at the time I didn't know what veganism entailed. I expected them all to be bloodless creatures—no personality," she said, laughing. In fact, she got along well with them and occasionally went to the pub with them after meetings. The agency warned her that they could be dangerous: "If I'd given them my telephone number or address and they found out who I was, [the agency said] I could have been under some threat. But in the end I found out that that wasn't at all the case." If anyone was out to intimidate Tiller, it wasn't the activists. A few weeks before she was due to give evidence in court, the agency she used to work for started following her around. A man who turned out to be Jack Russell, one of the four spies who gave evidence for McDonald's, called at her door while she was at work. Tiller said, "He asked my husband what time my train came in, what time I left work, what time I went to work—questions like that. Which was very unnerving. We were both quite worried about what the consequences might be—what he had in his mind to do." Tiller was given to understand that the agency did not like her appearing for the defendants instead of for McDonald's.

"I sort of dressed down"

London Greenpeace has never paid much attention to security or screening. The group has no formal membership; people get involved by coming to meetings and participating in events. This open way of working has made people from various backgrounds feel welcome. Several of the spies noted they had never felt really accepted because of their looks or age, but these things seemed to matter little to the group.

Frances Tiller explained her and Michelle Hooker's different approaches to presumed dress codes. The two would drive to the London Greenpeace office in Hooker's black BMW, parking a few streets away. "I sort of dressed down, wearing sandals and hippie-type clothes," Tiller said, "but she came along with quite flashy jewellery and long, tapered, painted fingernails and makeup. I thought that people would have suspected that she wasn't one of them, but in fact she got involved quite deeply afterwards."

Despite long-held suspicions, it was only during the preparations for the court hearings that London Greenpeace finally had its worst fears confirmed. "If you become too suspicious of new faces you can end up deterring people from joining and participating," said Helen Steel, who was concerned that an air of distrust was building up in the group. "We have tried to be aware of this, as McDonald's, other companies and the state would be very happy if groups become less active and effective because we all distrusted each other."[5]

"As the group was only involved in legal activities such as leafleting, picketing and demonstrations, we had no real reason to suspect that it might be infiltrated," says Helen Steel. But every now and then, someone would get the feeling that something was wrong. The high percentage of agents spying on each other undoubtedly influenced the atmosphere. Brian Bishop, for instance, had his doubts when he first met 'Shelley' (Michelle Hooker). "I reported on her as being a member of the group that I was a bit suspicious about. She was a bit too keen," he stated in court. Luckily for 'Shelley', her affair with Charlie Brooke allayed further doubts.

Suspicions were discussed outside the meetings. The campaigners even followed some of the suspected agents after a meeting, but discovered nothing that proved they were spies. "As we didn't have anything that solid to go on, there was not much that could be done," says Steel. "That is partly because we only thought about the risk of being infiltrated by the police or intelligence services. We never considered that they might be working for a company rather than the state."

Secret alliances

Sid Nicholson, McDonald's head of both security and personnel, told the court he would have the environmentalists behind 'What's Wrong With McDonald's?' identified "through whatever sources" he could. Private eyes were just one of those sources. The company also paid for the services of an extremely dubious information broker, made cloak-and-dagger arrangements with former colleagues on the police force and illegally exchanged information with intelligence sources.

The London Greenpeace leaflet came to Nicholson's attention in 1987 when it was sent to him by The Economic League, an organization which he described as aiming "to defend the interests of multinationals". In fact this group was generally regarded as extreme right-wing and obscure. The *Observer* newspaper called it "a secretive organization renowned for its blacklist of people it considers subversive." [6] The Economic League kept files on more than 22,000 people, then made them available to subscribers for vetting prospective employees. It disbanded in 1994 after complaints that some of its information was inaccurate. Under the recent British data law it would have had to open its files. [7]

According to Nicholson, The Economic League also "may very well" have sent McDonald's reports of employee involvement in union activities. In order to prove McDonald's was indeed exploiting its staff, the McLibel Two questioned him about employment conditions. His answers revealed intimidation and control to be basic assets in his department. Nicholson was responsible for both security and personnel, a combination of duties that apparently came in handy when he was dealing with union activities on the shop floor. Nicholson agreed that staff were not "allowed to carry out any overt union activity on McDonald's premises". He told the court that management would inform him when employees expressed interest in union representation. On several occasions, he visited stores accompanied by other management or security officials "to explain our point of view to" the crew. He denied people could have felt intimidated by his or his companions' presence, and said "nothing further happened" after the meetings.

Terry Carroll, the non-executive security chief whose job it was to deal with the environmentalist threat on a day-to-day basis, regularly sent instructions out to all McDonald's UK stores on how to handle a picket line. These instructions included taking photographs of protesters and sending them to him along with copies of any leaflets obtained. (He told the court "literally hundreds" of leaflets came in and his files became "unwieldy".) The purpose of gathering photographs was to identify a "hard core" of people carrying out protests around the country. But the company discovered instead that protesters were generally local people picketing their neighbourhood branch.

I scratch your back . . .

"All the [members of the] security department have many, many contacts in the police service; they are all ex-policemen," Nicholson told the court. If he wanted information about, for example, a protester, he would ask the local police officer on duty or "officers I used to work with, certainly". Prior to working for McDonald's, Nicholson spent 31 years on the police force, first in South Africa and then in London. He reached the rank of chief superintendent in charge of Brixton police station, a multiracial neighbourhood in the British capital. Terry Carroll, his second in command at McDonald's since 1984, had served under Nicholson in Brixton before becoming a chief superintendent himself elsewhere in London.

Nicholson also had "quite a lot of experience with the Special Branch", the intelligence department of London's Metropolitan Police. The court heard that Nicholson had been meeting Special Branch officers to discuss animal rights activities since 1984 in his role as McDonald's security chief. Specific details on the nature of and reason for the relationship were not made clear.

In 1987 the Special Branch founded the Animal Rights National Index (ARNI) to "monitor criminal activities of animal rights extremists and supply intelligence information to forces across the UK", according to a spokesperson. The first contact between the Special Branch and McDonald's relating to London Greenpeace took place in September 1989, when ARNI officers alerted Nicholson to an upcoming demonstration outside McDonald's headquarters. They asked for an observation post in the building from which to watch the protesters and take photographs. Nicholson was glad to help. In return, one of the Special Branch officers stood with him during the demonstration and freely passed on information about certain protesters. At least two of those identified subsequently received libel writs from the burger chain.

Nicholson said he had not wanted anyone at McDonald's to know he was talking to ARNI. He even kept his immediate junior Terry Carroll out of the infiltration operation for more than a year. He also said there was no formal working relationship between his department and Special Branch because it would have been impossible for McDonald's to use any information obtained that way. "They are an information-gathering organization who are involved in a lot of undercover working," he told the court. "Special Branch officers are extremely reluctant to disclose their identity, and dislike intensely having to attend court."

He forgot to mention that such collusion is also illegal. The police are not at liberty to disclose information from their files to anyone not involved in a criminal investigation.

Nicholson said the 1989 collaboration was his only contact with the Special Branch on London Greenpeace, but evidence suggested the liaison had continued. A memo signed by Terry Carroll and dated 22 September 1994 was read out in court. "I had a meeting with ARNI from Scotland Yard today who gave me the enclosed literature," it read. "Some of it we have, other bits are new." With the McLibel trial well under way, it seemed the company was still in close touch with ARNI.

Exchanging intelligence

After the verdict, the McLibel Two started proceedings against the London Metropolitan Police to expose the "political role of the police, the collusion between the police and a multinational corporation."[8] In September 1998 they claimed damages for malfeasance in public office, breach of confidence and breach of their right to privacy. This seemed the best course of legal action against the police for disclosing confidential, private and in some cases false information to McDonald's and its private investigators (PIs).

McDonald's admitted in the witness box that Special Branch officers had disclosed the names of several protesters to its security department. But Helen Steel says she had proof of more illegal information exchange. "The notebook of the spy Allan Clare revealed that on a separate occasion in June 1990 he had a secret meeting with police officers who told him where me and Dave lived, and also gave him other confidential information, some of it misleading and incorrect," she recalled.

Information collected by the private spies likewise found its way to the police and the Special Branch and, according to Steel, likely also to the Economic League or similar organizations. "The notes of Allan Clare show that he gave the police information about Poll Tax protests. He identified London Greenpeace activists in photographs that the police had taken at the huge anti-Poll Tax demonstration in 1990," she says.[9]

In July 2000, almost two years after the start of the proceedings, the police made clear they preferred to make the best of a bad job. In order to avoid what they called "a difficult and lengthy trial", they agreed to pay the McLibel Two £10,000 (more than $14,000) plus legal costs. The extraordinary out-of-court settlement also required the London police commissioner to remind all officers of their responsibility not to disclose information. Detective Sergeant Valentine even apologized for distress caused by the disclosure of claimants' personal details to the PIs.[10]

Further questions

One can only wonder why ARNI set its sights on London Greenpeace, as the former's official area of concern is "criminal activities of animal rights extremists". The simple answer would be that ARNI monitors all sorts of political activity, even when there is no hint of illegality. The revelations in the McLibel trial confirm this.

But there may be more to it than that. When Nicholson was cross-examined about his contacts with the Special Branch, he told the court they had initially exchanged information on animal rights issues, "of much more concern to me at that time". Unfortunately, nobody in the courtroom asked him to elaborate any further on this. If one takes into account this mutual worry about animal rights activists, it seems likely that ARNI would have considered how McDonald's infiltration of London Greenpeace might be useful for its own purposes. It may have used McDonald's private eyes as a stepping-stone to get introductions to people the Special Branch wanted to know better. And Michelle Hooker may even have been on a special assignment to become personally involved with Charlie Brooke in order to get to the alleged hardcore activists.

Through her relationship with Brooke, Hooker met a lot of other activists who were interesting to both McDonald's and Special Branch. Brooke worked with London Greenpeace part-time, and was more involved with Hackney and Islington Animal Rights, which also picketed McDonald's frequently. Hooker got heavily involved herself, joining pickets and handing out leaflets. One of the Hackney and Islington members was Paul Gravett, a vegan anarchist thought to be a linchpin in both the animal rights group and London Greenpeace's anti-McDonald's campaign. Another Hackney and Islington member, Geoffrey Shepherd, had been convicted for setting off sprinkler systems and destroying fur stocks at three Debenhams department stores in the mid-eighties. In the autumn of 1990, Hooker reportedly hosted dinner parties for both of them at Brooke's north London flat.[11]

Such an exercise of joint forces could have been coincidental, with McDonald's infiltrating London Greenpeace solely to sue it for the leaflet, and the Special Branch taking advantage of the opportunity while it was there. Or ARNI could have become more interested as the infiltration went along, and gradually come to steer the investigation from behind the scenes.

But if one speculates on a worst-case scenario, or just looks at things from a different angle, it seems plausible that the entire infiltration project could even have been an initiative of the Special Branch. In that case, London Greenpeace would have been used just as a means of access to other activists and people involved in animal rights. It wouldn't be the first time a police intelligence squad used a private company to do its dirty work.

Until we know the full extent of the infiltration of London Greenpeace—how many people were involved and who they were really working for—it is hard to draw definite conclusions. These speculations may seem far-fetched, but wouldn't the entire McSpy story be hard to believe if it weren't for all the evidence?

Of course, without the tireless efforts by the McLibel Two and their support group to uncover this intelligence operation, McDonald's information-gathering methods would never have been an issue at the trial. The cross-examination of the spies was entirely focused on their snooping on London Greenpeace and necessarily dealt with only the identified spies. Much information remained closed, because it was classified as privileged: documents were censored and questions refused. The hypotheses raised here were beyond the scope of the trial, which is a shame, because now we may never know what the bigger plan behind the infiltration was, if indeed there was one.

Epilogue

The McLibel trial is now generally seen as a major public relations disaster. In the courtroom the defendants found a new stage on which to criticize McDonald's in a more detailed way than they ever could have dreamed of. In the course of their attempt to prove the leaflet was not libellous,[12] they used the endless hearings to defend every single line of it, cross-examining scientists and top McDonald's officials. Eventually, even some expert witnesses called by the hamburger giant had to admit a number of the leaflet's statements were true.

The damage had been done. The launch of the McSpotlight website compounded the damage by making the London trial the virtual centre of a campaign against McDonald's worldwide (see Chapter 19, 'Net.activism').

McDonald's legal action backfired completely. The fact that Justice Bell's verdict was fiendishly complex—neither side could claim complete victory, although both did—was of no importance in the end. McDonald's won the court case, but the McLibel Two won in every other possible way.[13]

Thanks to Franny Armstrong, Dave Morris and Helen Steel for help with this chapter.

Chapter 10

Garbology: Activist Trash as Corporate Treasure

Eveline Lubbers

Going through your opponent's garbage to collect information—in detective slang, 'garbology'—is a particularly dirty kind of research. A Dutch information broker developed a new cover for the collection of waste-paper: its collector said he wanted it so he could sell it to recyclers to raise money for charity.

Activists, advocacy groups and NGOs in the Netherlands knew their trashed paperwork was being gathered, but not what it was being 'recycled' into: intelligence files for companies which those groups were boycotting. Little did they realize back then how interesting their paperwork could be— to the companies they campaigned against, the tabloids, and occasionally even the police, public prosecutor or secret service.

A company called ABC (the abbreviation for General Security Consultancy in Dutch) sent the spy, Paul Oosterbeek, to infiltrate a number of activist groups, posing as a volunteer who wanted to help them automate their data. Oosterbeek volunteered to do archival work and set up computer databases. He installed software and entered the contact addresses of new subscribers and possible sponsors. (Years after he was exposed, one group found its contact database software was registered to ABC.) To save time, he asked if he could take the groups' Rolodexes with him and finish the copying elsewhere. Meanwhile, he took advantage of his position to collect the groups' discarded paperwork, saying he wanted to sell it to recyclers for charity.

Buro Jansen & Janssen, an activist office for independent intelligence research, unmasked Oosterbeek in summer 1994. Earlier that year, some organizations he was working for had come to us, having become sufficiently suspicious about him that they wanted to take action. Oosterbeek had no activist background, and he was secretive about his address, phone number, motivation and interests—and every time people started asking questions, he disappeared for a while. We hadn't trusted him, either, when we'd encountered him at meetings years ago. So we launched an investigation.

We uncovered the waste-paper scheme in the course of exposing Oosterbeek as a spy. For more than eight years, we found out, he had been collecting paper from at least 30 organizations, from small radical activist groups to big church-affiliated research foundations, claiming he was selling it to recyclers to benefit a school in Amsterdam or an educational project in Zimbabwe. In fact, he was delivering the boxes of faxed originals, rejected photocopies and printouts to the offices of ABC.

Here, behind a high wall and a sharp-pronged iron fence and under the guard of security cameras, the loot was processed. Every sheet was carefully scrutinized for bits and pieces of information, from financial facts and figures to the ins and outs of internal strategy discussions. The special interests of groups' individual members were filtered out, as were interorganizational connections and personnel overlap. ABC thus fattened its numerous files on activists and NGOs, fleshing them out with information available from public sources. The office must have been flooded with subscriptions to every possible leftist magazine, human rights newsletter and special interest publication. ABC also collected annual reports and financial records of campaigning groups and thoroughly studied Chamber of Commerce records to check who was on their boards, make connections between them and see who funded them and for how much.

This chapter will look at what companies under fire can do with the information they buy from brokers, analyze how the spy in the Dutch case was able to hang around for so long, and discuss how groups might prevent such infiltration in the future.

Waste-paper service

With more and more companies selling brands rather than products these days, a company's image is increasingly vulnerable. Ethical entrepreneurship has become the way to present your company as being up-to-date.

Now that a company's reputation is its most valued asset, every company needs information on its market position. Business intelligence is no longer restricted to details about the world economy, faraway wars and news about the competition. It now includes assessment of the risks of becoming a target for campaigners, boycotters or net-activists. Publicly available information is no longer sufficient. Informal data, however obtained, can be worth its weight in gold. Desirable information is not limited to concrete action scenarios, but can be as broad (and vague) as discussions about long-term strategy, impressions of the atmosphere within a group, links between organizations, possibilities for networking, details of funding—the list is endless.

In this context, ABC's waste-paper service would seem to have been a logical activity of today's information brokerage business, albeit a niche one because of its cloak-and-dagger methods. The growth of the anti-globalization movement has resulted in renewed confrontations between activists and large corporations, and this phenomenon is bound to spread, creating new markets for information brokers like ABC and its successors.

Using inside information

Inside information gives companies a strategic advantage. Used at the right moment, it can be an effective weapon. It's no fun for critics to be confronted with an information leak during delicate talks with an adversary.

Wemos, a Dutch group that provides information on pharmaceutical companies and the aggressive marketing of infant formula products in developing countries, got a nasty shock when it found out a company had got hold of its internal documents. As Wemos tried in 1994 to convince the baby formula industry that it was not targeting specific companies, the company Nutricia (Numico) took the wind out of its sails by triumphantly producing a copy of a letter Wemos had sent to its partners in the Nestlé boycott campaign, which, in the industry's eyes, proved otherwise.

A year before, the industry had also got its hands on a request from baby formula campaigners for European Commission funding of a joint project. The English partner had faxed a draft to Wemos, a German group and the EC. Those were the only existing copies. None of the groups had anything to gain by leaking the information, and the EC insisted the proposal had not left its offices. But within six weeks of being faxed, the document was in the hands of the industry.

Wemos spent a lot of time trying to locate the leak. They wondered whether their fax machine might be tapped. But they didn't think of the garbage. Every incoming fax message was photocopied and the thermal original thrown away.

Incidents like these can greatly shake a group's confidence. The seed of suspicion is sown and can lead to serious accusations and doubts about co-workers' trustworthiness.

Companies don't always let on explicitly or immediately that they have inside information on their critics. Using it to anticipate future actions can be advantageous enough, since it takes away the element of surprise that campaigns against companies often rely on (stumbling spokespeople provide perfect soundbites). Using smooth, rapid, prepared responses in campaigner-like language, companies can confuse the public about whom they should believe. Of course, this kind of response can sometimes be more than a PR gesture, in which case it signifies a victory on the part of the campaigners. But often, slick answers are just manoeuvres used to avoid real change.

In 1990, the Clean Clothes Campaign (CCC) initiated a protest action against the clothing store chain C&A, in which customers were encouraged to ask at the checkout counter where their clothes had been manufactured. No sooner had the campaign begun than C&A came out with printed answer sheets. The company dealt with all questions promptly.

Until then, C&A had been known as a closed, family-run company that had no truck with prying outsiders. It didn't even publish annual reports. Its sudden flexible and open response to the Clean Clothes Campaign's actions was remarkable. With hindsight we can see that Paul Oosterbeek, then working for the CCC, was involved in preparing the action.

Just as the activists published their action leaflet, C&A put out a brochure responding to its arguments in depth. Under the slogan "C&A has nothing to hide", the brochure portrayed a company that was "vehemently opposed to degrading working conditions in the clothing industry anywhere in the world" and had been taking action against them for years. The brochure never directly mentioned the Clean Clothes Campaign, but its final sentence made clear to whom it was addressed: "An activist group might need a symbol to draw attention to its cause. But don't bark up the wrong tree and suggest that our customers are supporting exploitation: C&A wishes to sell only 'clean' clothes."

Less specific information, if interpreted correctly, can also be of interest. Non-confidential documents can reveal plenty about a group's activities when combined with other data, such as that found in annual reports and at the Chamber of Commerce. Stolen files can give insight into an organization's goals and its chances of success, information about its financial position, the size of its following or the strength of its alliances.

Some companies, it seemed, did nothing with the files ABC had sold them. Not all the groups Oosterbeek visited noticed their information had fallen into the wrong hands. Still, they were interesting enough to ABC's clients for the waste-paper man to pay them regular visits.

Media fallout

In Europe, the tabloid media have traditionally contributed to activist-bashing by publishing full-page mud-slinging articles. In the Netherlands, the main such paper is the daily *De Telegraaf.* The paper typically tries to discredit mainstream NGOs like Friends of the Earth or church-affiliated groups that support refugees or asylum-seekers by associating their activities with more radical groups or events.

Just before Milieudefensie (Friends of the Earth in the Netherlands) planned to launch balloons near Schiphol Airport in October 1996 in protest about the airport's expansion plans, *De Telegraaf* targeted the organization's campaign leader in two articles ('Secret service fears terrorist action at Schiphol' and 'Wijnand Duyvendak: a life of resistance'). Highlights of Wijnand Duyvendak's activist past were presented as facts that discredited him. On top of that, the paper claimed he had once been number four on a list of activist arson suspects. Ancient mugshots were provided as 'proof'.

In the midst of an interview about his group's actions, Duyvendak recalls, the *Telegraaf* journalist suddenly produced a stack of paperwork. "It was as if I was being questioned by the police," Duyvendak said. "He had a lot more information than he ended up using in his article. He had all sorts of internal documents, although they kind of jumped around in time. He was obviously trying to rattle me." In hindsight, Duyvendak believes ABC was the likely source of this information. "The only thing linking the documents he produced was the waste-paper affair."

Even after ABC was exposed, *De Telegraaf* published articles based on confidential material that could be traced back to the waste-paper affair. The newspaper suggestively presented facts and selectively quoted internal documents to suggest conspiracy by association. Waste-paper-based articles like these can do far more than damage an organization's image, as is illustrated by what happened to the left journalists' collective Opstand ('Revolt').

For 18 months, Opstand journalists Hans Krikke and Jan Müter were the victims of a miscarriage of justice. The prosecutor accused them of "intellectual involvement" in two bombings protesting about the Dutch government's asylum policy in the early 1990s. In September 1994, their homes and office were searched at dawn. Six months later, Krikke and Müter were arrested.

Police files given to the defendants' lawyers revealed that the major source of 'evidence' had been a full-page 1993 article in *De Telegraaf*. The story, written by the usual journalists and illustrated with a complicated diagram, suggested there was a direct link between 1970s armed resistance groups and 1990s radical activists. A number of organizations, the paper alleged, were forming an "underground network" based on solidarity with illegal refugees. In light of the bombings, the Secret Service was identifying the network as potentially terrorist, said the *Telegraaf*. Every group mentioned in the article could be found on Paul Oosterbeek's waste-paper collection list.

The article was filled in with thorough research at the Chamber of Commerce—another ABC speciality—and some laboriously gathered quotes. Opstand journalist Hans Krikke was one of the few people who spoke to the paper, and he would come to regret it later. His words came back to haunt him in the police file, albeit rather creatively quoted. The newspaper, the police happily state, quotes Krikke as saying he "doesn't rule out the practice of bomb attacks." The police conveniently left out the rest of the quotation—"in times of severe oppression, like World War II," which qualifies the statement somewhat.

In this case, the information was recycled twice, first by ABC and then by *De Telegraaf,* before going on to be used as evidence in a police investigation.

In the end, the case was dismissed, and together Krikke and Müter received almost $100,000 in compensation. But it was too late for Opstand. The collective had broken up as a result of the investigation, searches and arrests. Normal reporting and research operations became impossible, and then the incrimination began to take its toll and clients walked out.

The end of the story?

In summer 1994, Jansen & Janssen was forced to back off its investigation of the waste-paper affair slightly earlier than planned. After many weeks of us asking various groups about any leaks or suspicions, too many people had heard about it, and not all of them understood the need for discretion. Meanwhile, Paul Oosterbeek had got wind that we were on to him. A few days before a magazine broke the story, he told people in a few organizations he thought something was up. He never turned up at an appointment we had made at which we planned to confront him with our findings.

We had a lot of material incriminating Oosterbeek, Siebelt and ABC, and we wanted to take legal action. But although the evidence we had was more than circumstantial, it comprised a picture only when looked at together, like a reconstruction. Even when a group was confronted by a corporate representative about an internal document, as we weren't able to visit ABC's premises we couldn't get conclusive proof that it had got there via the waste-paper route.

Ever worse, there was no law against collecting waste-paper, even under false pretences, nor against the kind of espionage we could prove had occurred. Several of the groups involved sued the company and the infiltrator for 'fraudulent conspiracy', which was unfortunately the only possible legal action under Dutch criminal law. ABC Director Peter Siebelt and Oosterbeek were detained overnight and questioned, but the prosecutor decided not to indict in the absence of "legal and convincing evidence".

Oosterbeek has since vanished from the face of the earth. ABC all but shut down after we exposed them, but Siebelt now markets himself as a monitor of national and international activist groups. His speciality is still exposing networks between leftist organizations, albeit necessarily on the basis of increasingly outdated files.

The ABC material remains potentially dangerous even today, since it contains personal information about activists who need to be anonymous to do their work. The Fascism Research Collective (FOK), for instance, traces the activities of far-right splinter groups in the Netherlands. When a right-wing group accused the FOK of slander in 1998, ABC provided the plaintiffs' lawyers with the names and addresses of people whom its waste-paper said were members of the FOK. Fortunately, the material was never used in court, but being identified as an anti-fascist researcher in extreme-right magazines, as subsequently happened to those people, can have consequences too.

Lessons to be learned

The big question is how the waste-paper-gathering process was kept going for so long. Paul Oosterbeek kept his real identity a secret for almost eight years. Nobody knew his background or where he lived. This led to mistrust, but no real investigation; no group bothered to thoroughly check his credentials.

This had everything to do with his demeanour. He was elusive, missed appointments and generally didn't act like a 'typical' infiltrator. He never tried to gain access to 'core people' or any real secrets. He hardly ever went to meetings, never read the minutes and ignored incoming mail, which as a volunteer he would have seen. He was clearly investing in a long-term relationship, rather than collecting maximum information but risking attracting attention.

His computer expertise—still rare in the early 1990s—was useful. The groups welcomed him and it was easy for him to get in. So he continued to add more and more groups to his list in his quest for information via waste-paper.

Oosterbeek's understanding of the left's loose organizational structures paved his way. He worked for a great variety of groups. In radical circles he posed as a 'softie' working for a mainstream NGO. In more moderate ones, he hinted secretively at his 'heavier' contacts. Sometimes he made use of his connections, but often getting into a new group was as easy for him as answering an ad for volunteers. He exploited the fact that mentioning the name of a mutual acquaintance is the preferred access code in some circles.

As the piles of waste-paper began to mount, he almost blew his cover. He began turning up irregularly, failing to keep to the paper-collecting schedule on a leaflet he had handed out, and was unreachable at the numbers on it. And his odd preference for 'recycling' unsorted paperwork should have been a tipoff. He left behind boxes of outdated brochures printed on valuable paper—his car was too small, he said. We didn't understand until too late why he had persistently turned down the offer of a van: ABC wasn't interested in multiple copies. All these things should have given rise to suspicion, but they didn't—at least, not enough.

When the Clean Clothes Campaign and two other organizations did unite in an effort to investigate, in the early days of the C&A campaign, the waste-paper scheme nearly fell apart. They called the school named on Oosterbeek's leaflet and learned the paper was being stored at the premises of Siebelt Security (Siebelt's firm—he was founding ABC about that time) and no longer brought to the school. When the CCC confronted Oosterbeek about this, he changed his story three times. They tried to find out more about Siebelt Security, but since its phone number was not publicly registered, and nobody associated security companies with corporate public image management back then, the inquiry ended there, and ABC remained out of view.

It was only a few years later that it became apparent that a number of groups had felt uncomfortable about Oosterbeek. As they shared experiences, new light was shed on the various stories he had told. For instance, he had alluded several times to a family feud with some multinational company to explain his need to be discreet about his work, but nobody ever got the entire story. And he had sometimes pretended to be especially interested in a certain corporation or family business—which one varied depending on which organization he was working with (these companies were probably ABC clients).

Preventing future leaks

Openly bringing charges against an infiltrator poses an unwanted risk for a contemporary interest group: public association with espionage and other sinister goings-on is bad for a group's image. Most of the organizations Oosterbeek and ABC spied on remained reluctant to act even after the operation was exposed. Of more than 30 groups, only seven were willing to co-sign a complaint to the police against the information broker.

The others had been hurt by information leaks, and now they were understandably uncomfortable with the story being made public. Many of them depended on insider sources in their research, and they didn't want to be known as 'leaky'. They also wished to remain on speaking terms with the companies involved (even the ones that had them spied on). Many didn't want a public fuss to interfere with ongoing research or a pending grant proposal. But it is important that NGOs don't start valuing their relationships with business and government more than those with their radical counterparts. If groups allow their enemies to play them off against each other, uniting to expose corporate strategies will be difficult.

As activist groups institutionalize, they find it difficult to directly confront those who hire others to spy on them. Today's groups don't want to have anything to hide. Secrecy and suspicion belong to a radical past of which contemporary NGOs don't like to be reminded. Groups drifting towards a liberal 'insider' organizing model make security a low priority. It's much easier to attract volunteers if you display an open attitude, and you have to appear businesslike in order to be taken seriously.

In this context, some activists dismiss as paranoid the desire to deal cautiously with information and with new recruits. And the risk of information leaks is being underestimated, as we've seen in this chapter.

A few security measures, however, can do no harm. Screening new staff may not always be possible for practical reasons, but treating applications seriously and checking backgrounds and references are. Being careful with papers, locking filing cabinets, emptying desktops at the end of the day, and changing passwords regularly can all hinder covert information-gatherers.

Of course, we needn't be secretive about everything. But creating some kind of security awareness is essential. Just try to think like the company or institution you are campaigning against. What information would it be interested in? Not just papers and computer files but also conversations, meetings and emails can be significant. Information that might seem meaningless and general could become strategic later.

As companies do everything possible to protect their vulnerable reputations, their craving for informal information will only intensify.

Chapter 11

Private Spooks: Wackenhut vs. Whistleblowers

Sheila O'Donnell

Contrary to the saying "Any publicity is good publicity", corporations are always on guard for the negative kind. After the oil tanker Exxon Valdez ran aground in Alaska in early 1989 carrying a full tank of crude oil, not only were there negative comments, but the international press corps hurried to the once-pristine shores of Prince William Sound to photograph the disaster. The ship had spilled eleven million gallons of crude oil 25 miles offshore; the environmental damage and loss of sea life, and the attendant economic downturn, were devastating.

There were multiple investigations, the captain was accused of having been drunk on the job, and in 1990 the Alaska State Oil Spill Commission concluded that the spill was the result of "privatization, self-regulation and neglect. . . . The disaster could have been prevented by simple adherence to the original rules. . . . Concern for profits . . . obliterated concern for safe operations."[1]

Exxon executives were horrified at the bad press. Working with their public relations gurus, they put forth an affirmative defence as sea birds lay dying in the slick black oil spreading along the pristine coastline. Exxon's corporate press went to work on a huge and expensive media campaign as experts were flown in from around the world to clean up the spill.

The difficulty of cleaning up the spill created bad feelings in the local community, which was directly affected by the loss of fishing and hunting grounds and the huge toll on its subsistence economy. Whistleblowers and others criticized the way the corporation had handled the situation. People around the world cut up Exxon credit cards, and the company's name became synonymous with disaster, even as its experts supervised the washing of beaches and birds.

Former Army intelligence officer, Alaska senator's aide and independent oil broker Charles Hamel became a conduit for the whistleblowers. He also became one of the chief critics of Alyeska, the company that operates the

Trans-Alaska Pipeline System for a consortium of oil companies including BP, ExxonMobil and Phillips. The pipeline system funnels oil from the North Slope fields to the Valdez Marine Terminal, where ships like the Exxon Valdez pick it up for distribution.

Hamel claims he lost his business as a result of contaminated oil supplied by Alyeska. Since he gathered data about the pipeline company's environmental, health and safety violations, he was considered a significant threat. In the post-Valdez atmosphere, Exxon and Alyeska executives greeted his complaints with alarm. The last thing they needed was more bad press.

When Hamel began collecting health and safety complaints from Alyeska employees and submitting them to the House of Representatives' Committee on Interior and Insular Affairs and various regulatory agencies, the corporate leaders were concerned about exposure, so they hatched a nasty plan. Instead of cleaning up their act, they decided to target the whistleblowers and the committee chairman, Rep. George Miller. They hired the Wackenhut Corporation to help stem the flow of information from whistleblowers to the congressional committee. They also sought a way to bring charges against Miller. The committee, whose mandate is the protection of US natural resources, launched hearings in November 1991 into the Alyeska Pipeline Service Company and its owner companies' handling of the Exxon Valdez disaster and Wackenhut's questionable practices.

In July 1991, Hamel complained to the committee that he had been the target of an undercover sting operation conducted by Wackenhut on behalf of the pipeline company. Remarkably, he had documented a massive campaign of spying.

Dirty tricks

Wackenhut, Hamel found, had set up a bogus office to lure whistleblowers and others concerned about violations of law, as part of an effort to hinder the committee's investigation. The company had also illegally obtained telephone records, removed trash, done background investigations on many people (some with no connection to the investigation), and bugged hotel rooms—all in an effort to compromise and discredit whistleblowers.

The public record of the subsequent investigations and hearings shows how corporate spies plied their trade against a perceived enemy. While we rarely see such details exposed so publicly, we can rest assured that many other corporate executives view their critics with the same disdain Exxon displayed for Hamel and the committee.

What is remarkable here is that Exxon and Alyeska did not focus on mitigating the health and safety complaints brought by Hamel, but instead turned on him and Miller. Had they used the money on the environment instead, or on more secure tanker holds, they could have decreased the likelihood of other Valdez-like incidents in the future.

Exxon's choice of Wackenhut was significant, given the latter's history and connections. One of the largest private security firms in the world, Wackenhut has been at the forefront of corporate and government efforts to silence critics since 1965. It claims hundreds of millions of dollars worth of US government contracts every year. Wackenhut supplies security for US embassies and some of the country's most sensitive and strategic federal facilities, including the Hanford nuclear waste facility, the Savannah River plutonium plant and the Strategic Petroleum Reserve. It has also taken over the privatization of the US prison and detention system. Many consider Wackenhut comparable to a private Central Intelligence Agency.[2] Because it is a private corporation, its internal affairs are secret, protected by laws intended to allow unrestricted commerce.

Anatomy of a Sting

After the company hired Wackenhut, Alyeska's manager of corporate security set up a covert billing system for the investigation, intended to disguise the truth should questions ever be asked. Then Wackenhut laid its trap in the form of a bogus environmental litigation organization, The Ecolit Group.

The security company was so disrespectful of environmentalists that its brochure for the fake group contained grammatical errors, so that it would look less professional than a law office publication typically would. It described the group as "formed [by] a responsible group of individuals dedicated to the preservation and proper management of this planet. Towards that end, we are conducting specific and selected research to assist organizations in dealing with oil companies and other [sic] who have demonstrated little regard to [sic] live in sustained harmony with our planet's life support systems. . . . Our main objective, through litigation in every Court available, is the maintenance of essential ecological precocious [sic] and life support systems, the preservation of genetic diversities and the sustainable utilization of species and ecosystems."[3]

Wackenhut opened the fake Ecolit office in Miami in April 1990 with one desk, one chair, a telephone, an answering machine, a sofa, an end table, some environmental posters, stationery and brochures. Operatives began working there to make the organization appear real. They obtained computer records of long-distance calls made from Hamel's Alexandria, Virginia, home and identified four 'suspects' using the numbers on the bills. They also obtained records of calls to Frank De Long, a prominent oil industry commentator and

Fairbanks radio host, to Lois Simpson, secretary to Alyeska's general counsel, and to Alaska's 907 area code.

In August they established a second branch and set it up for surveillance. Operative Sherree Rich testified to Congress that she had been directed to set up the office, open a bank account in her own name with cheques that said 'Ecolit', and order fake business cards. She testified: "In order to appear legitimate I also received daily telephone calls from Miami, posing as if it was the Miami Ecolit office, as well as faxes and occasional letters. At about the same time, Mr Richard Llund, posing as Mr John Fox, rented a suite in the same location called Overseas Trading Company . . . (and wired the offices) for the purpose of recording all of the communications and transactions between Hamel and Black" (the director of Wackenhut's Special Investigations Division).[4]

In March, three Wackenhut operatives had travelled to Anchorage, where Hamel was attending an environmental conference. They had located his hotel and tried unsuccessfully to obtain his account information and a record of his telephone calls. One of them went to the office building of the public interest law firm Trustees for Alaska, shot photographs and took items from a trash bin. He also took pictures at a demonstration marking the anniversary of the oil spill, identifying people he believed to be key demonstrators, obtaining the organizers' names, and noting licence plate numbers to be traced later.

Meanwhile, the female operative was instructed to become familiar with environmental groups. She was provided with fake business cards and a fake driver's licence. She followed Hamel into a bar where he met another man, but she denied overhearing their conversation. Leaving for Miami, she ran into Hamel, who recognized her and invited her to sit with him on the plane. She later testified that she had given him her card and he had told her of his activities regarding Alyeska and Exxon. "Mr Hamel very candidly discussed many things of concern to him," she said. "He also mentioned that he had various sources inside Alyeska Corporation feeding him various types of sensitive information. He discussed secret meetings and even the suicide of one person involved."[5] Hamel told her he'd call her at the Ecolit office in Miami the following month.

Hamel began to work with the Wackenhut employees in the belief they were real environmentalists, sharing documents, information, strategies, tactics and information about sources. He told them about his own undercover investigation and the experts he was working with to document illegal dumping by Exxon and BP in Florida and California.

Meanwhile, two of the operatives returned to Alaska hoping to talk to Alyeska employees. They placed an ad in the *Valdez Vanguard* announcing Ecolit's interest in conducting confidential interviews with Valdez citizens about the oil spill and other environmental issues.[6] They placed similar notices on bulletin boards and car windshields. But there were no takers. Apparently a local joke was going around that the Drug Enforcement Agency or spies for Exxon were in town—a joke that turned out to be not so funny.

So that the trip wouldn't be a total waste, the operatives befriended a bartender, who filled them in on local people and the community. They obtained his credit report, vehicle registrations, driver's licence, police record and property records—just because they could. He had no involvement in what they were investigating beyond serving drinks to locals at his job.

They had rented two hotel rooms, wiring one with a hidden low-light monochrome camera and running wires to the other to monitor audio, video and telephone traffic. In June 1990, one spy secretly videotaped a two-hour meeting with Hamel in one hotel room while another operative monitored their conversation from the other room.

By August 1990, the Wackenhut employees had gathered information leading them to believe Hamel was having economic problems, and they decided to try to use them to compromise him. An operative met with Hamel on August 18, wearing a body wire, and a second one outside in a van recorded their conversation. The operative attempted to pay Hamel $2,000 for documents which he had received for free. But Hamel didn't bite. The next day, though, after a third offer of money, he accepted $2,000 for expenses incurred by his sources. It is unclear whether he handed over any documents.

The damage done

In late September 1990, Wackenhut's Director of Special Services Wayne Black finally briefed Alyeska's president, security manager, general counsel and other employees on the covert operation against Hamel and Miller. Alyeska decided to brief BP, Exxon and ARCO. The companies realized they had a problem.

Their lawyers were worried. The Wackenhut operation had been a gross violation of privacy. Exposure would not only greatly embarrass Alyeska, it could also cost the company a great deal of money in civil lawsuits and possibly make it vulnerable to criminal charges. The company could even be considered to have obstructed a congressional investigation.

The companies immediately ordered a halt to the covert operation and any plans to use the information. They discussed how to protect the documents, videotapes and other information from discovery if a congressional court of inquiry issued subpoenas. They also decided to hire a law firm to determine whether there had been any criminal violations and whether they were civilly liable for Wackenhut's behaviour. The Ecolit offices were closed, and Hamel was told the group had lost its funding.

In May 1991, an investigator working for Wackenhut's director of personnel looking into sexual harassment complaints against the chief investigator of the sting, Wayne Black, resigned. In the course of his work he found that operatives assigned to the Alyeska sting had been concerned about the propriety and legality of the surveillance techniques used in it. Observing that Wackenhut seemed to have no problem with any of it, the investigator resigned, obtained legal counsel, contacted Hamel, and told him of the sting. Hamel then told investigators for the Committee on Interior and Insular Affairs about the covert operation.

The committee held hearings in November 1991 to determine whether Alyeska's Ecolit ploy had been an effort to disrupt and compromise a source of information for the committee's ongoing investigation of oil industry practices in Alaska.

The committee found the sting to have been, at least in part, an attempt to obstruct a congressional investigation. It concluded the agents had "engaged in a pattern of deceitful, grossly offensive and potentially, if not blatantly, illegal conduct to accomplish their objectives . . . (in) Alyeska's disastrous campaign to silence its critics."[7] It found Alyeska partly responsible for Wackenhut's actions on its behalf. It also found that both Alyeska and Wackenhut had obstructed its investigation by withholding and possibly destroying and altering documents and records.

Alyeska admitted to hiring Wackenhut but asserted that it had done so to search for stolen documents it feared would fall into the hands of "competitors, terrorists or saboteurs".[8] Alyeska contended that it had only been trying to plug unlawful leaks. The committee found otherwise. Nowhere in the investigation did anyone find any evidence of stolen documents or of "competitors, terrorists or saboteurs". The only leaks found were in the form of oil destroying a delicate ecosystem.

Wackenhut was also found to have gathered information on other critics not known to be competitors, terrorists or saboteurs. It had spied on participants in a constitutionally protected demonstration, the Trustees for Alaska law firm, Alaska Department of Environmental Conservation employee Dan Lawn, marine pollution expert Dr. Riki Ott, and radio host and commentator Frank De Long. The information uncovered in regard to the breadth of the spying campaign leads one to speculate on who else might have been—and might be being—spied on.

The committee recommended that the government look into the environmental problems, keep an eye on the Alyeska terminal, and meet regularly with Alyeska employees. It also asked Alyeska and the pipeline consortium to look at the environmental problems discovered during Wackenhut's surveillance. It called on both the pipeline company and congressional committees to be more vigilant in their oversight, so there would be no more "outrageous" attempts to silence environmental critics. It took Alyeska and Wackenhut to task and asked for assurance that they would never do it again, and asked both companies to review their internal practices.

Wackenhut's chief investigator, Wayne Black, resigned under pressure. The company set up guidelines under which investigators cannot "remove or inventory garbage from an individual or entity; obtain or review financial or credit data without written permission from the subject; monitor any persons or entities with telephone, video or audio surveillance equipment without consent of all parties; review telephone records of any persons without consent; or install or utilize pen registers" (devices that record numbers dialled on a telephone).[9]

Vulnerability

We still need whistleblowers to provide information about dangerous conditions. In July 1999, seven years after the congressional reports were released, the *Guardian* newspaper published an update on the pipeline's continuing environmental problems and the harassment of its critics.[10] In it, Chuck Hamel was depicted as a model to embolden workers who have information to disseminate but face terrific obstacles from their corporate bosses.

But there has not been a really safe venue where these people can come forward—until cyberspace. The non-profit Government Accountability Project has a website (www.whistleblower.org) where people can report health, safety and environmental problems. And managers on the Trans-Alaska Pipeline System (TAPS) have set up their own website, at www.alaskagroup-six.org, which covers numerous issues specific to the TAPS' ongoing problems.

The internet makes it easy for whistleblowers to document their experiences for a broad audience without depending on the hard-to-access mainstream corporate media. But although the internet is an attractive forum for exposing problems without coming forward personally and making oneself vulnerable to reprisals, it must be used very cautiously. Transmissions should be made either from a public place or, better, from a secure computer. Most computers can be traced, so there is no guarantee that using cyberspace will keep you from being discovered (see Chapter 12, 'Cyber-surveillance').

But as the Alyeska case shows, it isn't only the whistleblower who's vulnerable. Corporations are ultrasensitive to exposure of malfeasance or errors of judgement. Even after bringing in Wackenhut's big guns to manipulate its critics, Alyeska saw its operation uncovered, and now it functions as a clear example of a corporate body using a counter-strategy to try—unsuccessfully—to silence its critics.

| Chapter 12 |

Cyber-surveillance

Eveline Lubbers

"One of the major strengths of pressure groups—in fact the levelling factor in their confrontation with powerful companies—is their ability to exploit the instruments of the telecommunication revolution," said the organizer of a 1998 European PR conference on the dangers of pressure groups. "Their agile use of global tools such as the internet reduces the advantage that corporate budgets once provided."[1]

Since the internet has indeed increased the power of anti-corporate campaigners, big companies today are increasingly hiring cybersleuthing services to monitor their brand positions. This chapter explores the field of online business intelligence activity by profiling two companies Shell hired after its Brent Spar PR disaster. It also looks at what happens to those who become the targets of cybersnitches, ideologically and technically, and what they can do about it.

The internet as a barometer

Shell was one of the first companies to take a hit in the new-media war. The company was surprised in 1995 when a campaign by Greenpeace succeeded in preventing it from sinking its redundant Brent Spar drilling platform. Greenpeace spread enough bad publicity with the help of the internet that Shell felt forced to shift ground, surrendering a position it had held to fiercely. The company had done too little too late to defend itself, refraining from publicly explaining why dumping was the best solution, which only reinforced its image as arrogant in the eyes of the public.

At a conference held in the aftermath of the Brent Spar affair to comprehensively examine 'the PR disaster of the century', the company's new internet manager, Simon May, added a new perspective to the many analyses of the crisis. Shell, he said, had been wrong about its own influence on the media and had completely overlooked a new factor in the game: the internet. "There has been a shift in the balance of power; activists are no longer entirely dependent on the existing media," May said. "Shell learned it the hard way with the Brent Spar, when a lot of information was disseminated outside the regular channels."[2]

After the execution of Ken Saro-Wiwa and eight other Ogoni opposition leaders a few months later, the company was criticized again, for its intimate links with Nigeria's military regime. This situation also prompted what May called "a massive online bombardment of criticism".[3] A third disaster would not be allowed to happen.

Shell International's internet manager helped the company formulate an online strategy, which included monitoring what was being said about Shell in cyberspace. May's personal motto: "You need to keep track of your audience all the time, since you may learn a lot from it."[4] The company hired specialized, external services to scout the Web daily, listing all the places the company was mentioned, and in which contexts. May explained in 1998: "We use a service which operates from the US, eWatch, who scan the Web worldwide for references to certain key words and phrases we supply to them. In the UK we use a company called Infonic, who does the same thing from a European perspective."[5] Shell also uses so-called intelligent agents: search programs that can be trained to improve their performance over time.

This monitoring cannot be 100 percent effective, but must be carried out nonetheless, according to May. "The online community should not be ignored," he said. "There are pressure groups that exist only on the internet. They're difficult to monitor and to control. You can't easily enrol as a member of these closed groups."[6]

Shell's impressive website, too, launched in early 1996 to complete a PR offensive trumpeting its change of heart (manifest in a new charter of business principles including a comprehensive code of conduct with due allowance for human rights), is being used as an agent of surveillance. The ostensible basic tenet of www.shell.com is the company's new philosophy of "openness and honesty": dialogue is the core concept, and sensitive issues are not sidestepped. But a closer look reveals that the site's openness is mostly for show. Behind the façade, the site is keeping an eye on the audience.

On the discussion forums, organized by subject, anyone is allowed a say about Shell's practices, uncensored. Besides that, an email facility has been set up to answer every message personally within 48 hours. In the early period Shell proudly claimed it was receiving 1,100 email messages a month. But however open this may sound, the company's responses remain private. The forums are not intended for people to question Shell directly, its internet manager admitted; the email facility is provided for that purpose. May denied that the forums were merely window-dressing, but said, "of course they function as a barometer for what certain people think, although it is not their primary aim."[7]

Online detective agencies

The number of Web detective agencies—which now include Nichols-Dezenhall, iDefense, Cyveillance, NetCurrents and CyberAlert—has grown since the early days of the internet, as has the wide range of services they offer. The two May mentioned in 1998, eWatch and Infonic, have since developed into completely contrasting companies, illustrating opposite ends of the spectrum.

eWatch appeals to the bunker mentality most multinationals opt for when first faced with online activism. The terminology it uses to promote cybersnitch services that help companies identify and "eliminate" online activists is pure Cold-War-framed hostility. The language of London-based Infonic, on the other hand, reveals an almost holistic approach. It claims to exist "to help companies understand and engage with the growing living space that is the internet. Smart companies recognize that the internet is redefining relationships between companies and their stakeholders. We are a new kind of business for a new world." Besides the ways these companies profile themselves, there is much to learn from the different ways they react when their activities are exposed.

eWatch

eWatch pioneered internet monitoring in 1995, scouring online publications, discussion forums, bulletin boards and electronic mailing lists for customers, looking for certain references. By the end of 2001, it claimed to be continuously scanning more than 4,700 online publications and 66,000 Usenet groups, bulletin boards and mailing lists.[8] A growing number of large corporations (more than 900 by late 2001) use this virtual clipping service, which focuses on topics like reputation, rumour, stock manipulation and insider trading.

eWatch launched a short-lived service called CyberSleuth in 1999 especially to counteract online anti-corporate activism. The promotional website was explicit about the services for sale. First, if a corporation wished to know who was behind a given screen name, the service would provide a complete dossier in seven to ten days. The price for targeting individual users: $5,000 per screen name. "Identifying these perpetrators is done using a variety of methods such as following leads found in postings and websites, working (sic) ISPs, involving law enforcement, conducting virtual stings, among other tactics," the website said. Then, depending on the seriousness of the offence, the site promised appropriate counter-measures would be taken. "These may include everything from simply exposing the individual online, all the way to arrest. In some cases, the perpetrator is an employee of, or contractor to, the targeted company. In these cases, termination of employment is customary." And if that wasn't enough, CyberSleuth would make sure no further damage was done. "We can neutralize the information appearing online, identifying the perpetrators behind uncomplimentary postings and rogue websites," the company said on its site. Info-cleansing was an essential part of eWatch's containment policy: "This may mean something as simple as removing a posting from a Web message board on Yahoo! to the shuttering of a terrorist website." CyberSleuth claimed a success rate of more than 80 percent at rooting out online offenders.[9]

Though the website overtly promoted CyberSleuth, eWatch's owners went ballistic when the service's existence was exposed in a *Business Week* column in July 2000. The article basically reproduced the website's promotional text and backed it up with quotes from the company's product manager, Ted Skinner.[10] The story caused quite a stir online after being sent around by privacy activists. The damage control operation that followed raises questions about what was really going on under the CyberSleuth flag.

First, eWatch owner PR Newswire asked *Business Week* to publish a correction. But it refused—the author, Marcia Stepanek, had her facts straight. Claims about "errors" and "misquotes" were easily countered with printouts of the website. When the company disavowed Skinner's quotes, Stepanek produced notes from Skinner himself.[11] Ever since, PR Newswire spokesperson Renu Aldrich has gone after anybody who dares quote the article online or in print. eWatch is nothing but a clipping service, she states over and over, denying the company conducts any of the other activities the article said it promoted.

In autumn 2000, as I was researching this chapter, my inquiries into the CyberSleuth past still clearly touched a nerve.[12] My mere mention of the *Business Week* article infuriated PR Newswire's spokeswoman. She warned me not to use it as a source and tried to convince me it consisted of "lies and misinformation", denying the CyberSleuth website, the article's prime source of information, had ever existed, which I knew was untrue.

Asked why eWatch no longer offered the CyberSleuth product, Aldrich declined to elaborate at first, saying, "We just decided to take a different approach." eWatch, she said, now refers companies wishing to investigate anonymous screen names to the licensed detection firm internet Crimes Group (ICG).[13]

One could get the impression PR Newswire no longer wanted to be associated directly with CyberSleuth and thus had had another umbrella constructed for the same snooping product. International Business Research, a company already involved in Web investigation, set up ICG as a special subsidiary in January 2000, the same month PR Newswire purchased eWatch.

ICG's "investigative service to uncover identities of malicious attackers" comes with a complimentary 30-day subscription to all eWatch monitoring services.[14]

Before answering any further questions, Aldrich issued a statement saying, "eWatch has never done more than provide monitoring reports or refer people to ICG. eWatch has never nor will it call an ISP or otherwise try to alter or delete posts or websites for its clients." When she finally consented to go into details, her answers were revealing. Asked why licensed detectives were necessary, she said, "We wanted a partner who would be beneficial to our clients and do proper investigations legally and above board as well as successfully." Had eWatch ever got into trouble with the methods it had used to identify the people behind screen names? "Not that I am aware of; certainly nothing untoward has occurred since PR Newswire has owned eWatch." She was unwilling to provide more details.

ICG's directors proudly identify themselves as a former British intelligence officer and an ex-FBI agent. They have confirmed in interviews that they use the full range of investigative tricks, from lurking in newsgroup discussions to creating hoax identities—attractive females if necessary—to seduce culprits into traceable statements or actions. Their ideas, too, smack of CyberSleuth rhetoric. Discussing constitutional rights with a reporter from the online publication *WebWatch*, one ICG director said bluntly, "Anonymity does for the internet poster what the white robe does for the KKK."[15]

Infonic

At the other end of the spectrum, Infonic's business philosophy could not be more remote from that of its competitor eWatch. "It is not that the internet has an anti-corporate culture; it is people who have that culture. What internet has allowed us to do is simply to see the scale of that anti-corporate culture," Lipski says. "We stress that companies should be grateful to the internet for enabling them to get closer to their stakeholders; we believe that too many companies are locked into a defensive mode that prevents them from realizing the full potential of the Net. We need to remember that the internet frees companies as well as their critics from some of the historic constraints on the scope of their communication and interaction."[16]

And that's where Infonic, which calls itself an internet research and communication firm, comes in. The actions and opinions of online communities are beginning to have a serious impact on public relations, investor relations and corporate brand management, according to Managing Director Roy Lipski. He says he believes progressive corporations are taking this opportunity to make serious changes, and Infonic aspires to facilitate this process by distilling and communicating these passions and opinions (and rumours) to empower organizations to make informed choices.

"We see our role as providing lubrication to the communication between pressure groups and consumers and large corporations," Lipski says. "We are seeing the death of 'spin' as major corporations are forced to become more and more transparent, and it is becoming harder (and less beneficial) to conceal their weaknesses." [17]

Lipski sounds like a modern internet guru. Consumers, he says, now want to buy more than just a product with certain features; it has to be manufactured with ethical and environmental concern. "The internet has developed at a time characterized by increasing suspicion of corporate behaviour and growing willingness to scrutinize what companies say and do." Cases like the Exxon Valdez, the Brent Spar, animal testing and BSE have contributed to the development of a credibility gap between corporate messages and public perception, he says.

What exactly is the company selling, apart from cyber-religion? Its main service is technology-enabled research which Lipski describes as "more than a clippings service"—it also involves "a distillation of online opinions and activity". Infonic also helps businesses with "online communication plans", which involves "understanding online communities" and helping clients "connect with their audiences in a positive, proactive way". Infonic claims to be successful at understanding how online communities "develop and grow, and translating this understanding into an effective path to effective communications." This was about as concrete as the company got when asked to describe the services it offers.

Leaked counter-strategy

A Sony document leaked onto the Web in summer 2000 gives an indication of how companies might like Infonic to fulfil their needs. The document, entitled 'NGO Strategy', was made as part of a presentation given at a meeting of EICTA, a powerful IT association that lobbies against health and environmental laws in Europe. It outlined an "action plan for counteracting the efforts of several domestic and international environmental groups". [18]

The document disclosed names and contact information for groups which allegedly posed a threat to the IT industry, from Greenpeace and Friends of the Earth to the tiny Silicon Valley Toxics Coalition. Sony characterized the groups as "highly active" and "well-organized" with a "global reach", successful in their efforts to expose human health hazards. The presentation suggested that the meeting attendees develop a unified counter-strategy for the industry, including hiring rapid press response units exclusively for environmental criticism and pre-empting future legislation by working with NGOs on localized recycling campaigns. Sony exhorted other electronics firms to establish relationships with "reliable NGOs" and noted there were "tax rebates in some Member states for doing so".[19]

The presentation further suggested the industry "set up a detailed monitoring and contact network (on) NGOs". It recommended Infonic be used to keep tabs on environmentalists who were pushing for regulations to make electronics manufacturers responsible for their own toxic waste. What was more, other recommendations in the leaked presentation showed great similarity to Infonic's mantra of getting closer to stakeholders.[20]

The expected criticism followed, and Infonic rushed to engage in damage control, in a joint venture with Sony. Roy Lipski was not amused: Infonic does not like to be portrayed as a company that spies on activists. He claimed Infonic had nothing to do with the action plan beyond providing its standard information pack. As he put it, "One representative within Sony had misinterpreted what we do and had presented ourselves in a manner which suited their own objectives, without our knowledge or consent, and which did not reflect what we do or believe."[21]

Even Sony attempted to dissociate itself from 'NGO Strategy', telling a *Wall Street Journal* reporter that although the company's name was on the document and an employee had written it, it wasn't a Sony document since it had been created on behalf of EICTA.[22] At a meeting in Brussels with a delegation from the activist groups named in the document, Sony explained it had merely mentioned Infonic as an example of a service other companies might want to use, and denied hiring Infonic itself.[23]

Coincidentally or not, Infonic paid an unusual amount of attention to Greenpeace in the months prior to Sony's July 2000 presentation. Greenpeace Web statistics show Infonic was among the ten most frequent visitors for six months in a row, with an average of 300 to 450 visits a week.[24] Infonic alone entered the Greenpeace site more often than all the Google or Alta Vista users combined. This intensive monitoring started in December 1999 and ended in the week the Sony presentation was held.[25]

Infonic was obviously closely monitoring Greenpeace. Of course, Greenpeace campaigns on other subjects besides toxic waste. And since other campaigning groups didn't keep track of similar statistics, it is too early to draw further conclusions.

Before the ranks closed, however, Sony executives freely acknowledged the company was tracking environmental groups. "We are obviously concerned about our image," Sony's vice-president of environmental, and health and safety issues told the news agency IPS, which first exposed the strategy paper. "If Greenpeace is pushing something, we want to be on top of it." He admitted the 'NGO Strategy' presentation had not been put together in the "most tasteful" way, but said it had not been meant for public release.[26]

The big question raised here is why Web intelligence agencies would be so allergic to publicity about their work. Both eWatch and Infonic were extremely touchy about being exposed, even though what was said and written was not particularly damning or detailed. Apparently the new masters of intelligence prefer to remain on the dark side—whatever they are doing, they want it kept out of public view.

Private justice

The potential consequences of being labelled a "perpetrator" by eWatch (or a comparable service) are illustrated by the following case—probably the first time people who openly grumbled about their employer on a public website became the target of a far-reaching investigation.

The *Business Week* article quoted eWatch's manager Ted Skinner on a recent success story: in early 2000, CyberSleuth had helped Northwest Airlines track down the alleged organizers of an employee 'sickout' that had nearly halted flights over the Christmas holidays. The company had fired the alleged organizers, and a court had upheld the legality of the action. Northwest had been using eWatch ever since to help it finger fed-up flight attendants—for "re-education", as Skinner explained.

The target of the surveillance was a chat room on a flight attendants' website where Northwest employees discussed work-related issues, including a long-running dispute between the airline and its 11,000 flight attendants. The end of 1999 marked a year with no negotiation on working conditions or new contracts.[27] The posts included some from disgruntled employees advocating sickouts and strikes, as well as others discouraging such actions.

The court granted Northwest a temporary injunction prohibiting the union from encouraging its members to participate in a sickout or other illegal activity. Then the company obtained a court order requiring 43 named defendants to turn over their office and home computer equipment to the accounting company Ernst & Young for "purposes of examining and copying information and communications contained on the computer hard drives." After conducting an enquiry, Northwest Airlines fired more than a dozen employees in March 2000, saying they had participated in a sickout.[28]

The effect on employees' use of the website forums has been marked. Posts critical of Northwest have dwindled, and most messages are now posted anonymously. But besides threatening freedom of speech, and perhaps also the freedom to organize, the case marks a shift towards private justice. The company used an online intelligence firm to track down employees who expressed support for a strike from their home computers, and an accounting company reviewed the evidence. In the end, the company's lawsuit was dropped as part of a collective bargaining agreement to improve working conditions. The discovery and investigation were never judged, the accusations never proved, the employees never tried in a court of law. But they got punished anyway—they were fired.

Technical tricks

Even within the limits of simply monitoring the Net, eWatch discovered ways to hinder activists' Web presence. The following examples show how eWatch uses technology to sabotage critics of large companies online. You might call it reverse net-activism.

Mark Gold's Aspartame Toxicity Info Center website provides information about the dangers of NutraSweet, Monsanto's artificial sweetener.[29] In autumn 1999, Gold noticed eWatch was monitoring his site. "Instead of accessing my website once per day, like they are doing now, their software was accessing my site constantly, every minute or so." This caused him several problems. His hosting service charged him large amounts of money for exceeding the monthly limit on bytes transferred. The constant accessing of the site also tended to slow down his computer, which may have discouraged some people from trying to download larger files. Furthermore, journalists often asked Gold how many people were visiting his site and from where, and the constant connections by eWatch were skewing the results. "In order to provide at least some accuracy," he says, "I had to get eWatch to stop the spamming." In this case, informing eWatch.com's ISP put a swift end to the attacks.

eWatch also used a more complicated form of harassment against Gold that involved exploiting the bidding wars at www.GoTo.com. GoTo (since renamed Overture) is a search engine that allows site owners to select search terms relevant to their sites and choose how much to pay when users click on their listings. The higher you bid, the higher your site appears in the search results. GoTo became popular when other big search engines including AOL, Netscape and Lycos started listing the top two or three results from GoTo first. That was when Gold started to notice attacks in his log files.

"One person would first go to five different GoTo.com-affiliated search engines, then search on a particular term that I bid on to continue to click on my particular link, causing me to be charged anywhere from $0.08 to $0.50 per click," he says. "I could tell they were doing this because my log showed that they were coming from the same IP address. They were using various search engines, but the same search term and all of the accesses were within a few seconds of each other. They would do this over and over again."

Fortunately for Gold, GoTo used software to catch such abuse and prevent customers from being billed for it. But he suspects it would be easy for sophisticated users to make the clicks on those links come from different IP addresses.

Countersurveillance and exposure

Without a doubt, these technical tricks mentioned here are not the only ones services like eWatch could use to undermine their targets. The problem is that most such techniques are neither very visible nor widely known. It would take special attention from a skilled webmaster to reveal them. Meanwhile, to keep an eye on frequent visitors, it's a good idea for website owners to subscribe to a web server statistics service (most are free). Nowadays there is also software that alerts you when certain known visitors show up.

After its webstats showed lots of hits were coming from BP, Greenpeace had a great idea. It set up a detection system that served up a special pop-up page to BP employees. Knowing BP's Alaska project was controversial within the company, Greenpeace encouraged staff to come forward with any inside environmental or safety information they felt the public needed to know. Webmaster Brian Fitzgerald says, "We didn't get anything we could use publicly, but part of our intent was to reach inside the corporate structure and try to prick a few consciences and to make BP more accountable to their own staff." Targeting pop-ups at specific visitors using domain tracing is one relatively simple way to fan the flames of existing controversy inside a company and increase a project's liability. Brainstorming further along this road should give rise to many others.

Of course, more detailed countersurveillance is too complicated and time-consuming for most understaffed low-budget NGOs and activist groups. Perhaps a more systematic way of dealing with such issues could be developed. Imagine a network of countersurveillance services, for instance connected to the independent media centres, that would specialize in countering all kinds of Web surveillance. Using the latest software, realizing such a fantasy might not be so far off after all.

Or might the time be ripe for another idea that has popped up among Net activists? After *Business Week* exposed eWatch, an activist using the name Knightmare called for the formation of an "Internet Liberation Front". "The ILF should work outside the bounds of the internet and hacking, and take inspiration from other like-minded groups (ALF, ELF). Instead of liberating animals, they would liberate information."

Exposing the activities of Web intelligence agencies and confronting the companies that hire them should always be a prime goal. The campaigning organizations targeted by Sony wrote a letter to the CEO to express their disappointment with the exposed strategy plan, suggesting Sony could better direct its energy and resources toward helping the environment instead of trying to undermine critics.

Corporate stalking is designed to put an end to uncensored communication. It is intended to make you afraid to speak up because you know you're outgunned and out-financed by a corporation's legal team.

But freedom of speech is just one issue at stake here. Users' messages have been removed, and others have seen their content destroyed or removed without notice after corporate lawyers threatened their ISPs. Users can also be banned from using certain online services. But some have also been harassed by powerful entities without due process. All this has been made possible with the help of online intelligence services. Most Western countries guarantee citizens a speedy and public trial, but the Northwest employees did not get one, nor were their houses and personal effects secured against unreasonable searches.[30]

Even if a corporation doesn't send you a cease-and-desist order, you should never censor yourself because you know it might. Only by exposing counter-strategies and using the available technology to tackle them will we be able to foil the cybersnitches.

Chapter 13

Corporate Intelligence

Eveline Lubbers

"The idea was to do for industry what we had done for the government."
—*Hakluyt co-founder Christopher James*

The boundaries between corporate intelligence and government snooping are getting blurred. Previous chapters on monitoring and surveillance have stressed the need to recognize the difference between secret service informers and their counterparts working for big business; now it is time to highlight the relationships and the overlap between them. Though their goals may differ depending on their clients' needs, business intelligence agencies often use much the same surveillance *modus operandi* as do governments.

Once a group is thought to pose a serious threat—whether based on a realistic assessment or an unfounded fear—it is at risk of falling prey to special operations orchestrated by its opponents. Know thine enemy! In the past, state intelligence programmes have tried to undermine successful campaigns or destabilize activist groups. Now private or privatized spy shops can access the same tools, sometimes even in co-operation with the state secret service.

Most of the big business consulting firms have for years had departments dealing with political risk management; recently the number of specialized business 'intelligence' firms has been growing. This chapter will show how a private intelligence firm linked closely to MI6, the British foreign intelligence service, spied on environmental campaign groups to collect information for oil companies. It will also explain how growing resistance against economic globalization provides a new field of activity for Western secret services. The FBI's inclusion of 'anarchist groups' like Reclaim the Streets within its definition of terrorism opens the way for a crackdown on political activists. Finally, this chapter will explore the dangers of corporate special operations for anti-corporate campaigners. Although it is almost impossible to effectively arm yourself against such operations, it is nonetheless important to be aware of their existence.

Intelligence for sale

Hakluyt & Company Ltd, a London business intelligence bureau named after a 16th-century geographer and economic intelligence specialist *avant la lettre*, was founded in 1995 by former members of the British foreign secret service. The idea, to quote one of its founders, was "to do for industry what we had done for the government".[1]

Hakluyt fills a niche in the intelligence sector by specializing in upmarket business, with which it has been very successful. The company started in a one-room office in 1995; in 2001 it claims its clients include one-quarter of FTSE 100 companies. In its brochure, Hakluyt promises to find information for its clients which they "will not receive by the usual government, media and commercial routes". The company tries to distinguish itself from other business intelligence consultants, spinmasters and clipping services. "We do not take anything off the shelf, nothing off the Net—we assume that any company worth its salt has done all of that," Hakluyt's Michael Maclay explained at a 1999 conference in the Netherlands. "We go with the judgement of people who know the countries, the élites, the industries, the local media, the local environmentalists, all the factors that will feed into big decisions being made."[2]

Manfred Schlickenrieder apparently was one of those people who "knew the local environmentalists". For years, he posed as a leftist sympathizer and film-maker while working as a spy for Hakluyt. His cover was blown when the Swiss action group Revolutionaire Aufbau began to distrust him. In the investigation which led to his exposure, the group uncovered a large pile of documents. Many were put online at the beginning of 2000 (www.aufbau.org).These documents prove Schlickenrieder was on Hakluyt's payroll—and indicate strongly that he was working for more than one German state intelligence service.

Among the documents was detailed email correspondence between Schlickenrieder and Hakluyt. There was also a DM20,000 ($9,000) invoice to Hakluyt for "Greenpeace research" including expenses, "to be paid according to agreement in the usual manner". Confronted with this material, Hakluyt reluctantly admitted having employed him. When *The Sunday Times* broke the story in Britain in July 2000, both BP and Shell acknowledged having hired the firm, but claimed they had been unaware of its tactics.

Schlickenrieder's exposure put the spotlight on an firm that prefers to operate highly discreetly in the shadowy area of former state intelligence specialists-turned-private spies. Members of Parliament accused MI6 of using the firm as a front to spy on green activists.

Analyzing archival material found in Schlickenrieder's house teaches us much about how he did his work for Hakluyt, and about oil companies' current intelligence needs.

Schlickenrieder traded on his image as a long-term devoted activist to get various information-gathering commissions. After the Brent Spar PR crisis and the death of Ken Saro-Wiwa in Nigeria, he made an inventory for Shell International of the activist agenda.[3] Posing as a film-maker making a film about the anti-Shell campaigns, Schlickenrieder travelled around Europe, and managed to interview on film a broad spectrum of people campaigning for the Ogoni people in Nigeria. He spent months questioning all sorts of groups, and wrote to organizations ranging from Friends of the Earth to the Body Shop asking about their ongoing campaigns, their future plans and the impact of their work. The project eventually resulted in a documentary video, *Business as Usual: The Arrogance of Power*, which gave a rather superficial insight into the European campaign against Shell. But it was only a byproduct of the investigation: every worthwhile detail was captured in a report for Hakluyt and subsequently channelled to Shell International.

Other oil companies were scared to death, too, of becoming Greenpeace's next target. BP turned to Hakluyt for help after it got wind that Greenpeace was planning its Atlantic Frontier campaign to stop oil drilling in a new part of the Atlantic. The company asked Schlickenrieder to deliver details about what was going to happen as well as assess how Greenpeace might respond to possible damage claims that could be used in an attempt to paralyze it.

Hakluyt used material from other sources to complement the information about Greenpeace's plans Schlickenrieder provided. It claimed to have laid its hands on a copy of 'Putting the Lid on Fossil Fuels', the Greenpeace brochure meant to kick off the campaign, even before the ink was dry. BP used this inside information to polish its press and PR communications. "BP countered the campaign in an unusually fast and smart way," Greenpeace Germany spokesperson Stefan Krug told the German daily *die tageszeitung*. Since it knew what was coming in advance, BP was never taken by surprise.[4]

It also used Hakluyt to plan a counter-strategic lawsuit against Greenpeace. In a May 1997 email message to Schlickenrieder, Hakluyt's Director Mike Reynolds inquired about the possible impact of suing the environmentalists for mounting a campaign like the Brent Spar one. He asked his German spy for information on whether Greenpeace was taking legal steps to protect its assets against seizure in the event it was sued by an oil company.

The answer to that question is not among the exposed documents. However, when BP's Stena Dee oil installation in the Atlantic Ocean was occupied two months later, the company sued Greenpeace for DM4.2 million (almost $2 million) in damages, insisting its work was being delayed. BP got an injunction to block Greenpeace UK's bank accounts, which caused the group serious financial problems. (This was one of the first times an injunc tion was used to threaten activists with possible arrest. It has since become an increasingly popular way to stop a campaign.)

Oil activism was not Schlickenrieder's only field of activity. The Aufbau group discovered leads about research he did for Hakluyt on banks and financial takeovers. And in 1996 he started mapping resistance against Rio Tinto, which calls itself the "world leader in finding, mining and processing the Earth's mineral resources."[5] He continued to bill Hakluyt for this research until at least spring 1999.[6]

A freelance spy

Schlickenrieder had apparently built up spying experience during years of working for Germany's domestic and foreign intelligence services, Landesamt für Verfassungsschutz and Bundesnachrichtendienst.

Documents found at his home indicated he had had access to reports from them as well as the French and Italian secret services. None of the spy agencies acknowledged publicly that Schlickenrieder had been working for them; however, informed sources agreed that the agent's exposure had been a blow for the German intelligence community, as several serious papers reported. Furthermore, the Schlickenrieder case was discussed in the prime minister and parliamentary committee's weekly meeting with the German secret services—a meeting of which no minutes are ever published.[7]

Though there is evidence that they paid him, it is not known whether he was actually on the payroll; he may have been a freelance spy. The fact that he wrote detailed proposals for the government, suggesting new fields of research within the radical leftist movement, points in this direction. Whichever it was, the rewards of espionage seem to have included a spacious flat overlooking a park in Munich and a BMW Z3, the model of sports car driven by James Bond in *Goldeneye*. His monthly expenses were calculated at $4,500.

He became good at delivering different kinds of intelligence, from broad overviews to assessments to insider mood reports. Taking advantage of activists' trust, he developed a knack for piecing together bits and pieces of information to compile a fairly accurate picture.

He frequented meetings of radical leftist groups (including the Red Army Faction) from the early 1980s until his cover was blown, and he made a documentary about violent resistance with solidarity groups and relatives of convicted comrades which featured the RAF. Another film, about Italy's Red Brigades, on which he had been working since 1985, was never finished. But stills from his video footage served as a photo database, accompanied by personal details about everybody he had met.

His ways of working for state and business were similar—there seemed to be no boundaries between the two. He sometimes compiled reports for Hakluyt without being asked. For instance, in a September 1997 email to Hakluyt, he explained how he had "used the opportunity of visiting Hamburg to talk to two separate people within Greenpeace". In closing, he wrote: "That was your free 'mood report' supplement from Hamburg."

The MI6 connection

News clippings provide revealing details on the background of Hakluyt's founders. Christopher James and Mike Reynolds are both former members of the British foreign service. Ex-MI6 chief Spedding is said to have given his blessing to Hakluyt as a company, as is the foreign secretary.[8]

Reynolds founded MI6's counter-terrorism branch and was the foreign service's head of station in Berlin. This explains his impeccable spoken and written German and may also be the way he got to know Manfred Schlickenrieder. The newly appointed head of MI6, Richard Dearlove, is a close friend of his.[9]

James led a section of MI6 that liaised with British firms. Over his 20-year career he got to know the heads of many of Britain's top companies. In return for a few tips that helped them compete in the market, he persuaded them to pass on intelligence from their overseas operations, industry sources told *Management Today*. After the Cold War, James argued that MI6 should expand this role. But others in the organization feared this could be mistaken for 'economic espionage'. He left MI6 in 1995, taking his intelligence work private.[10]

Hakluyt's management board is a display case for the kind of reputation the company is aiming for. One member was Ian Fleming's model for James Bond—the former soldier, spy and diplomat Sir Fitzroy Maclean. And the company is linked to the oil industry through Sir William Purves, CEO of Shell Transport and chairman of Hakluyt; Sir Peter Holmes, former chairman of Shell and current president of the Hakluyt foundation (a kind of supervisory board); and Sir Peter Cazalet, the former deputy chairman of BP, who helped to establish Hakluyt before he retired in 2000. BP itself has long-standing ties to MI6: its director of government and public affairs, John Gerson, was at one time a leading candidate to succeed Sir David Spedding as chief of MI6.[11]

It is important that NGOs and other pressure groups trying to assess possible threats remember the close ties between risk assessment companies and the government intelligence community. Some larger and older companies, such as Control Risks, may have grown away from direct links to government,

which could explain the market for new agencies with more recent connections, like Hakluyt. Such firms have the necessary knowledge and techniques
at their disposal, either through their own experience, their staff's experience,
or direct contacts. This can have consequences for the way they investigate
their clients' adversaries; as in the Schlickenrieder case, they might use infiltrators posing as activists or dedicated journalists, and they might have access
to classified intelligence information. The specialism of privatized spying
shops goes beyond PR consulting or spin doctoring into the rather vague
terrain of intelligence operations, which can be used in both gathering information and setting up stings.

A new terrain for intelligence

With the growing success of the anti-globalization movement, state authorities are showing increased interest in it. Seattle was the turning point: a large
number of demonstrators and broad scope of presentation combined with the
use of sophisticated methods and technology effectively shut down the WTO
Ministerial Conference. More importantly, state and private security agencies
were caught off guard.

Some governments now see anti-corporate activities as a serious threat to
social stability. And their intelligence services see securing that stability as a
primary task.

The first indication of this interest was a widely circulated secret report
by the Canadian Security Intelligence Service (CSIS), 'Anti-Globalization—A
Spreading Phenomenon.'[12] The CSIS report became famous because it used
quotes from Naomi Klein's No Logo in an effort to assess the threat posed by
anti-corporate protests to the Summit of the Americas in Quebec which was
coming up in April 2001. Klein was not amused to be used as an informant,
but noted the CSIS had done more than paint activists as latent terrorists
(though it did that too): "It also makes a somewhat valiant effort to understand the issues behind the anger. These observations are made in the spirit of
know thy enemy, but at least CSIS is listening."[13]

One of the first public reports of state intelligence units' gathering information on anti-globalization militants appeared in May 2000 in the France-
based periodical Intelligence Newsletter and was based on information from
sources close to the spying community. During the 17 April 2000 World
Bank protests in Washington DC, the newsletter said, the US Army
Intelligence and Security Command and the Pentagon helped the police keep
an eye on demonstrators.[14]

Perhaps when the US Attorney's office praised the DC police for their
"unparalleled" coordination with other police agencies during the spring

2000 IMF protests, it was thinking of these bodies. The FBI reportedly had held seminars on the lessons of Seattle for police in other protest cities to help them prepare for demonstrations. Now it had paid off. "The FBI provided valuable background on the individuals who were intent on committing criminal acts," the US Attorney's office declared, according to an article by Abby Scher in *The Nation*.

Scher warned of an intensifying crackdown on opponents of corporate globalization, pointing to unusually close collaboration between police and intelligence services including the FBI before and during the DC protests.[15] This collaboration harks back to the heyday of J. Edgar Hoover and his illegal Counter Intelligence Program (COINTELPRO). Back then, the FBI relied on local police and even private right-wing spy groups for information about anti-war and other activists. The FBI used that information and its own *agents provocateurs* to disrupt the activities of the Black Panthers, Students for a Democratic Society, Puerto Rican nationalist groups and others.

Targeting organizers and letting activists know they are under surveillance are two time-honoured tactics of local intelligence units and the FBI. Preventive detention, spreading fear of infiltration, and disseminating false stories to the press were also used during the dark days of COINTELPRO. Now, the first reports of comparable police strategies aimed at the movement of movements in 2000 and 2001 have been collected and published.[16]

Whether (and if so, how) the Justice Department or the FBI plotted to crack down on protesters is the type of information often only revealed by chance or long after the fact. COINTELPRO was famously exposed in 1971 when activists liberated documents from an FBI office in Media, Pennsylvania. Details of the programme's reactivation in the 1980s, targeting the Central America solidarity movements, came out after a whistleblower exposed his work targeting CISPES (Committee in Solidarity with the People of El Salvador), which supported resistance against the military regime, under the Freedom of Information Act.[17] Other groups, including some involved in the Puerto Rican independence movement, have been targeted too. As Scher concluded, "The process of uncovering the government's recent attempts to suppress dissent has just begun."

Unsettlingly, in 2001 the FBI listed "anarchist and extremist socialist groups" such as the Workers' World Party, Reclaim the Streets and Carnival Against Capitalism as a "potential threat" to the United States.[18] Reclaim the Streets (RTS) is actually more a tactic than a movement or organization. In 1996, activists in England decided to hold the first RTS 'street party', a daytime rave with a political spin, complete with sound system, dancing, and party games, in the middle of a busy intersection. The party aimed to temporarily 'reclaim' the street from cars, and point out how capitalism and car culture deprive people of public space and opportunities for festivals.

The fact that dancing in the street could become terrorism in the eyes of the FBI can only be explained by the aftershock of Seattle, where, according to the FBI, "anarchists, operating individually and in groups, caused much of the damage." This statement, made on 10 May 2001, mentioned these groups as part of "The Domestic Terrorism Threat", soon after a section on "The International Terrorist Situation" featuring Osama bin Laden and individuals affiliated with al-Qu'eda. After the attacks on the World Trade Center four months later, the lack of proportion between the two 'threats' goes without saying.

Categorizing "anarchist groups" like Reclaim the Streets as terrorist organizations can be seen as a way for the FBI to justify its interest in anti-globalization from a legal standpoint. Although inclusion on such a list can be taken to mean such groups are gaining influence, it also increases the likelihood of government-sponsored involvement, such as infiltration or frame-ups based on planted evidence.

Intelligence agencies in most Western countries already had broad powers to track and monitor suspected activists and political organizations. But the events of 11 September 2001 triggered further anti-terrorist legislation everywhere that all but encouraged repressive police and intelligence tactics. Only the future can tell how these new laws will affect the manoeuvring space for anti-corporate activism and campaigning groups.

The Department of Dirty Tricks

Besides being spied upon and having information leaked, activists risk being manipulated or threatened, too. Consulting companies like KPMG and security firms like Control Risks Group have reasons to monitor NGOs, as an article in *Intelligence Newsletter* stated: ostensibly, corporate clients want to be informed of destabilization campaigns that could affect them well in advance. "But they also want to fend off indirect attack," the magazine went on. "To be sure, some firms feel a strong temptation to 'channel' the fury of NGOs like Export Credit Agencies, Public Citizen or ATTAC towards some of their business competitors," the magazine said.

It quoted intelligence expert Roy Godson as predicting that manipulating NGOs would become one of the most effective means for companies to destabilize rivals and adversaries in the future.[19]

Intelligence Newsletter hints at the endless time and effort NGOs spend in the perpetual quest for 'ideal' companies to take on. "Only by targeting a known corporate name can they be sure to enhance their own profile, distinguish from other NGOs and compete with them for media attention." Apparently this early stage of campaigning is seen as the best moment to intervene.

How? One possibility that springs to mind: imagine your group gets a dedicated new member who has convincing ideas for a new campaign against a company you haven't paid much attention to so far. Perhaps he's been sent by another company you've been successfully campaigning against for years, or are intending to target in the near future.

NGOs' taste for media attention can be their Achilles' heel, which makes it relatively easy to feed them (dis-)information that they'll rush to publicize. The East German secret service apparently understood this back in the 1970s: Godson claimed it used this weakness for publicity against Amnesty International during the Cold War. This is another kind of manipulation which it is easy to envision a company using.

Manipulating internal differences is another strategy that can cripple the power of an activist coalition. Reporting on the planning of protests against the November 2001 WTO trade rounds in Qatar, the consulting firm Strategic Forecasting (STRATFOR) emphasized the threat of a split between anti-globalization forces.

After the 11 September attacks and the authorities' subsequent zero-tolerance policy, the movement had been discussing how it could show force without being labelled as unpatriotic. STRATFOR warned its readers in business and the press against the rise of "a more violent radical activist faction" unconcerned about a possible backlash from "mainstream activists who fear the anti-globalization message would be tarnished".

The STRATFOR report was written as a warning, and is full of exaggerations. But with its detailed predictions ("A vocal, extremely aggressive faction of activists will soon emerge in the United States and pursue a different form of more direct action") the report can be read as strategic advice for the corporate world.

Someone wishing to make trouble could, by fuelling the discussion within the movement on the use of violence, effectively cripple the movement's resurrection at this point in time. Heating up the violent faction by using *agents provocateurs* to incite violence, as reportedly happened in Genoa in July 2001, could effectively destroy the coalition, or groups which are part of it.[20]

Companies can also simply try to persuade NGOs outright to stop campaigning against them, such as McDonald's did when it offered to settle its court case against the McLibel Two. A few months into the trial, the company understood the suit was backfiring and offered to drop it and donate a substantial sum to a third party if the defendants agreed never again to publicly criticize McDonald's. (They refused.) There are also reports of other entities trying to bribe campaigners to stop their work in a similar fashion.

When your group is targeted

The smaller a campaigning group is, the more promising it might seem for a company to bribe its key people into giving up their work in exchange for money. Relatively isolated groups, or people acting more or less on their own, will be the easiest targets of such operations.

It is hard to tell whether the *Intelligence Newsletter* predictions will come true. And detecting such efforts at manipulation would be extremely difficult. However, the past has shown that targeting and terrorizing specific people can make them stop their campaigning activities as well as scare off others around them. The authors of *The War Against the Greens* documented cases of activists, often female, working alone and as members of groups in relatively isolated parts of the United States, being harassed in the 1980s.

Once a company's off-the-record efforts to effectively stop a campaign fail, it can shift into threat mode. From then on, it will be hard to distinguish actual attacks from coincidental accidents within the same time frame. When campaigners are confronted with night-time visits, telephone death threats and near-accidents with cars forcing cycles off the road, it is hard to judge whether out-of-order phones, missing mail and malfunctioning fax machines are part of the same scheme.

Terror induces fear, and fear spreads like a virus if not stopped in time. To separate unfounded paranoia from vague unease that may later prove to be well founded, it is strongly advisable to keep logs of strange incidents, debunking any suspicions that are possible to debunk. It is important that people who are targeted are taken seriously within the organization, and their suspicions researched and followed up on with the necessary security measures, up to and including calling the police or hiring a private detective. If not, these people are likely eventually to lose confidence, have a nervous breakdown, or leave activism altogether.

If the stakes are high enough, targeted companies can resort to special operations. It will be very difficult to expose this kind of counter-strategy, because it is often almost impossible to prove your organization is being manipulated. Even more difficult would be distinguishing the possible involvement of an official secret service from that of a private intelligence company. But it is essential that groups that suspect they are being targeted come forward with documented examples, if only to warn potential future victims.

Part Two

Battling
Big Business

Chapter 14

Investigating and Exposing

Nicky Hager

The long campaign to end the logging of public rainforests in New Zealand was at its lowest ebb by the end of 1998, worn down by a nasty counter-campaign by the main logging company. Yet less than a year later, that company had been publicly discredited and all logging on New Zealand public lands was being shut down. A large part of the reason for this turnaround can be traced to a single event in early 1999, when an employee of a public relations company agreed to leak me copies of the logging company's aggressive anti-environmental strategies.

At the end of 1999, after two years of investigating, Bob Burton and I published *Secrets and Lies,* a book exposing a large-scale anti-environmental campaign co-ordinated by the US-owned public relations company Shandwick.[1] The truth was much worse than my original suspicions. The PR campaign included infiltration of environmental groups, a systematic effort to discredit and discourage these groups and their supporters, legal threats against critical journalists and cultivation of friendly ones, orchestration of a 'community' pro-logging campaign, secret government lobbying by PR people on behalf of the government's own company, and more.

What happened after the book's publication shows the kind of impact investigations like ours can have. Its two major effects were to unmask sophisticated PR strategies and to cause a political upheaval that shattered the prime minister's position and ultimately resulted in a reversal of logging policy.

Until the book was published, most journalists uncritically reported press releases orchestrated by the PR company. The main pro-logging spokesperson they quoted was part of a phony community group set up as a PR strategy. They reported stories and incidents manufactured to discredit the environmentalists—such as unflattering personal revelations, and a fake bomb—often uncritically. By and large, reporters acted as channels for PR rather than questioning and scrutinizing it.

With time, persistence and some tricks of the trade, a sensible person (or group) can, as we did, investigate and expose the kinds of subject ordinary journalists rarely uncover. In this chapter, I introduce some powerful tools journalists and activists can use to dig out useful and important information in order to expose wrongdoing and empower the public.

Smelling a rat

The first steps in my research into anti-environmental public relations were based on the vaguest of hunches. The mainstream news media in New Zealand had been reporting on the public conflict between environmental groups and the state-owned logging company. But there seemed to be a more interesting story going on behind the news. The aggressiveness and persistence of the pro-logging campaign reminded me of stories I had heard about organized anti-environmental tactics in the United States. I wondered if similar tactics might invisibly be at work here as well.

So the rainforest controversy was on my mental list of interesting subjects worth following up. I did some exploratory probing into the subject by asking a member of Parliament to ask official questions about the logging company's PR activities. In many countries this is a quick way to access government information. The government provided details of Timberlands' high level of PR spending and noted that a company called Shandwick (which I had never heard of) was providing "communications advice" to the company. But it quickly became clear they were not going to release any information beyond that.

The subject then went on to another mental list of those subjects that needed inside sources before I could pursue them further. I would keep my ears open for news of someone involved in the PR campaign who might talk to me quietly about it.

I have a personal motto concerning research. It is that nearly every piece of information in the world is accessible—no matter how secret it appears at first—and just carries a 'price tag' of hours. Some information is quick to find. Other information is much harder to get, but, as I learned through years of studying military and intelligence subjects, there always seems to be a way if you are able and willing to spend enough time. Some information might not be important enough to justify the time it would take. But when the information matters, again and again this motto proves true.

Breaching the walls

I believe secrecy is, in many cases, an abuse of power or a cover for activities people would be ashamed to do publicly, and in those cases using unauthorized ways to get information can be justified.

But where do you start? Institutions that control information often appear hopelessly impregnable. The information is inside the walls and we are outside. The more secret the information, the thicker the walls and the tighter the security. But security is always more impression than reality. At every government agency and private company, no matter how strict the security, the secrets walk in and out every day as people go to and from work.

Finding an insider willing to help you get information is a matter of persistence and luck. Never assume that organizations are homogeneous, where everyone thinks alike and blindly supports everything the organization does. Most organizations contain a mixture of people, including some at least as concerned about wrongdoing and ethics and willing to act in the public interest as you are. They may be senior or junior staff. Senior staff often treat lower-paid workers as if they are invisible, blind or stupid—but they may well know exactly what is going on. The challenge is finding the right person and winning his or her trust.

The most successful way to find people is by word of mouth. Most of my inside sources on many subjects are people whom a friend of a friend told me about. All it took was asking around. More specific leads can come from someone you know in a related university department (e.g. languages, mathematics or computing, in the case of intelligence agencies), elsewhere in the same profession (e.g. another PR company) or the trade union concerned (e.g. a public service union). They may well know of someone who recently left the very place you are interested in. The key is simply to start looking.

Remember, too, that the particular secret information you are seeking is usually located in several different places, not just the obvious ones, and some of these may be more accessible than others. The first thing I try to get when studying an organization is an internal phone directory or staff list, which provides a window into the organization and shows who works on what (in some cases, I have a series of staff lists covering many years so that I can see people come and go).

The Timberlands leak

With the Timberlands PR story, it took over a year of casual asking around before I found someone willing to help. I never telephone a potential source the first time, as it is too hard to establish trust and not scare them off. I usually visit the person's home—turning up on their doorstep—and introduce myself and explain what I am trying to achieve. Only one person has ever acted annoyed at me for turning up, and a few have politely said no. But I am still amazed at the way that most people, by far, have been willing to help.

I cannot say how I heard about my Timberlands source, but we met the first time in an out-of-the-way, very unfashionable café where we were unlikely to meet anyone we knew. I explained my suspicions about the PR campaign and said I was looking for evidence so I could write about it. It was like a floodgate opened. I suddenly began hearing an outpouring of indignation and stories about activities I had never even imagined were going on. It often happens like that. People work in secretive jobs they don't feel comfortable about and yet would probably never take the step of approaching someone like me. But once approached, they are clearly relieved at having someone to talk to.

On our second meeting, at the source's home, I started taking more methodical interview notes. The material was fascinating and provided lots of leads for further investigation, but it did not solve the problem of proof. There's not much point in writing a detailed exposé if it can simply be dismissed as a conspiracy theory. It is harder to ask someone to take confidential papers away from their work than just to speak to you, but luckily the person was again willing to help.

We agreed to meet for the third time one evening soon after. I went out to dinner with a good friend and told him I would appreciate his help with an unusual evening out. We filled in time going to an early film (*Enemy of the State*, of all things!), and then, joking away Hollywood-induced paranoia, went to meet my source.

We met at a friend's office where we could use a photocopier without being disturbed. I would have been thrilled with two or three good inside documents. My source arrived with two enormous boxes crammed with files. We took turns sorting and photocopying them. By midnight, I was tired but excited, as I copied more and more proof: the minutes of all the weekly PR teleconferences, the detailed PR strategy plans and much more. And we were only partway through the boxes. We were still photocopying by the time it got light. My body ached from standing up all night. I went home through the bright early morning, not quite believing the thousands of pages I was carrying.

I was in the middle of some other writing, so I hid the leaked papers, telling no one about them, and spent several weeks wondering what I should do with them. During this period something rather unsettling happened. Out of the blue, I received a terse one-line email from the chief executive of Shandwick suggesting we meet for a cup of coffee. I couldn't believe it—I'd been sprung! I replied politely that perhaps we could meet, but that I would like to know why first.

To my immense relief, it had nothing to do with the real leak, which was still smouldering away waiting to be used. It turned out he was feeling indignant about my approaching a former Shandwick employee some months

earlier to ask about Timberlands. This potential source, the brother of a journalist friend, had mass-produced pro-logging letters to the editor for
Shandwick—but he had said he would rather not talk.

I wrote back to the Shandwick boss saying that, since he was a former journalist himself, I thought he would regard it as perfectly legitimate for me to be
pursuing a story. I said that if I could find the information, I intended to write
about his company's PR campaign for Timberlands. Confident that they were
protected by secrecy, he never suspected that I was already well on the way.

At this stage, I realized there was so much material it should become a
book. I invited my Australian journalist friend Bob Burton to collaborate,
since he had far more experience writing about public relations than I had. It
was he who had introduced me to the idea of deliberately anti-democratic
public relations, leading to my suspicions years later about the Timberlands
campaign. Six months of intense work began.

Logjamming

Because of the risk of legal action, *Secrets and Lies* was written, printed and
distributed in complete secrecy, with no publicity until the day it was in the
bookshops. I did tell a few journalists, including a TV current affairs reporter
who quietly prepared a documentary on the book. The day before it was
released, he interviewed the head of the logging company, Timberlands, who
sincerely told the camera that his company had never lobbied nor tried to
interfere with the environmental campaign. The reporter said, "Can you give
me your word on that, Dave?" He said, "I certainly can, yeah."

The book came out the next morning. The reaction to it surprised everyone, including us. It quickly became lead news, and the prime minister, who
had been a staunch supporter of Timberlands, found herself in the middle of
a controversy over the state logging company's dirty PR tactics. She changed
her story three times during the week after the book's launch, looking increasingly exasperated at the bad publicity. Journalists later cited the controversy as
one of the three issues that had dented her credibility and helped her lose the
national election later that year.

In the wake of the publicity about Timberlands' tactics—and especially its
covert activities to pressure the opposition Labor Party to support logging—
the Labor Party leader personally pushed through a new policy ending all
rainforest logging. When she became prime minister a few months later in
late 1999, one of her new government's first acts was to begin cancelling
logging approvals and preparing to make the forests national parks and
reserves. In March 2001 the government formally agreed to transfer all public
rainforests to the Department of Conservation.

Non-secret detective work

I would not like to give the impression that investigative research is all about secrets and leaked information. In some cases, like this one, there is no other way forward. But most investigative work relies on a much wider set of tools and approaches, and involves locating non-secret information that otherwise would simply remain scattered and unpublicized. This kind of detective work can be just as exciting, satisfying and productive as finding secret sources.

Although we had piles of internal Timberlands documents, I suspect that if I had just passed them on to mainstream journalists they would not even have seen a story there. The shocking and incriminating parts were mostly small sections of larger documents, like "Anti-NFA letter-writing campaign (stock letters). . . NFA lies" mentioned in the minutes of a planning meeting (Native Forest Action was the leading rainforest conservation group). Without context and background, they had little obvious significance. We had to use many other investigative tricks of the trade to explain what the papers revealed and tell the story.

This job of uncovering stories, explanations and truths that are not obvious is the role of the investigative journalist. I believe journalists and researchers have a special role in democratic society far beyond the commercial one of finding stories that are interesting and help sell the surrounding ads. That role is to uncover news those in power would prefer remained secret or unnoticed, to alert the public to important issues, and to scrutinize the versions of truth being broadcast by vested interests through the media. I call this being a 'democratic agent': helping enable the public to play a serious role in politics. This role is similar to that of public interest groups (civil rights and environmentalist groups, for instance), which also uncover important issues, alert the public and challenge the statements and actions of the powerful.

The first thing an investigative journalist brings to the job is an ability to ask the right questions: What lies behind this press release? Is this really true? Who arranged for that statement/information/event to transpire now, and why? As I said, *Secrets and Lies* came about because we wondered what lay behind some attacks on environmentalists.

In the case of public interest groups, I think members should repeatedly ask themselves, "What information, if we had it, would make a huge difference to our campaign?" That is the information they should be seeking. Key information includes the kind that allows a group to make news and set the agenda on an issue (plans, official information, statistics, opinion polls, and so on); the tactical kind about who's making what decisions when, which enables public input; and the factual kind, which people can use to reply to the arguments or expose the untruths of political opponents.

The breakthrough in research often comes when we suddenly realize where we should be probing. In my intelligence research, for instance, I conducted extensive interviews in the assumption that I understood roughly how Western spy agencies co-operated. In fact, I had not really considered that the interception facilities in my country and elsewhere might be integrated into a global system. I simply had not thought to ask about that, although I was talking to people who used the system every day—and so I nearly missed the key to understanding modern electronic spying. Then one day I was discussing a draft section with an intelligence officer who said, "That's not how it works!" That was the day I heard my first description of the Echelon system and realized what I should be investigating.

Open sources

I usually find the best way to start any new investigation is to read through all readily available public information on the subject. Generally, if you have not got to know a subject by means of this slog through the open sources, you will be unable to notice the good stuff when you find it (or even know what to look for).

These open sources include annual reports, all manner of special reports, parliamentary questions and inquiries, official websites and industry and professional magazines. I regard these boring-looking sources—which often almost no one reads or even knows exist—as research gold mines. Wherever possible, we should start with these original documents (not other people's articles about them or quotations from them), as secondary sources can miss interesting clues and even get things wrong. One of the key differences between investigative journalists and garden-variety ones is this return to primary documents. The average newsroom has virtually no files apart from the 'morgue' of past stories. Information is reused from old stories without being checked, so inaccuracies and PR spin can be recycled over and over, with journalists lending their authority to the 'facts'.

A good way to save time is to ask around to find researchers, campaigners or academics who know the topic and can recommend people, publications and collections of information you can consult directly. In articles or books, footnotes or endnotes are often the most valuable part. They can point you to exactly the source you need. And despite the convenience of the internet, don't assume you only need to look there. It is a wonderful tool (for basic information on individuals, companies and organizations, for instance) but can also waste heaps of time in fruitless searches. For many subjects, most information sources are not online. One reason is that many sources more than a couple of years old have either never been placed online or already been taken off again. Specialist libraries and the files of specialist organizations are often more useful. Companies, government departments, research institutes and public interest groups often have libraries you can use if you ask. A day spent reading old files in the national archives can likewise be productive. And whatever the institution, the librarian is the researcher's friend.

This first search does not entail weeks of work. It involves locating the most promising sources and having a first dig. This background allows you to decide where it might be worth looking next: circumstances that look suspicious, an interesting statistic that we decide to compare with figures from other years, and so on. Careful reading of original sources often provides surprises. For instance, while carefully reading the (obviously little-read) legal document that authorized Timberlands' controversial logging, I noticed that a much-quoted key phrase had been handwritten by an official *after* the document was signed. As was subsequently confirmed in a court case, the supposed authority for the logging was invalid.

Some simple sources were invaluable in researching *Secrets and Lies*. For example, I read three years of newspaper clippings on the forest controversy (all carefully collected in New Zealand's Ministry of Forestry library) from beginning to end. This not only allowed me to identify incidents corresponding to ones mentioned in the leaked PR papers, but also let me see, for instance, where officials had changed their stories over time. Reading through the environmental groups' campaign files likewise provided lots of useful material and questions.

Good things take time

The vital investigative attributes I have described so far can be summarized as nosiness, curiosity and an awareness of the diversity of sources available. The next crucial thing we bring to the job is time. Many journalists would like to pursue stories and probe more deeply but their news organizations do not allow them the time. (As a result, some journalists do their most important and rewarding work in their spare time.) Other people can afford the time for investigative research because they are employed by an academic institution or special interest group. However, most people I know of who do this work have adjusted their lives to allow for it, choosing a non-extravagant lifestyle in which part-time paid work allows them to pursue rewarding but often unpaid work in the rest of their time. To them, meaningful work more than compensates for not earning a high salary.

One thing that takes time is waiting for answers to letters requesting information. We can seek official documents using freedom of information laws and use parliamentary processes to gather lots of detailed information, but as replies can take weeks or longer, these methods are of little use to daily news reporters. If we have sufficient time, though, the biggest limitation to what we can find using official questioning is our own ability to think up lots of questions.

We can also interview officials and business people to gather non-secret insights into issues. Note also that retired politicians, government officials and businesspeople—who might not have talked to us while in their jobs—are often quickly forgotten by their old colleagues once they cease to be powerful and useful and are pleased to be interviewed about their experiences and insights. (Just after a 'restructuring', layoffs or a change in government, is a good time to find people willing to talk.)

The key to getting information from people is being brave enough to ask. I find that most people are willing to help. This should be your assumption. Two or three phone calls are often all it takes to locate someone who can help you on the way to the information you are looking for. Once I start asking around, information usually pours in, often in unexpected ways. During the *Secrets and Lies* research, I phoned a woman in a small town who I had heard knew about an arson threat against environmentalists. After talking for a little while, she said, "It's really my husband you should be talking to. He's in Coast Action Network." I waited apprehensively for him to come to the phone: Coast Action Network was a pro-logging group that had been set up as part of the PR strategy. He turned out to be one of the local people who had joined the group in good faith, and he was soon telling me how he had left in disgust when he realized that all the group's activities were being planned at the Timberlands headquarters. He became one of my best sources.

Another time, I phoned an environmentalist who suggested I talk to a woman he went to university with who had a curious story about the Timberlands issue. This woman, it turned out, was being courted by a young man who had confided in her about an exciting job he had had: infiltrating an environmental group for $50 an hour. I checked and found out that he had indeed joined the group and asked lots of questions at meetings, that he had had no involvement in environmental politics before or since, and that he was the son of a senior Shandwick New Zealand employee.

Time allows us to locate helpful people and chance upon bits of luck like this. Time is also what allows us to check whether official facts are true. Sadly, with politicized issues and vested interests, we cannot assume any of the supposed facts are true. Many times I have forgotten this and assumed facts stated plainly by people in positions of authority were more or less true, only to find later that they were not. In the course of writing *Secrets and Lies* we found that nearly all the 'facts' in the pro-logging PR material turned out not to be such, or else told a different story when put into context.

The power of exposure

The anti-environmental campaign described in *Secrets and Lies* might have made depressing reading, showing how secret tactics and constant lies could be used to undermine genuine community groups relatively easily. They were caught out this time, but lots of other times such tactics succeed. Still, I believe the lessons of the Timberlands case are positive and hopeful.

The best defence against these kinds of PR tactics is to know about them. Recognizing them is the first step in exposing them.

Intimidating legal threats, front groups, systematic attacks on critics: when community groups can identify these, and cry foul when they are used, it helps to reduce their power. There has been more public discussion about public relations in my country (including among PR professionals) since the book's publication than ever before.

Perhaps the most powerful lesson in this case study is that when companies and governments resort to unethical tactics, they wield a double-edged sword. The dirtier the tactics, the more damage they do to those responsible if they are exposed. Timberlands' reward for using these tactics was that it was seriously discredited. At the time of writing, the government is discussing disestablishing the company.

The Timberlands case turned out to be a spectacular example of how exposing corporate PR activities can help to undo dirty strategies. Most investigative work, of course, does not have quite such dramatic and immediate effects. But it is still fascinating and very satisfying. I wish more people would do it. There is lots to be done.

Chapter 15

Digging up Astroturf

Claudia Peter

You could say that Monsanto invented astroturf.[1]

Originally, astroturf was artificial grass for playgrounds and sports fields. But the term is also used to describe the artificial grassroots organizations corporations create and send into battle against their activist critics. John Stauber of the Center for Media and Democracy described astroturf as "the appearance of democracy bought and paid for with millions of dollars from wealthy special interests".[2]

For companies, pseudo-grassroots front groups are a bargain. They cost less than PR departments, and enjoy much more prestige in the eyes of the media, and sometimes even politicians, who are afraid of the power of the people. PR departments are reduced to issuing dull press releases, but these freewheeling front groups can employ Greenpeace-like civil disobedience tactics sure to put them in the national media spotlight.

Astroturf lobbying is not restricted to Anglo-Saxon countries. It is alive and well in Germany, where it has been tailored to fit the local political system. The 1990s saw a virtual flood of astroturf groups in Germany. This chapter describes some of their methods and shows how they moved from aggressive anti-environmental tactics to a softer approach which is slowly changing German power brokers' attitude to environmental protection.

Journalists and NGOs can expose astroturf tactics through investigation of their founders, funding and connections. This can send these groups up in smoke quickly.

The Waste Watchers

The first anti-environmental group in Germany to resort to astroturf methods carefully chose its name to resemble that of a well-respected NGO. They called themselves Waste Watchers, luring people into connecting them with Helsinki Watch, Americas Watch and other respected human rights groups.

The group watched waste all right—protected it, one might say. At its first public appearance, at an environmental fair in Ulm, it diligently assembled a mountain of waste. Signs on top bore the names of five leading German environmental organizations. The argument: those irresponsible environmentalists were causing waste to pile up by opposing incinerators.

The incinerator debate loomed large in Germany in the early 1990s. Federal and state governments promoted incinerators heavily. But environmentalists argued they were dangerous because they emitted dioxins and unknown quantities of other dangerous compounds. They also said burning waste would fuel the throwaway consumer society. They advocated recycling technologies instead, or, where recycling wasn't possible, letting waste rot away in a protected environment. Their arguments met with increasing success, especially at the local level. No community wanted an incinerator in its backyard. Instead of being drowned in lawsuits with angry constituents, local politicians preferred to find common ground with an environmentally aware citizenry.

So the incinerator industry was in danger of losing business. But packaging manufacturers that produced drink cartons and cans had a problem too. These packaging materials were hard to recycle and easy to burn. Environmentalists had already proposed an additional tax to make producers and consumers pay for their disposal.

Waste Watchers' arrival on the scene produced a media stir. Here was a group that challenged the environmental movement's position from an environmentalist point of view—or so it seemed.

But doubts arose quickly when journalists took a closer look at the group's origins. Waste Watchers was founded in 1992 in Hamburg. Spokesman Manfred Geisler-Hansson had quit his job as head of the Tetra Pak press office weeks before. Tetra Pak, a Dutch company, was and is Europe's leading manufacturer of soft drink cartons. It has a reputation for greenwashing in both Europe and the US, where it ran into problems when its ads falsely claimed recycling a Tetra Box was "as easy as recycling a sheet of paper".[3] The same campaign hit Europe in winter 1992, with no reaction from any national authorities. But the European Union fined Tetra Pak a record 75 million ECUs (about $96,915,000 in 1992) for aggressively pushing competitors out of the market.

Geisler-Hansson was silent about Waste Watchers' financial sources. One thing was clear, though: he had a lot of cash. He had an office suite in an upscale area and five employees. In its first year, Waste Watchers claimed a membership of 300, and DM20,000 ($12,377) in membership fees. But it also said it spent DM600,000 ($371,310) that year.[4] Where had the other DM580,000 ($358,933) come from?

Geisler-Hansson finally admitted his organization was "co-operating" with industry. But he insisted Waste Watchers had no financial connections to Tetra Pak. "We asked, but they declined," he said.

It was clear at the beginning that the prime goal of Waste Watchers was not about waste disposal policy, but discrediting the environmental movement. Its technique was simple, but effective at first. It hailed itself as the only voice for "responsible" waste management. Opponents of incinerators were "irrational" and "antisocial".[5] In fact, because of their positions on waste disposal, environmental organizations were a danger to society.

A special target was the German branch of Friends of the Earth (FoE), the Association for the Preservation of Nature and Environment (BUND), which Waste Watchers accused of "scheming for the collapse of society" and painted larger than life. Politicians, Waste Watchers argued, were easy prey for the "pressure that BUND groups exerted in nearly every field of policy on a daily basis." [6]

Geisler-Hansson started a newsletter, *Federal Environmental News Service*, whose stated purpose was to publish inside information on environmental organizations which those organizations preferred to keep hidden. Its primary source was said to be a confidential telephone hotline.[7] The result was a collection of short news bites, most credited to unnamed sources. From August to October 1994, Waste Watchers published three issues of this newsletter. One-third of 37 total news bites were about BUND. Subscriptions for journalists were supposedly DM180 ($111) per year, but hundreds received the newsletter for free, unasked.

But Geisler-Hansson went too far when he personally targeted the CEO of BUND Baden-Württemberg, Erhard Schulz, accusing him of taking bribes from companies at an environmental fair he organized each year. Waste Watchers offered no proof these allegations were true but promised readers it was "investigating".[8] Professional journalists should have recognized the scam immediately, but the rubbish made it into print. Weeks later, Geisler-Hansson told reporters he was still "investigating". Schulz sued for damages, saying his reputation had been tarnished.

In spite of all the ruckus, Waste Watchers' actions did little to divide the environmental movement or weaken its position with policymakers. So the group tried a different approach, introducing another organization with similar views. Out of the blue, Ehrliches Müllkonzept ("Honest Waste Concept") appeared. The name was no surprise: it echoed that of a genuine organization, Das bessere Müllkonzept ("Better Waste Concept"), which had become popular in Bavaria for successfully using grassroots lobbying tactics against incineration and nearly winning a referendum on alternative waste disposal. The campaign of the fake group, Ehrliches Müllkonzept, on the other hand, was unimpressive, consisting mainly of passing around brochures with pictures of incinerators and marvelling at their beauty.

The group's leader turned out to be Rüdiger Polster—a freelance journalist and a Waste Watchers founder. And some investigation in Hamburg revealed further surprises.

To celebrate its birth, the group had held a press conference in January 1992. All its members had turned up—all seven, the smallest number required to found a Verein, a registered and tax-favoured group. But four of the seven were foreigners. Why were they interested in the intricacies of German waste policy?

One, the Danish businessman Ove Hansson, was Geisler-Hansson's father-in-law. Another, Briton Maggie Thurgood, was editor-in-chief of the British waste journal *Warmer Bulletin*.[9] The publication was owned by the Paris-based World Resource Foundation—whose name called to mind the scientific research organization World Resources Institute. One of Thurgood's bosses proved to be Hans Rausing, member of the board of trustees of this noble foundation—and chairman of Tetra Pak.

When Waste Watchers' board members' ties to Rausing and Tetra Pak were revealed in the book *Deckmantel Oekologie* ('The Ecology Disguise'),[10] and later in the weekly *Der Spiegel*,[11] the group was finished. On top of all that came the verdict in the Erhard Schulz libel case. Waste Watchers was ordered to pay DM25,000 ($15,471) in damages. To everybody's surprise, they paid. But when *Der Spiegel* tried to reach them for an interview on their Tetra Pak ties, it found the group's phones were disconnected.

Waste Watchers has not been active since. The group failed not only because of its immense stupidity but also its ignorance of the German political system and mentality. Its cheap slander was strongly reminiscent of the methods of US right-wing conspiracy groups. It held up environmentalists' skepticism about incineration as proof that they wanted to rule the country. Germans were unused to these methods, and didn't like them. In two decades, the environmental movement had built a reputation as one of the most credible institutions in German society. US-style environmentalist-bashing was no way to beat it.

Tilting at windmills

Much is at stake for German utility companies in the debate over wind farms. By law, utility companies must subsidize their wind-electricity-producing competitors. The German government designed this law to reduce the use of nuclear and fossil-fuel energy in favour of renewable energy. Large utility companies see it as an obstacle to business and free market forces.

Out of nowhere, a self-proclaimed 'environmental' organization calling itself the Federal Organization for Landscape Protection, abbreviated BLS in German, started complaining that wind energy companies were profiting from the law. Suspicions quickly arose that the BLS was an astroturf outfit designed to simulate local resistance against wind energy and cause unrest and debate. The unmasking of Waste Watchers served as a blueprint for journalists to evaluate the BLS for what it was.

Just east of Munich, the tiny village of Neufarn boasts one hill, about 500 feet high. Two years ago, a company set its sights on this hill, looking to erect an environmentally friendly electricity-producing windmill. The Social Democrat mayor was excited and spread the news around town. But then the storm set in.

Out of the blue, a citizens' group appeared, arguing against the "madness" of the windmill. It was much too high, they argued. Its shadow and noise would "terrorize" the neighbourhood. It would kill birds by the hundreds. And it would almost certainly devalue property. The group borrowed its arguments from BLS propaganda, according to journalist Michael Franken, as did several dozen similar anti-wind-farm initiatives around Germany. The BLS almost never acted under its own name at the local level. Every campaign was "an initiative by Village X against the terrible wind farm threat".

Neufarn held a highly emotional city hall meeting. Afterward, the wind farm's few proponents couldn't walk down the street without being called names, and anonymous callers threatened to kill the mayor.[12] The project was cancelled.

Across the country, in the town of Ahlerstedt near Hamburg, conservative councilman Luder Pott was also arguing for a local wind farm. He told Franken some people had held him up on the street and threatened him, saying the wind farm would raise energy prices and he would pay dearly. "It's like a civil war," he said. "Daughters are not talking to their fathers any more; sons don't say hello to their brothers on the street."[13]

The two stories are remarkably similar, and the same name often pops up in both: BLS. Founded in late 1994, the group opposes the building of wind farms from the North Sea to the Alps, handing out pre-packaged 'Anti-Windfarm First Aid Kits' for people to use in starting clone campaigns across Germany.[14] Local mouthpieces are almost always citizens of towns near proposed wind farm sites. But BLS representatives also busily tour the country giving talks, fuelling local anger and sometimes even personally distributing lengthy 'scientific' papers to everyone in a community.

According to the Federal Association for Wind Energy, the BLS has caused the abandonment of projects worth more than DM500 million (about $225 million). In most cases, creating a groundswell of negative public opinion was enough. Local politicians dropped the projects voluntarily, sometimes wasting years of planning. Unanimous support for projects among council members changed almost overnight into strong majorities against them.

The BLS insists it is an association of normal citizens with no links to industry. But contrary to this professed modest status, the group seems to have enormous amounts of money and time. Wherever a plan for a new wind farm is made public, the group shows up within days, distributing leaflets and lengthy 'scientific assessments' throughout the community, free of charge. From the beginning it has styled itself like a large NGO, dividing the country into several regions and—in a stunning flashback to Nazi language—placing a 'Gruppenführer' (squad leader) in charge of each.[15]

For a long time its background was mysterious. The association is registered in the tiny seaside village of Niebüll. It publishes no financial records or information on who its members are. This lack of transparency in itself raises suspicions. Though not legally obliged to do so, most genuine German NGOs freely share information on their financing, members, donors and sponsors to head off suspicion they are pawns of other political actors. The BLS routinely sues those voicing doubts about it—but it never actively tries to counter or disprove those doubts.

For years, even insiders could do no more than voice their suspicions about industry sponsorship. The group's arguments were remarkably in tune with those of conventional energy giants. And not surprisingly, the industry warmly recommended BLS material as a source of further 'information' on wind energy. But there was no proof of any direct link between industry and the BLS.

Then one little fax number on BLS documents distributed by its lawyer Thomas Mock gave the group away. That number led journalist Michael Franken to damning information about the 'grassroots' BLS: the fax machine belonged to the aluminium producer Vereinigte Aluminiumwerke (VAW), which Mock admitted he worked for. VAW's then-parent company, VIAG, made most of its profits through conventional and nuclear electricity.[16] Mock said the fax number had been an oversight and his work for BLS was entirely private. But if that's true, the company must be a generous employer, since Mock spends several days a week on the road for the group, according to Franken.[17]

Franken publicly revealed the conventional and nuclear power industry's involvement in BLS in an award-winning TV report. For instance, he told how the group's propaganda was routinely mailed in envelopes bearing the postal stamp of another company, HochTief, part of Rheinisch-Westfälische Elektrizitätswerke (RWE)—another large energy producer. Asked about the mailings, HochTief claimed they were private acts by an employee. Others familiar with German office procedures also doubt the truth of this—in Germany sending private mail using a company's franking machine is a grave offence normally followed by dismissal, and no dismissal or disciplinary action was ever mentioned.

He also showed how the BLS used deceptive tactics to get its message out. In the town of Reuth, lawyer Mock started a petition against a wind farm project, but the mayor sued him for tampering with the petition's text after collecting signatures.[18] Even his environmentalist opponents were surprised that a lawyer would resort to such an act—and get caught.

The BLS's website lauds "sister organizations" in countries including Britain and Denmark.[19] According to Greenpeace, the British group Country Guardian is the baby of Sir Bernard Ingham, former press secretary to Margaret Thatcher and secretary of an organization called Supporters of Nuclear Energy.[20] The three "sister" groups' websites use the same frightening pictures: windmills blown up to the size of cathedrals, accompanied by the menacing prediction that they will change the landscape forever. (Coal mines and nuclear power stations alter the landscape much more, but these organizations have never been spotted protesting about them.)

The BLS survived its humiliation on national television. But at the time of writing, economics and politics seem to be accomplishing what environmentalists couldn't—putting the BLS out of business. Wind farms have become so profitable that large utility companies like Siemens and RWE are building them instead of fighting them. "They are more liberal now than their own front group," Franken says. "In time the BLS will be nothing but a big embarrassment for companies."[21]

Weeding out astroturf

The unmasking of Waste Watchers served as a blueprint for the future evaluation of astroturf groups. Answers to a few questions can reveal whether a group is genuine. How deeply is it rooted in the community—does it have local and regional chapters, or is it just a tiny outfit claiming national importance? How open is it about its funding and membership? Do its leaders have a credible record of previous grassroots work? Do its expenditures match its resources? Where these questions lead to less than satisfying answers, activists can alert the media. They can now voice legitimate doubts about a group's grassroots origins.

But that's just the first step. If a group seems to be an industry front, the next question is: exactly who is funding it? With Waste Watchers it was easy; all the signs pointed to Tetra Pak. But newer groups in Germany learned from the Waste Watchers affair to hide their ties to industry. The BLS—founded in 1995, the year journalists forced the Waste Watchers out of business—hides its financial records from public scrutiny (as is legal under German law), and its key figures are careful not to display any financial interest in opposing wind farms.

Such groups make artful use of citizens' freedom to organize: posing as grassroots groups, they are accountable to no one but the local tax office. Their bookkeeping is amateurish and their tax returns are hardly checked since they appear to be nothing but concerned citizens. And they have learned to call less attention to themselves by being less aggressive, since there is no pre-existing public anti-environmental sentiment to be preyed upon in Germany.

The current set-up stretches the powers of investigative journalists to the limit. Newspapers and TV shows don't accept stories on astroturf groups if their ties to industry can't be shown through bank accounts. Successfully uncovering such a group usually requires a combination of meticulous research and sheer luck. You have to trace a lot of faxes before you hit the jackpot.

Lonely fighters can't easily do this. Journalists like Franken—often self-employed—must go out on a limb to pursue these stories. They carry the legal risks, with no financial, nor sometimes even moral, backing. And even large organizations like Greenpeace shy away from the task. A big group could put its own researchers onto the task of uncovering astroturf groups, but since such tiresome background work doesn't impress donors, it is rarely under-taken, at least in Germany.

Astroturf seems to be working better than ever. Environmentalists must continue to spread the word—this organization is astroturf, here's how it works, and the mainstream media had better believe it—but it's important that they communicate and organize more effectively, too.

Franken blames wind farm companies' and environmentalists' lack of organized opposition. "The BLS employed exactly the same methods at dozens of sites. The professional engineers and the wind farm lobbyists should have been better prepared. They failed to set up any kind of public relations on the ground. If you start working with the population and stifle arguments against wind farms before they are even made, you're sure to win," he said.[22]

NGOs must keep fighting to uproot new patches of astroturf, since the new methods are more sophisticated than old-style badmouthing and pre-sumably have a better chance of success. Far from the spotlight, such simu-lated concern could slowly change public attitudes.

Chapter 16

Obstructing the Mainstream: Lessons from Seattle

Kees Hudig

"They've got the guns, but we've got the numbers."—The Doors

Until recently, resistance to neoliberal policy and the power of business was still weak and fragmentary, but it now seems as though the powers that be are being forced more and more on to the defensive. Wherever businesspeople and politicians gather, they hold their meetings with difficulty, surrounded by barbed wire and heavily armed police forces while being besieged by enraged crowds. Fukuyama has swiftly had to swallow his thesis about the "end of history".

The mass blockade in Seattle caught the local guardians of law and order totally by surprise, as did the fact that classical means of repression failed to work. Amidst a cloud of tear gas and pepper spray, the WTO Summit was suffocated by waves of protesters. What's notable about these spectacular events is not only that thousands of people took part, but that they refused to limit themselves to demonstrating. They developed effective strategies to prevent or impede the meetings of institutions they criticize.

From a distance, the blockade actions in Seattle, Washington, Melbourne and Prague[1] may have looked like simple, somewhat spontaneous affairs—with enough people, you can take over the city. But in reality, they were extremely complex operations preceded by months of hard work. They succeeded only through clever organization that made use of a decentralized concept.

The events in Washington and Seattle were based on broad coalitions of various kinds of NGO (chiefly those concerned with debt, the Third World and the environment), unions and activist groups. They grouped partly around a clearly stated criticism of the institutions and a number of radical demands. The central manifesto was accompanied by websites giving more detailed background information. But it was made clear to all that the block-

ades needed to be effective: not just a symbolic demonstration, but a deliberate attempt to stop the meetings. This unique blend of widely shared criticism
and activist attitude may be the new movement's biggest 'secret'.

After the core coalitions were formed, the activists did a lot of work and
held a lot of meetings dealing with money, pamphlets, posters, websites and
the initial infrastructure, in order to make the actions a success. Websites
played an important role, enabling information distribution, discussion,
fundraising and expansion of the coalition.[2]

A big blockade is usually accompanied by seminars, workshops and discussions on the background of the protested institution that attract hundreds
of people. A non-commercial journalists' network and central office are set
up. Articles, photos, radio reports and short videos are placed online, and the
network is able to produce instant video reports for viewing around the
world. The commercial media are making increasing use of this information.
But the Indymedia sites' chief purpose is to allow people around the world to
follow the events, even when official media coverage is skimpy or poor.[3]

Forming base groups

A central gathering place ('convergence centre') plays a central role at a big
blockade. People can go there during the run-up to the actions for information, workshops and food, and to form 'affinity groups', which are akin to the
'base groups' of the European anti-nuclear movement in the early '80s. An
organizing platform asks everyone who wants to join the blockade to organize
into groups of up to a few dozen and report to the centre.

The groups practice things like effective blockading and resisting police
attacks. Organizations like the Ruckus Society and Direct Action Network
(DAN), which specialize in training activists in methods of non-violent direct
action, help.[4] Every affinity group is asked to send a representative to the daily
planning meeting. The representative presents decisions made there to the
affinity group.

At the April 2000 IMF/World Bank meeting in Washington, about 600
people attended a public meeting on the evening between the two days of the
blockade. Officially, only affinity group representatives could speak and vote,
but control was impossible and not really attempted. It was more or less left
up to the participants to keep things from disintegrating into chaos, which
worked reasonably well. When the participants were unable to agree on a
unanimous plan for the second day, they divided into two groups, and each
made and carried out its own plan.

Naturally, this structure was highly vulnerable to infiltration, and not
much could be done to prevent it. People continually reminded each other at

the public meetings that 'they' were listening, and naturally any infiltrators found would have been removed, but mostly people were just advised to work out the details of actions within the affinity groups.

Piece of pie

In Washington, as in Seattle, the area around the World Bank and IMF buildings was divided into a large number of 'pie pieces' and the hundreds of small groups were distributed over the intersections. Some people formed 'flying squads' that could speed to weak points in the blockade or places where the police were trying to break through. They could also surround busloads of meeting participants on their way to the summit.

The road-blocking groups sat all day, beginning at 5 a.m., often chained together. Some groups were divided in two so people could work in shifts. Group members agreed in advance who was willing to be arrested and who preferred to operate in the background. It was also decided who in a group would stay outside to take care of other chores like providing food and drink, 'coaching' in panic situations, and trying to negotiate with police.

The central organization arranged for people available at each blockade point to keep in touch with headquarters, first aid workers and attorneys by mobile phone or walkie-talkie. 'Spies' also circulated on foot and by bicycle and car, observing police activities, checking on blockade points and reporting arrests and incidents.

The demonstrators brought along a remarkable number of subversive decorations. Every blockade point overflowed with banners and posters; giant papier-maché figures were on display, chants were repeated. Even 'flying squads' carried drums made of garbage cans, wore fake shark fins on their heads (IMF as 'loan sharks') or dressed as businessman caricatures. A group of university students sang a special song to people being arrested, informing them of their rights. 'Radical cheerleaders' danced around encouraging the blockade groups. And even the fearsome-looking Black Bloc—one of the most effective flying squads, with 300 people—had an 'anarchist marching band' in its ranks.

Forging agreements

The organizing coalition had not only clearly formulated criticisms and demands but also agreed on action methods. The blockade needed to be effective and non-violent. But Seattle had proved that formulating a few sentences wouldn't cut it. After a small group of organized anarchists unleashed their fury on selected banks and multinationals, acts of enraged retaliation issued from the ranks of the fundamentally non-violent, to the immense pleasure of the press. Instead of going along with the post-Seattle hysteria and committing themselves to strict non-violence, the Washington DC organizers and participants held a fruitful discussion to deal with the problem in a practical way. They agreed the upcoming blockade would be non-violent but also worked out in detail what would and would not be considered 'violent'. It was decided that spray-painting slogans on company buildings and building barricades would not, and that demonstrators had the right to defend themselves from police attacks. This flexible position was met with an unspoken agreement by the more radical visitors not to go overboard smashing windows under cover of the crowd. The Black Bloc busily barricaded intersections in the early morning hours, and police were pushed back several times when they tried to attack blockade points.

There were no clear common standpoints about how exactly to carry out the blockade. But it was agreed that no one would be let through, including the press. Everyone knew the agreements made by the members of the organizing umbrella in discussion with the affinity groups. A programme booklet summed up the plans, and included advice on preparing for action, such as wearing a helmet and bringing along vinegar-soaked cloths to use against tear gas or pepper spray, and what to do in case of arrest.

The issue of violence

But the successful formula used in Seattle and Washington does not always lead to the same results, as activists learned in Prague.

At the IMF/World Bank Summit in September 2000 in Prague, the organizers of the actions tried to get all the participants behind a common idea of non-violent blockade. The organizers, many from the US, did not realize the North American non-violent blockade model could not be indiscriminately transferred to Europe. Many activists, mostly from autonomist and anarchist groups, did not feel bound to the agreements and tried to access the conference centre by militant means. And at the EU summit in Nice, France, in December 2000, some activists resorted to attacking the police lines which cordoned off the summit site.

Relationships are different in Europe, for various reasons. Some activist groups, clinging tight to their roots in 1980s radical movements, embrace street confrontation. The squatters' and anti-nuclear movements then powerful in many cities regard their 'right to resist' as of great importance, and reject the state's monopoly on violence. They are also extremely suspicious of the big NGOs they consider 'reformist'—more part of the system than agents of change. The gap between the direct-action activists and the big NGOs is probably wider in Europe than in North America, as Northern European social-democratic government structures have co-opted larger sectors.

Another difference in Europe is that there, trade unions generally take more of a wait-and-see approach, so the coalition is less broad. The European anti-globalization movement seems to have less to lose if things escalate, since its members don't rely on the support of organized labour. In Southern Europe (especially France, Italy, Spain and Greece), the co-optation of critical organizations is less a part of the political system, and large trade unions are an important part of the movement. They have a tradition of militancy and are not easily scared off by skirmishes with the police.

Actions by autonomist groups threaten to further narrow the 'movement', by putting off less militant demonstrators and moving moderate organizations to refuse to take part in umbrella activist platforms. These people may also be forfeiting the sympathy of those members of the public who deeply respect deliberate non-violence, especially when the state is clearly using violence, as it did in Seattle. But militant activists defend their position by arguing that the commercial media always blame protesters for riots, even those caused by police or provocateurs. All in all, with many NGOs openly distancing themselves from violence and few structures bridging the two sides, the radical cocktail we have seen in other parts of the world seems less promising in Northern Europe.

In addition, blockading the meetings was not a realistic option in Prague, for several reasons. Many activists would not arrive until the delegates were at work, and many delegates were staying in a gigantic hotel next door to the meeting centre and inside the zone secured by police.

The conference centre was in an easy-to-shield valley, and participants were brought in via the metro system, which had a stop underneath the conference centre. This had also been a problem in Washington, where many delegates could reach the meeting centre via tunnels without running into activists. Those who weren't fundamentally non-violent argued that surrounding the meeting would have to be mainly symbolic because of this setup, but many people came to try to impede the meeting anyway.

Another problem was that the Prague authorities had prohibited demonstrations during the meeting, granting permission only for a manifestation on a square far from the conference centre. In order to protest and blockade the meeting, the activists would have to approach the conference centre against the will of the police.

The solution was a sort of compromise, which offered a way forward but not a unified strategy. It consisted of the unexpected breakup of the central manifestation into three separate ones that would move toward the conference centre along different routes. These smaller demonstrations differed in character, so everyone could join in the form of action that suited them.

In this way, militant and non-violent activists took to the streets together. A necessary condition for this is that the two camps respect and tolerate each other. This approach has worked for more than 20 years in the German anti-nuclear movement.

The militant demonstrations in Prague had the unforeseen effect of prematurely ending the IMF-World Bank meeting. Though the institutions' spokespeople tried to create the impression that nothing was out of the ordinary, it was clear that pressure from 'outsiders' had played a crucial role. Summits like this one don't happen only inside the official meeting centre. The thousands of participants also go into the city for various sessions, meals and recreation. In a Prague swarming with enraged and inventive activists, they could not do so. On the first night of the meeting a classical concert was cancelled when thousands of demonstrators surrounded the opera house, and small groups of activists also gathered outside hotels where delegates from rich countries were staying.

Another lesson from Prague, then, is that activists can frustrate a summit from points other than the central meeting place. The big question after Prague and Nice is whether the movement will splinter further or keep its focus on discussion, consensus and building up the broadest and biggest possible front.

Summit-hopping

Another recent debate concerns 'summit-hopping'. Critics say too much attention and energy goes into the big blockades of multinational summits, which activists travel to get to. This, they say, comes at the cost of developing an infrastructure for local and daily struggle against the power of big business. The critics charge that people are blinded by the spectacle of the official summits, though often all they are is festive signing ceremonies, the decisions being made elsewhere. They also say summit-hopping is a form of action that excludes the main victims of globalization, who are unable to get to such events.

But most people who participate in large-scale protests also belong to organizations that are active at the local, everyday level. A considerable number of the demonstrators in Washington were members of local chapters of Students Against Sweatshops, a group that protests against universities' ties with multinationals that treat and pay their workers poorly. And it cannot be denied that the spectacular joining of forces at these summits has had a magical effect.[5]

Still, it is clear that this movement which has applied itself to the media-sensitive spectacle of international summits should work on developing a worldwide network that offers a perspective for local, everyday action. Both the media and the critics of summit-hopping fail to see that important movements in the South took this step long ago. The Zapatistas, the MST landless workers' movement in Brazil, and farmers' movements in India that oppose activities including dam-building and genetic manipulation are based in strong local practice but also consider themselves part of a worldwide resistance movement and actively contribute to the formation of international networks.

Another new development is the designation of international days of local action during important summits. The June 1999 G-7 summit in Cologne, Germany, was accompanied by demonstrations, occupations and blockades all over the world. In London, for example, the City was occupied by thousands of protesters festively and effectively.

The law enforcement counter-offensive

The developments since Seattle not only paint a gratifying picture of growing international resistance against 'corporate' globalization. We have also gained insight into methods being used to throw sand in the protest machine.

Abby Scher's article in *The Nation*, 'The Crackdown on Dissent', shows how secret services and police forces have mounted a counter-offensive to prevent future Seattles—by nearly any means available. Infiltration, criminalization and arrests of peaceful activists are part of the daily routine. The guardians of order have also figured out the importance of the infrastructure for the actions. Police closed the convention centres in Washington, Philadelphia and Prague. They jammed mobile telephones, detained people with key positions in communication and independent media, closed radio transmitters, raided banner- and puppet-making workshops and interfered with websites.

At the FTAA summit in Quebec in April 2001 (on expanding the NAFTA trade zone across the Americas), the jaw-dropping precautionary measures included fencing off a huge no-demonstration zone in the city centre and clearing a 600-place jail for demonstrators. In Quebec, activists faced a dilemma similar to the one in Prague—with all the hotels and meeting places blocked off, an effective blockade became impossible. Militant demonstrators focused on attacking the fence, but police used copious amounts of tear gas and other weapons to keep them at bay. Many analysts, however, have concluded that the critics scored publicity points and the authorities paid a heavy price for such tactics.

Crucial to the success of the actions in Quebec was the concept of 'diversity of tactics'. Militant and non-militant activists gave each other space. Instead of wasting time criticizing each other, they formed separate platforms that worked together on organization and publicity. The activists also contacted and consulted local residents' organizations far in advance, so they would be less easy to play off against each other when the time came.

Activists now know to set up flexible structures that enable quick substitutions and detours. But that is expensive and confusing, for it is difficult to communicate with thousands of foreign activists when your meeting centre is closed and alternative means of communication are blocked.

Increasing numbers of foreign activists are also being turned back at international borders by authorities armed with lists of the names of people arrested at earlier summits. Hundreds have been arrested at mass arrests during the summits, usually without any legal grounds. One reason seems to be that it allows them to be registered. The vast majority are not convicted.

Clearly these mass arrests are also intended to scare away demonstrators. And that is threatening precisely because the movement is such an international phenomenon. No distinction is made on the lists between the convicted and the acquitted; just having been arrested in Prague or Seattle could get you turned away at the border on the way to the WEF meeting in Davos or the FTAA summit in Quebec.

But there is reason for hope: activists are developing new means of organization and communication. They are refusing to be intimidated by mass arrests, and jails are becoming new sites for mass action. The relatively new strategy of 'jail solidarity' is being used more and more often. It goes further than refusing to give your name and making a statement to police: in Seattle and Washington those released refused to leave their cells until everyone was let go. For the same reason, large numbers of people also refused to pay a $50 fine that would enable them to go free, ultimately leading to mass releases without people having had to give their names or pay.

Sit-ins and other actions are also being deployed more quickly around the world in demands for the release of people arrested. In place of 'convergence centres', activists are opening multiple small independent media channels as a more flexible replacement. And when police block off a summit meeting centre, demonstrators blockade the hotels, or organize a football game on an unblocked piece of freeway. Those resisting a world in which only corporate rule would apply are beginning to realize that it's all about who has the most endurance and ingenuity.

Breadth: a strength and a weakness

Another visible trend is the attempt by the powers that be to create ruptures in the informal network. The beleaguered institutions have been courting the more moderate organizations, even inviting them to take part in their programmes in exchange for the organizations' distancing themselves from more radical activists. This, of course, is not new. And the fact that powerful institutions are opening their doors to selected critics shows how effective recent actions have been. Still, we are in danger of returning to the days when there was a clear difference between the proper, law-abiding lobbyist NGOs and the wild hordes of activists whom it's OK to abuse and arrest.

The movement giving so much grief to world leaders lately is a multifaceted community of groups which are far from agreeing on every point and even stand in polar opposition on some. No rigid structure unites them, and in that sense this cannot really be called a movement. These people found each other mainly because they have a common enemy—corporate globalization (though there is disagreement on how to define that enemy and whether to call it 'globalization', 'capitalism', or something else). But the breakthrough since the 1990s has been that people now seem to be more willing to give differences—within certain boundaries—a subordinate role, 'to agree to disagree'. The breadth of the spectrum, in terms of ideology as well as political strategy, is what makes up the 'movement's' strength, and what makes it so difficult to fight. Its lack of central authority or hierarchical structure means that no roundup or imprisonment can spell its death blow. And fruitful cross-pollination between the different organizations is also taking place. The radicals are using the expertise of the established NGOs that have thoroughly researched the problems the activists are targeting. And the NGOs (or unions or environmental organizations) are catching the infectious perspectives and methods of the groups devoted to direct action. Of course, this whole informal network is constantly under tension, and it will only exist as long as the participating organizations refrain from condemning each other.

As moderate groups have increasingly lost faith in parliamentary politics, groups that once refused to co-operate, or were uninterested in each other, have come together. After years of working like mad on the lobbying level, many moderate groups have openly concluded that such work yielded little or nothing.

The shift of power on to the corporate level in the last 10 years has evidently begun to accelerate and, maybe even more provocatively, it is generally doing so with the consent of politicians in rich countries. In accepting the superiority of the neoliberal model and continuously emphasizing a belief in 'the market' as a regulating phenomenon, established politics "committed suicide", as the masked Zapatista spokesperson Subcomandante Marcos put it. Politicians and their parties are increasingly seen as the stooges of big business, as the differences between progressive and conservative political parties steadily evaporate.

For organizations that want changes that do not coincide with the interests of business, and will certainly not be provided by 'the market', it makes sense to concentrate on action methods that route around parliamentary politics and directly confront corporate interests. And a more confrontational attitude has yielded visible results, if only in terms of media attention.

The institutions being taken to task for their international economic decision-making are steadily gaining centralized power, and thus affect all sectors of society. AIDS activists, feminists, union members, environmental activists and solidarity groups meet on the street as they demonstrate against the common enemy: the WTO, the IMF, the EU, the WEF or one of their clones. Here, too, we see fruitful cross-pollination: all kinds of single-issue groups are discovering their problems are connected to those of other groups, and getting to know those other groups' activities and members at demonstrations and anti-conferences.

Naturally, this breadth of the ideological spectrum could become a problem. A growing issue is that some groups are forging connections with shadowy conservative groups that oppose globalization mainly for xenophobic and nationalistic reasons. An ongoing honest discussion, in place of the traditional sectarian denunciations by radical groups and haughty unaccountability on the part of big NGOs, should determine the boundaries of coalitions.

The key question is whether it's going to be possible to develop networks broad enough to include and mobilize substantial sectors of society but at the same time powerful enough to exact structural changes. And those networks will also have to be resilient enough to exist for longer than one summit or campaign, and not fall apart along traditional dividing lines at the first criticism.

Strangely enough, the fact that the movement, or 'network of networks', has become an undeniable power also constitutes a threat to it. Many social-democratic political parties and NGOs are coming forth to claim leadership, such as at the World Social Forum in Porto Alegre. There is also an unmistakable flood of commercial interest in the increasingly popular movement. Commercial media and publishers are jumping on the bandwagon, creating the spokespeople and 'leaders' that had been lacking, and politicians rush to 'debate' them.

The escalation of police violence in Gothenburg and Genoa in 2001 has pushed the boundaries; no easy answers have yet been found, but the discussion is heated. One of the most important questions is how protests under such circumstances can still take place without falling back on militaristic reactions.

The coming challenge will be not so much to maintain the growth of the critical movements, since that seems to be continuing, but how to keep surprising—and throwing sand in—the neoliberal machine. Sometimes it takes a while before new answers are found, and we must have the patience to let them develop. For now, luckily, the development of more colourful protest groups shows no signs of slowing down. The practical experiments carried out at the big summits show that we are learning more and growing stronger every day.

Chapter 17

Communication Guerrillas: Using the Language of Power

autonome a.f.r.i.k.a. gruppe

The best argument is useless if nobody wants to hear it. The world knows the planet is warming up, but that didn't stop George W. Bush from blocking the limits on emissions fixed in the Kyoto treaty. Everybody knows people in the global South are forced to work in sweatshops under terrible conditions, but this knowledge has done little to improve workers' rights or wages.

With political rituals like trashing a McDonald's or blocking a nuclear waste transport or a neo-fascist meeting, activists often become the state's included 'other': the roles are set, the militant ritual fails to communicate its political message. The state, in fact, needs radical leftist rituals to provide symbolic balance against the extreme right and justify new repressive laws.

A few years ago, the German-based autonome a.f.r.i.k.a. gruppe started to think about ways to break out of traditional approaches to political articulation which rely on counter-information and confrontational action. In *Handbuch der Kommunikations Guerrilla* (Handbook for the Communication Guerrilla) we collected and analyzed methods which leave aside the logic of 'us vs. them' trench warfare and distort the channels and modalities of communication.[1] By playing with the discourses and representations of power rather then banging their heads against them, activists can 'redesign' public space and turn a spectacle of power into a backdrop for their own message.

We interwove interventions with theoretical analysis, looking at the practices of dada, the situationists, the Dutch Provos, the Italian Indiani Metropolitani, the various psychogeographic societies, the German Spaßguerrilla, the US Yippies, and many other freaks, pranksters, fools and culture jammers.[2] We scammed anything that could be useful in distorting the unwritten rules of the cultural grammar and subverting the powerful machinery that constantly produces the acceptance of existing power relations and a certain kind of normality.

This kind of creative political articulation is becoming more popular among artists/activists. How do these playful attacks on multinational corporations, politicians and other authorities work? Here are some recent examples of such actions, along with insights into aspects of communication guerrilla theory which they exemplify.

Taking PR a step too far

The image of Lufthansa—and that of every other airline—is based on the fantasy of a world without borders, open for unlimited excitement and adventurous explorations of its hidden treasures (or business opportunities). The reality of migration and border regimes, with all their deadly consequences, however, grossly contradicts this ideological image. This reality constitutes what Slavoj Zizek calls a "hidden reverse": a cynical self-contradiction of the ideology of globalization which is hardly ever spoken aloud.[3]

Lufthansa's image relies on the implication that it makes the pleasures of travelling available to every customer, that it can take you to the remotest parts of the world at any time. Not articulated is the fact that Lufthansa also coerces unwanted immigrants to go where they definitely don't want to go— the countries they left for political or economic reasons, or even places they have never been.

A campaign by the German anti-racist network 'kein mensch ist illegal' ('no one is illegal') against the deportation of refugees and immigrants articulates the aforementioned internal contradictions and hidden reverses of globalization ideology in many creative ways.

In its first leaflet in spring 2000, 'kein mensch ist illegal' produced a fake leaflet advertising the airline's new 'Deportation Class'.[4] The leaflet featured the company's colours and typography and looked exactly as if it was produced by the airline. It also read like an original, since the customer-friendly corporate language was also copied. Moreover, the content overidentified with the logic of profit. The leaflet explained Lufthansa was obliged to carry out deportations for the German government. Yet the company knew handcuffed people with helmets on their heads and tape over their mouths reduced the comfort of paying passengers, especially if the deportees resisted. To compensate for this inconvenience, the leaflet said, the airline was launching lower-priced Deportation Class flights.

The leaflet was left at Lufthansa counters in airports, at tourist fairs and at travel agencies. The logic was credible enough: customers, journalists and others believed the airline capable of such cynical marketing and started attacking it. Lufthansa published a statement distancing itself from the leaflet. But the company found itself in a bind: it couldn't deny that it was carrying out deportations, and that this inconvenienced customers, but it was offering them no compensation.

The Deportation Class logo was taken from the winning entry in the campaign's poster competition, which called for detournements* of Lufthansa branding that made connections between deportation and the ideology of free travel. An exhibition of the entries was shown in many museums. Interestingly, Lufthansa didn't object until October 2000, when it discovered the entries could be viewed on the internet. Then it threatened to sue the owner of the website. He refused to back down. Within a few days, dozens of sites were mirroring the exhibition. Lufthansa ended up looking like a Web neophyte with no respect for the freedom of art.

The company faced 'tactical embarrassment' and interventions on many other fronts. The passenger lobby group Fair Fly staged 'invisible theatre'[5] performances about deportation at airports and tourist fairs. Plastic bags bearing the deportation alliance logo and filled with information about deportations were distributed at the Hanover Expo on 'Airline Day'. In summer 2000, an investor at the annual Lufthansa shareholders' meeting pointed out the financial risk involved in deportation. Several deportations were stopped through direct action. *The Wall Street Journal* even wrote an in-depth article on Lufthansa and the ethics of deporting refugees.[6]

The campaign had swift political results. Lufthansa successfully negotiated with German Home Secretary Otto Schily to be released from transporting passengers against their will and publicly announced it would no longer do so. The activists never could have achieved this result through direct negotiations with Schily. Attacking Lufthansa was a clever move which exploited a conflict of interest between Home Secretary and airline, between political and corporate logic. For the former, deportations are good—they increase the number of votes. For the latter, deportations are bad—they pollute the company's image, its most precious asset.

Detournement and overidentification

The Deportation Class campaign is an example of the sophisticated use of two of the main principles of guerrilla communication: detournement and overidentification.

By depending on the elusive power of signs, companies have made themselves especially vulnerable. Multinational corporations furiously defend their territory of images, colours, music and logos. With marketing strategies increasingly shifting from selling products to selling lifestyles, brand must be

---

* a Situationist term, meaning to subvert the meaning of a sign or text.

defended at all costs. Image has become capital, and on the terrain of image, communication guerrillas can easily subvert the messages of power.

Subvertisers like Adbusters and the anti-Nike campaigners communicate counter-information on issues as broad as the injustice of existing power relations and as specific as devastating conditions in sweatshops by using the first principle of guerrilla communication: detournement.[7]

By distorting or adding to the signs and symbols of corporate self-representation, subvertisers suggest a more realistic reading of advertisements. The simple detournement of a billboard—'Shell' becomes 'hell'—creates a moment of surprise and confusion in the receiver and brings out meanings other than those intended by the advertisers. The effect of detourning a mythical figure like Bill Gates by throwing a pie at him, is that he appears less god-like: he is human like the rest of us, vulnerable and thus not untouchable. Needless to say, this also works on politicians, philosophers and other representatives of power. With wit and humour, detournement creates distance between a message's sender and receiver.

'Overidentification'—the second principle of guerrilla communication—rests on Zizek's idea that every ideology has a hidden reverse, something that must not be articulated under any circumstances, a taboo. Overidentification means articulating this hidden taboo in the language of power itself, more clearly than the opponents do, but in a perfect imitation of the tone of their voices and the look of their symbols.

In a way, the anti-deportation campaigners kidnapped the Lufthansa brand, reinventing it as even more customer-friendly and thus challenging Lufthansa to live up to its implicit promises, and simultaneously pulling the hidden cynicism of its deportation practice into the open territory of marketing.

In the first fake leaflet, the campaigners secretly switched the sender: what read like a statement by the airline itself was in fact the campaigners' over-identification with Lufthansa's corporate logic, their adoption of its discourse of power. Being forced to deal publicly with its inherent contradictions, Lufthansa became an unwilling temporary ally of its critics.

Yet, as happens in guerrilla war, victory in the Lufthansa campaign has been limited. Refugees and immigrants are still being deported, increasingly via charter flights. Stopping a state from fortifying its borders calls for more than communication guerrilla tactics. Still, the agents of power can never be sure where the guerrillas will strike next.

What the French philosopher Michel de Certeau says about the "tactics of everyday life" also applies to communication guerrilla tactics. Lacking its own place, a tactic "operates in isolated actions, blow by blow. It takes advantage of 'opportunities' and depends on them, being without any base where it could stockpile its winnings, build up its own position, and plan raids. What it wins it cannot keep. This nowhere gives a tactic mobility . . . It must vigilantly make use of the cracks that particular conjunctions open in the surveillance of the proprietary powers. It poaches in them. It creates surprises in them. . . . In short, a tactic is an art of the weak." [8]

Intervening in an official spectacle

In October of 1999, the year NATO bombed Serbia, Germany's Bundeswehr military forces staged a public celebration on the Schloßplatz in the southern city of Stuttgart. Young soldiers publicly swore their loyalty to the Constitution. Since military parades have been unpopular in Germany since World War II, these celebrations were invented as a substitute, staging the soldier as 'citizen in uniform'. The last one in Stuttgart, in the early '80s, had turned into a massive riot. Now, almost 20 years later, the authorities were trying again.

A broad alliance of local anti-fascists and pacifists didn't like this demonstration of militarist ritual, and took action—but not quite as the officials expected. The campaign, which involved counter-information and communication guerrilla action, went by the informal name of 'GelöbNIX'—a pun on the word for a public loyalty oath, *Gelöbnis*. The detournement 'GelöbNIX' denotes something like "promise nothing". The activists organized a series of talks against militarism and war and publicized them at local social centres and in the media.

A leaflet announcing the protests used the official city logo, hinting at the style of the coming interventions. Later, another official-looking leaflet turned up in households and at official information points. It used slightly distorted replicas of the graphics and language used in official publications. An iron cross (a Nazi military symbol) took off spacecraft-like from a globe icon set against a friendly Stuttgart-yellow background. The slogan "Think globally, act locally" became "Think locally, act globally", with reference to the global activities of the German army. Inside the leaflet was a message from the mayor which made use of a potpourri of catchphrases and buzzwords that had become fashionable during the NATO bombing: "taking responsibility", "facing worldwide challenges", "defending the values of civilization".

The leaflet announced a series of municipal events. The Red Cross offered personalized blood donations ("your chosen soldier will be available after the ceremony"). A local resident who had won the 1998 Olympic 5,000-metre race reminded citizens of their responsibility towards their own bodies and invited them for a communal jog. The Green MP was to chair an air force pilots' panel discussion, explaining why German history shows that the military must attack civil targets to avoid confrontations with military forces. The public transport company announced it would offer free rides on the day to make up for delays. Finally, the leaflet mentioned a special hotline people could call to reserve seats.

The speakers and organizations, of course, learned only from a rather amused report in the local paper how the anti-militarist communication guerrillas were expecting them to participate. Only the city council member for safety and public order knew beforehand, since the 'hotline' was his phone number and never stopped ringing.

By then, people had started talking about GelöbNIX and wondering what would happen. Rock fans were looking forward to a free concert by famous bands, also advertised under the city logo. The media reported that one of the bands didn't appreciate the fake gig and had threatened to sue the designers.

To alert the police, someone set up a dangerous-looking—but little-known—website featuring militant action methods ("How to throw an egg") and a call for punks and anarchists to invade Stuttgart. Even the image of dangerous troublemakers was turned into a useful element. The stage was set: the police and city council expected a riot, the media were questioning the use of public displays of military power, and activist groups were hoping for as many police officers as possible to play with on the day.

The game worked well. The soldiers took position in front of Stuttgart's New Palace, surrounded by three rings of riot police. Shoppers and cars were searched ("Anything dangerous in that bag?") and traffic came to a standstill. The papers later commented on this: Did it make sense to demonstrate the integration of soldiers in civil society if the army had to be protected so heavily from the public? The expected battalions of anarchist thugs, however, remained absent.

Instead, figures in white anti-virus suits and masks erected a barrier of white material, of human height and long enough to encircle the police encircling the soldiers. Against the green lawn the barrier looked like some kind of hygienic device. Another leaflet explained why this precaution was necessary: "Violence is contagious!" This time, the layout was inspired by the publications of public health organizations and insurance companies: bulleted lists, FAQs, authoritative warning icons. At-risk groups were listed, symptoms were identified: extensive consumption of violent TV programmes and alcohol, exaggerated need for security, pathological group formation through the wearing of uniforms. In an authentic case study, Johanna H. from "Mothers Against BW (Bundeswehr) Syndrome" explained "How my son got BW". The "Association for a Safe, Clean Stuttgart" invited people to help build a security wall against the dangerous virus—hence the white fence.

Using overidentification, GelöbNIX redefined a spectacle of power. Police, soldiers, activists and city users were included in the choreography of the happening; the boundaries between actors and audience were blurred. Long before the day, the expectations of the audiences—public, administrators and police, activists—were raised through the use of their own respective languages and media. The popular memory of rioting at the last such ceremony was exploited to create a diffuse, ambiguous mixture of expectations. The state provided the scenery: large numbers of uniformed officers against a background of national flags and the lawn of an 18th-century chateau. From long experience, the GelöbNIX crew knew the police would close off the space. The best way to deal with this would be to help them in their effort.

A strong visual image was needed to subvert the meaning of the gathering. White contrasted well with the green of lawn and uniforms, and as a non-colour, a negation of anarchist black, it made a powerful non-statement. White set off a chain of connotations: cleanliness, hospitals, germs—and the violence-enhancing Bundeswehr virus was invented. The hegemonic concept of 'violence' often deployed against demonstrations was turned against the state itself. The white safety fence also played with the racist discourse of fear of being flooded and invaded by uncontrollable dangers—viruses, vermin, foreigners. GelöbNIX did not stop the aggressive activities of the German army, but it opened up a discursive space where at least it was possible to question them.

Over the next few days, the public discussion of displays of military power continued. This time, the discussion did not degenerate into a condemnation of the rioters. Journalists and readers expressed doubts about the army's use of public space, exchanging arguments that shifted the discourse from empty words around responsibility and security to more tangible concerns about who should use public space and how.

Using the symbols of power

Summer 1998. A sunny day in the Stuttgart pedestrian zone. People were bargain-hunting at the summer sales, flâneurs were strolling across the Schloßplatz, passing the punks using the space as a summer residence. A Peruvian band played. Homeless people asked for change.

Then, suddenly, an obstacle appeared. A large empty area was fenced off with red-and-white plastic ribbon. Ten men and women secured the designated test area. Green berets and black jackets that said 'Security' identified them as members of one of those now-familiar private security services. They denied access to the space to anyone without a permit. To apply for a permit, one had to fill in a questionnaire, available from the formally dressed representatives of the research group "Future with Security", who staffed official-looking desks at both entrances to the fenced-off area. Desks, leaflets and staffers' white T-shirts all bore the Future with Security logo.

The research team explained the project to passers-by. Responding to an offer by the city, a local company, Firma Biehle, was considering buying the entire Schloßplatz for private business use. Future with Security had been commissioned to test potential control of the square and check out its users' consumer profile.

Citizens were asked to fill in the professional-looking questionnaires with information such as gender, age, purpose of visit, place of residence, and how they were paying for their purchases. They were asked if they approved of the privatization of the square. Then they received either a "Welcome-to-the-test-area" leaflet or a "Sorry-not-eligible" leaflet, each complete with corporate-looking logo and formal typography. No one would have suspected the two versions were handed out completely at random. At the end of each leaflet, the project's real purpose was revealed: a critique of the privatization of public space.

Two policemen were suspicious about the project, which had not been registered with the local authorities. But when they were told it was an art event and not an unauthorized political action, their suspicion turned to confusion and they left without interfering.

Was this political art, or political activism using art as camouflage? The artists, group 01, were not interested in definitions. The piece, Horror Vacui, was merely a local intervention commenting on the increasing private control of public space.

Since the 1980s, city councils in Germany and elsewhere have been reshaping public space according to the needs of consumerism, industry and profit. From a position of power, they work with architects, designers, businesses and artists to reshape inner cities according to the demands of a symbolic economy that satisfies the needs of potential investors and customers.[9] This process produces a globalized architecture of restaurant chains and fashion shops, multiplex cinemas, museums, art objects and malls, promising entertainment and the pleasures of consumption undisturbed by social struggles.

To keep this promise credible, inner cities must be made 'safe'. Urban development has many ways of complying with such requests. Benches are removed to discourage the homeless and other unwanted people from relaxing without consuming. Entire streets are sold off to warehouse chains and transformed into shopping malls. Communicative spaces are transformed into expensive museums. The marble, glass and steel aesthetic of malls, museums, banks and houses of parliament is so intimidating that no one would dream of sitting down on their steps to rest or play guitar. If they breach the aesthetic fence, homeless people, immigrants, people of colour, punks, buskers and anyone else who disturbs the clean, rich image can easily be removed. Police and private guards patrol the streets to protect shoppers and businesses.

Yet public space is not fully determined by the strategies of power. It is also shaped by the feelings and desires of ordinary city-dwellers. People constantly develop practices to use space in ways other than those intended. An expensive new pedestrian zone becomes a skateboarders' playground, a renovated building turns into a canvas for graffiti, enclosed ATMs become preferred party zones. Central streets and freeways have been collectively occupied for Reclaim the Streets parties and taken over by cyclists from Critical Mass. These tactics were not invented from scratch. The material provided by the symbolic economy is already in place. But users and inventors of such temporary autonomous zones can never expect to remain in one place for long—they are not in a position to define the space permanently.[10]

Horror Vacui condensed signs and symbols connoting privatization and control: security guards with uniforms and decisive body language and the precise lines of familiar red-and-white tape reflected an aesthetic of authority and legality. Neatly dressed staff combined service-industry friendliness with academic authority and the popular appeal of market research. Local characteristics added further credibility: the name 'Firma Biehle' connotes a specific type of local mid-sized business, and the promise of "a safe, clean place" reflects the regional obsession with cleanliness. To their own surprise, the artists of group 01 used the voice of power so well that the police left Horror Vacui alone. Group 01 had hit on the cultural grammar of urban control.

Group 01 used art as camouflage, as a way of creating an image to attract people: here, overidentification was merely a way to get out as many leaflets as possible.

Horror Vacui did not cross the border from counter-information to communication guerrilla action. Though the first part of the leaflets could easily be read as corporate information, the second part uncovered the purpose of the action. Group 01 also revealed its identity in a press release to the local paper, which announced the intervention as an action against privatization, not a project of Firma Biehle. Visually, the overidentification with security-firm discourse succeeded in bringing out the absurdity of inner-city privatization. But the unmasking of the action meant the initially distorted codes were put back in place. What could have created a local scandal and forced the city council to deny it was planning to sell off the square remained instead in the space of 'creative action'.

Expanding political space

Horror Vacui, GelöbNIX and Deportation Class were explicitly situated within a wider critical discourse articulated by social movements whose strategic demands included free access to inner cities, Germany keeping its soldiers out of Kosovo, and open borders. Yet these actions were not confined to designated political space as marked by a culture of political parties, demonstrations, information booths, frustrating meetings and the language of morality.

The communications guerrilla adopts a tactical approach to political action: paradoxically speaking, s/he attempts a 'strategy of tactics'. 'Tactics of everyday life' express desires other than those included in strategic planning, and in this way often acquire a subversive meaning. Blagging,[11] fare-dodging and skateboarding in posh places are not necessarily meant to be political interventions but can end up being such. Taking this idea of tactics further, contextualizing political issues in unusual ways and refusing clear definition, can help broaden political space.

Detournements, happenings and similar interventions can bring the political into daily life, if organizers use their own local knowledge and experience with public space. When you go shopping in the city, you don't expect the police to search your bag. During GelöbNIX this searching distorted the positive image of police as people there to protect 'us' and only bother 'others'.

Ideally, activists can draw on local knowledge, anger, pleasures, and secret subversive desires. For example, quite a few citizens used the free public transport tickets in the GelöbNIX leaflets, though they might easily have realized it was a prank (and maybe they did). The local paper mentioned the leaflet with amusement—another sign it had met with local interest. Only if an intervention works locally can it become relevant in a broader context.

A focus on images and playful forms can create new alliances. If agreement on every detail of political analysis is not required, actions can be more inclusive. The art and activist scenes are beginning to overlap; a new arena of political articulation is opening up. In using images, music, bodies and performance, activists are rediscovering the pleasures of aesthetic experience as part of political speech.

Outlook

Times have changed since the *Handbuch der Kommunikations Guerrilla* was published. Then it was the early '90s, the West was at war with Iraq, and the decade's political depression was at its height. Political space seemed barren and closed.[12]

Although the changes in social and economic power during the last decade have not been in our favour, a surge of energy is noticeable among activists in urban areas. This is most visible in the new global movement protesting against organizations like the World Bank and the International Monetary Fund.

Large numbers of demonstrators, new/old forms of protest like carnivals, creative interventions and direct actions, and, maybe, Web hype too, have put this movement on the mainstream media agenda. The appropriation of information technology has facilitated the creation of a worldwide activist network and rapid communication. In this sense, the conditions of struggle have improved, certainly in the space of representation—people know there is a new, globally connected movement.

Yet in provincial areas, local neighbourhoods, small towns and border zones, we are smaller in number than the images from Seattle, Prague or London would suggest. Locally, we continue to rely on molecular communication guerrilla tactics, the kind of actions anyone can stage without the backup of thousands. Large mobilizations may be highlights on the activist calendar, but communication guerrilla actions are effective interventions in local public space—ways to annoy the conservative hypocrites, ordinary racists and apostles of normalization, but also ways of taking our own pleasure and fighting the frustrations we face in daily life.

But what about the use of communication guerrilla tactics at mass events? Being a communication guerrilla means distorting the rules of normality and challenging hegemonic discourse. The new global movement attacks neoliberalism and economic globalization, and communication guerrilla actions could help challenge the legitimacy and quasi-natural status assumed by present-day worldwide capitalism.

But the difficulties in preparing for the anti-IMF protests in Prague, for example (see Chapter 16, 'Obstructing the Mainstream: Lessons from Seattle'), show that co-operation across differences still needs a lot of work. The global mobilizations rely on 'political tourists' from all over the world, people who bring their own cultures of resistance with them. Is it possible to communicate local knowledge effectively so a larger community of activists can use it? Does it make sense to transfer specific actions?

Continuous communication, as it happens in many of the current interconnected networks, would be crucial to this process. We might find ways to plot stylish, decentralized actions that leave space for the creativity of autonomous affinity groups yet provide an effective political focus that can link a variety of actions into one compelling, empowering image.

Neither the global days of action nor the local communication guerrilla interventions have, so far, attempted permanent, strategic change. Yet such interventions could be part of a 'strategy of tactics' capable of expressing the widespread dissent with the new forms of global and local governance, without falling into the old leftist error of claiming for itself the possession of the one and only truth.

| Chapter 18 |
Virtual Sabotage
Florian Schneider

Wednesday 20 June 2001. At about 10:15 a.m., Klaus Schlede, spokesman for the board of directors, opens Lufthansa's annual general meeting in the Kölnarena (Cologne Arena), speaking in his usual penetrating tone before a few thousand shareholders. He wants to appear in control, but he knows what he will have to face: protests by critical shareholders, activists from the 'kein mensch ist illegal' ('no one is illegal') network and the deportation.class campaign, who will—as they have at every meeting for the past few years—voice their demand: no deportations on scheduled Lufthansa flights.

In front of the hall, 'stewards and stewardesses against deportation' are providing the shareholders with newspapers, flyers and plastic bags. Next to them, performance groups are acting out the deportation procedure, in particular how passengers and crew can stop deportations even at the last minute. At the door, security checks this year seem aimed at preventing critical information from being brought into the hall and at confiscating deportation.class plastic bags carried by shareholders. The bags are thrown into waiting garbage cans.

Meanwhile, inside the inevitable is happening: CEO Jürgen Weber's speech is being interrupted again and again by heckling and banners in front of the podium. Security staff, obviously becoming increasingly nervous, drag activists out of the spotlight five times as various TV stations' camera operators film it all.

The meeting continues with activists, lawyers and more and more shareholders approaching the microphone to criticize the board for maintaining deportations on Lufthansa flights. Finally, it all ends in the usual way: the exhausted board make fools of themselves by trying helplessly and incompetently to evade their critics' convincing arguments.

So far, so good. Even with the hardened position of the board of directors, it can be assumed that these rituals will probably overshadow next year's general meeting as well.

There was, however, another action taking place—not in the hall or in front of it, but in the virtual world. Weeks before the shareholders' meeting, media reports about it were full of mentions of an upcoming online demonstration, already officially registered with the municipal authorities and the police. At exactly 10 a.m. the virtual protest was opened outside the arena with a symbolic mouse click. Lufthansa's Web server was to be disturbed so massively that by noon it would no longer work or at least be noticeably slow, at the same time as the protests were going on in the hall.

The demonstration was a kind of premiere, although it was not the first time the expression 'online demo' had been used for an electronic gathering. It was a software-supported mass protest that people from all over the world could take part in with the click of a mouse. It was a sort of denial-of-service attack, except its aims, motives and date had been openly announced and it was restricted in time and space. It aimed not to cause maximum damage, but to be a symbolic act of compression: the long-awaited and long-desired synchronization of the online and the offline. The action had aimed to realize the wish, which never could have been so widely distributed and mediated by traditional means, to test a form of action both highly debatable and highly promising, which both virtualizes and globalizes resistance: a hybrid of immaterial sabotage and digital demonstration.

The outcome of such an unconventional enterprise necessarily escapes simple interpretation. From a technical point of view, the effects can be seen as favourable from both sides. As usual, both sides speak of the success of their tactics. The organizers of the online demonstration stress that Lufthansa's home page was unreachable for the planned two hours, and have pretty diagrams to prove it. Lufthansa concedes there were bottlenecks, but says its strategies against the protesters succeeded because it managed to provide for additional capacity. At the same time, all access from networks where the critical requests were believed to originate seemed to have been denied. The logical conclusion was that those who protested from there had succeeded, even if that success might have been noticed only by themselves.

On the symbolic level, too, there were two winners. The online demonstration, which had aimed at garnering publicity for the cause, attracted enormous and even international attention, which could not have been obtained using traditional methods. Articles in publications including *The Washington Post* rapidly spread the news around the globe; television and print media outlets constructed great debates in online forums. Almost every magazine, online news and local newspaper report on the Lufthansa meeting led with the catchy opening, "online demo".

But Lufthansa network technicians can also say they succeeded at least in limiting the attack, which from their point of view had been aggressive. The server didn't crash, against the expectations of many virtual demonstrators, though parts of the site were unreachable and the online booking system was out of order for some time. Even the immense costs Lufthansa had to cover were probably worth it: the corporation had demonstrated more or less involuntarily a certain competence in dealing with new challenges.

The good thing about making moves in the virtual environment is that both sides can claim to have success—a 'win-win situation'. The New Actonomy, however, is not just about translating political metaphor as understandably and consistently as possible from offline to online reality, in order to yield propagandistic added value. The real challenge of virtual forms of resistance exists in an utterly pragmatic dimension: the materiality of virtual resistance results in an interactivity, a communication between activists who are connected to each other, who not only take part but also organize.

The members of the deportation.class campaign have devoted themselves to a difficult task. 'Denial of service' is at least a *double entendre*: the campaign is aimed at making Lufthansa refuse to transport passengers forcibly: at 'denying service' to those who deport refugees and migrants.

* * *

So what's new about a virtual action like this one? Perhaps not the fact that people have begun demonstrating on the screen instead of the street, though that plot had plenty of news value for the mainstream media. This effect will wear off and be of little importance next time. What might prove to be much more interesting instead is a new definition of sabotage.

Historically, sabotage was a particularly appropriate, though illegal, means of struggle within factories when workers were robbed of their right to strike. During the New York waiters' strike at the end of the 19th century, waiters so disgusted customers merely by speaking indirectly but freely about working conditions that the industry quickly had to give in to the demands of these very badly organized workers.

The traditional Protestant understanding of militancy included a certain amount of pathological self-destruction: pricking the other's conscience, burning down the neighbourhood, demonstrating puritanism for once without having to think or communicate your ideas.

Sabotage refers to a social antagonism and to the realm of production, and constitutes a collective process of appropriation of knowledge and power. Today, various movements must communicate and reach out at the level of production, no matter where it takes place and no matter whether they are 'old' or 'new'.

Direct action nowadays is re-presenting sabotage. It's a direct application of the idea that property can claim no rights. But sabotage in the new, immaterial context is defined differently from the traditional, destructive meaning of the word (damaging property), and gets a new meaning as a constructive, innovative and creative social practice. Such a constructive approach results in a movement 'without organs' or organization. It is conducted from a variety of perspectives—self-determined cybernetic thinking that spurs on different approaches and connections. The sabotage concept is a reverse-engineering of an open source idea. Sabotage is radically antagonistic to the representative discourse of the institutionalized contexts of working-class and social movements. Those representative forms have always referred to a nation-state; spontaneous, unorganized or better-organized forms of resistance have instead expressed a global class-consciousness.

Sabotage, as its pragmatic counterpart and as a means of direct action, picked the corporate pocket in order to realize certain conditions. Immaterial sabotage aims at 'polluting' and obstructing the corporate image. Unlike boycott campaigns of the social and environmental movements in the 1980s and 1990s, which held activists captive in their status as pure consumers voting with their purses, immaterial sabotage explicitly encourages creativity and productivity, the collectivity and collaboration of roaming, unseizable, but interconnected activists. The number of people taking part in today's redefinition and recapitulation is as irrelevant as it was in the 19th century. The overall goal is not to convince and organize as many allies as possible, but to make a precise difference, an immediate change. It seems effective to use various tactics and methods to put pressure on the weakest link in the chain: the enemy's brand, its corporate identity.

For more information see www.deportation-class.com, www.deportation-alliance.com, www.go.to/online-demo, www.noborder.org and www.make-world.org.

Chapter 19

Net.activism

Eveline Lubbers

The internet has proved important for activists in enabling networking and facilitating platforms for both organizing and publishing. In large part, the rapid growth of the 'movement of movements' (to avoid the unworthy term 'anti-globalization movement') could not have happened without the internet. Mobilization for summit protests and days of action, and all the practical connections needed to bring a lot of people and stuff together so that these events can be successful, would not have been the same without it.

But the Net has also changed content radically. Online connections between otherwise isolated activities and initiatives have painted a broader picture of resistance and strengthened the motivation of those involved. The ability to publish background information outside the regular channels proved a powerful tool, both for reaching larger audiences and providing sources for mainstream media.

The political movement that is growing out of diverse campaigns, from fighting Nike to confronting Third World debt, shares a belief that the disparate problems they are wrestling with all derive from global deregulation, an agenda which is concentrating power and wealth in fewer and fewer hands.

Naomi Klein calls this movement—whose hubs and spokes and hotlinks, and emphasis on information rather than ideology, reflect the tools it uses — the "Internet come to life". Those pictures meant to represent the internet, showing scattered single points that converge in places into big black blobs, resemble the pattern of the movement with its scattered local campaigns that join forces on common themes and meet at summit protests, and go back to working separately on the local level afterwards.

The question this chapter addresses is not simply how the internet can best be used to support activism, although it would be valuable to discuss how to improve facilities to benefit the movement of movements: to draw together its potential while at the same time avoiding institutionalization through email lists, info sites and Independent Media Centres (IMCs).

Instead, I aim to describe the concept of net.activism by presenting an inspiring series of examples, and to look at what it would take to improve conditions for practising net.activism. I think it is possible to use the Net and other modern tools of communication to develop new and unique prototypes of activism.

Using the Net to pose a threat does not equal net.activism

To focus on corporate campaigning, the subject of this book, every website or mailing list criticizing a company is interpreted as a threat to that company. Nowadays corporate identity determines the value of a business over its actual products or services. As we have seen again and again, companies are increasingly vulnerable to criticism and other attacks on their image. Consumer criticism on mailing lists, rumours that evolve into urban legends at astonishing speed, companyXsucks.com sites that catalogue bad experiences—all these frighten companies because they are forced on to the defensive, and have a hard time controlling the damage.

Such naming and shaming is a familiar move; the new tools just mean it can be done faster, with a greater reach, much greater impact, and the ability to do more damage. The same goes for email and website calls for petition signatures or letters of protest.

The growing amount of PR advice on the subject (brochures include 'Cyber Activism', 'Managing Activism: A Guide to Dealing with Activists and Pressure Groups' and 'Using the Internet in a Corporate Public Affairs Office') would have you believe any Web-based action network represents a major threat to any company targeted. But I think net.activism is much more than just posing a threat using the internet.

Net.philosopher Geert Lovink agrees: "We could say that activists are no different from other Web users. They all build sites, set up lists, have their own online events, just like the motorcycle gangs, video game fanatics and those interested in exchanging Indian cooking recipes. They all form virtual communities and create both group and individual identities," he says. "I think it should be the task of activists to go beyond the user level and question the workings of net subjectivity. I would hope that activists are more aware of the underlying power structures of the information economy. Armed with this critical knowledge, net.activists can go beyond the status of merely using applications. By questioning the way existing network architectures work, new strategies come into existence, both on the aesthetic level of the user interface and (on the level of) software."[1]

Finding new ways to free information while intervening in a political debate

When I started to write about net.activism in 1996, I was a true believer.[2] I honestly worshipped the idea of a form of activism that could only exist by the grace of the Net. My conviction was born of the success of a project I had been involved in, in the early days of the internet.

I work for buro Jansen & Janssen monitoring police and intelligence activities in the Netherlands. In 1996 a Dutch parliamentary research commission revealed that police were setting up drug lines as part of a strategy to fight organized crime—'Set a thief to catch a thief.' After months of televised hearings, the results of the research were published in thirteen volumes (more than 5,000 pages) and sold as a boxed set for about $700. A CD-ROM with the same information was also available. As the paper version had no index whatsoever, people were in fact forced to buy the package at a cost of more than $1,000. These prices caused much controversy, as these documents were in fact reports of parliamentary proceedings, which are supposed to be freely available.

With a little help from some techies, we cracked the CD-ROM and freed the texts from the layout, which was copyrighted by the newly privatized state publishers. We published the texts at www.burojansen.nl. The site was an instant hit in the Netherlands. "This is what the internet was meant for," people wrote to us. "An important contribution to democracy."

Without the internet, we could not have broken the information monopoly so easily without legal trouble. This action was a coup because it highlighted a new use of the internet: making information public that should have been public in the first place.

Net.activism is connecting to an ongoing campaign

Net.activism should be based in, and aim to promote, a real-life campaign, by either providing information in support of it or drawing attention to it through surprising, groundbreaking interventions. In anti-corporate campaigning, the best example is still McSpotlight (www.McSpotlight.org). When the site was launched in 1996, and for a long time thereafter, it was innovative on various levels. It contains a lot of information and resources and is attractive and professional-looking. It combines the virtues of investigative research and exposure, outreach and publicity PR work, and activist networking.

Non-virtual activism laid the foundation for McSpotlight's success, but it was through the site that local campaigning against McDonald's gained global momentum for the first time. McSpotlight started as the website accompanying McDonald's libel trial against Dave Morris and Helen Steel (see Chapter 9, 'McSpying'). The trial became the virtual centre of activism against the hamburger giant. Through the McLibel mailing list, campaigners from all over kept each other up to date on activities around the world—suburbanites against drive-thrus, looters in Copenhagen, Gandhi-inspired Finns holding discussions with their local McDonald's, India against invasion by McDonald's—all connected through the internet.

McSpotlight published the transcripts of the hearings and complemented them with information about the case, the company, the resumés of all the people involved in the trial and the media coverage. In the Campaign section, groups from all over the world can present themselves and their material. A current anti-McDonald's leaflet can be printed out in various languages. McSpotlight was in effect the first worldwide activist manual.

Also new was the site's innovative use of technological tools. The Guided Tour, narrated by the McLibel Two, takes visitors around key parts of the site. An especially inspiring feature is the use of frames to hijack McDonald's own corporate website. On one side of the screen you can call up McDonald's shiny, expensive website, while on the other you see McSpotlight's detailed deconstruction and criticism.

This example is aging and suffering from overexposure, and this raises the question of why this very effective strategy was never repeated elsewhere on the same scale. Apparently, such a project can only crystallize at a special moment in time: some plan of the company must be thwarted, and the right tools must be in the hands of the right team devoted to making something of it. The combination of technical skills and political cleverness is a treasure. In this case, both virtues were found in most people on the McSpotlight team—and that is exceptional.

Exploring the back alleys of the internet

Searching for secret information to expose online is still an underdeveloped strategy. In October 2001, the GATSwatch research group revealed that the UK government and the London financial services lobby were colluding through something called International Financial Services, London (IFSL).

By accident, GATSwatch had found a set of internal minutes on an unlinked part of the IFSL website that showed how government and business had jointly planned a campaign to defeat civil opposition to the WTO services negotiations earlier that year. This unique source material was there on the Web just waiting to be found.[3]

In a similar action against the OECD's Multilateral Agreement on

Investment (MAI) in 1997, activists posted the provisional agreement on the internet while the MAI was being negotiated. The posting of the agreement led to a huge victory: the downfall of the MAI, in one of the first campaigns to gain global momentum through email and websites. The leaking of the draft and its broad distribution on the internet helped campaigners build political pressure in the various countries. The long lists of exceptions to the treaty proposed by various governments, after citizens pointed out various limitations the MAI would impose, ultimately frustrated the negotiations.[4]

A fertile exchange between techies and activists (not to mention artists)

Collaboration between techies and activists can lead to spectacular events like the redirection of Nike's corporate website to one run by the Melbourne S11 Web Collective. Hundreds of thousands of would-be visitors to Nike were greeted with the message "Global justice is coming—prepare now" and sent to www.s11.org, an Australian activist site about the then-upcoming World Economic Forum Asia-Pacific Economic Summit.[5]

Hits on the S11 site skyrocketed from a low of 57 an hour before the Nike site was hacked, to a high of 66,000 an hour during the hijacking. By the time the summit took place, the S11 Web Collective said hits had gone "through the roof", with more than 880,000 since the redirection. The redirection was a big success at promoting the demonstrations, both by leading unsuspecting Nike visitors to a different site and by garnering plenty of publicity.

To the surprise of all parties, Nike's internet service provider could do little about the hijacking. The redirection was accomplished by modifying the DNS entry at Network Solutions, a company that manages the database which links URLs with content. By the time Nike's ISP had the entry changed back, the activists had already succeeded in their goal. By literally linking the long-running campaigns against Nike sweatshops to the critique of the Economic Summit in an original way, the redirection connected anti-corporate campaigning to a broader critique of economic globalization.

Tweaking the corporate imagery

Spoof sites are another way of confusing the audience. The best examples copy the style or layout of the original site, replacing the original message with something quite similar but ironically critical.

The site for Insanex Genomix, a fake life science company, presents Insanex as a proud member of the real lobby group EuropaBio, grateful for that group's achievements in moulding European Union biotech legislation to the interests of its member corporations.

Made by Danish activists, it is a brilliant example of creative internet activism, incorporating the now broadly accepted greenwashing house style of biotech companies, which present themselves as saviours of the human race. At first sight, it looks like a typical glossy company site. Indeed, many visitors will probably think Insanex Genomix is real.

The 'products' offered mirror what the near future might bring as a result of the lax regulations being promoted by the biotech industry. For example, Insanex Genomix takes the visitor a step into the future by offering human cloning services directly to customers. "Spend a second honeymoon at The Future Resort®. Enjoy the sun and entertainment at our luxury resort in the Caribbean while we work on creating your dream child. Your personal counselor helps you select the right characteristics for your future child. Pain-free extraction of gametes (cells) from you and your partner. Implantation of the genetically improved fetus before your week-long stay at The Future Resort is over." [6]

In October 2000 EuropaBio hired a law firm and threatened the webmasters with a lawsuit if the site was not shut down, but nothing has happened since.

Crossing the boundary between the virtual and the real

While the Insanex site was made for a 'company' invented out of the blue for activist purposes, www.gatt.org is a painstaking copy of the real WTO site. Using a domain name based on the pre-WTO General Agreement on Tariffs and Trade, the phony site mimicked almost every detail of the official WTO site (www.wto.org), down to the front-page warning about a fake site masquerading as the real thing. Though the layout was eventually changed to avoid copyright problems, the content remained the same, conveying the WTO's message more bluntly, as the site's creators, the Yes Men, declared.

The site links to WTO-related activist websites and specially produced content, but sometimes original WTO material and other primary sources are enough. In an item called 'Qatar Saves the Day', the fake text explains how happy the WTO is to hold its next Trade Round in Qatar, where "the sort of lobbying seen in Seattle, Quebec, Davos, Prague, Barcelona, and elsewhere is strictly illegal and heavily punished, and come November 5, the security forces of Qatar have vowed to protect our freedoms with all means at their disposal." This 'news' item is linked to the State Department's genuine travel advisory, highlighting the country's human rights records, which needs no further explanation in this context.[7]

The Yes Men are a loose-knit group of anti-free-trade activists who view hoaxes as a legitimate weapon of protest, as *The New York Times* wrote in what it described as "a cautionary tale about gall and gullibility in the information age".[8]

After the first gatt.org site was launched in March 2000, the Yes Men were offered an opportunity they couldn't pass up: to speak before an international group of distinguished lawyers on the ideology of the World Trade Organization . . . as representatives of that agency. Through the contact link on their site, the Yes Men received a speaking invitation for WTO Director-General Mike Moore. They offered to send a replacement.

It was the beginning of a 'long and winding cyberhoax', a unique example of online political theatre seamlessly blending into real-life performances and back, and endless online correspondence tweaking the WTO. The fictional substitute, one Herr Dr Andreas Bichlbauer, arrived at the conference and proceeded to tell delegates that the WTO found Italians "work-shy", and that it was proposing the US allow people to auction their votes to corporations. All this caused barely a ripple in the audience. Only weeks and many email exchanges later, after the Yes Men announced that Herr Dr Andreas Bichlbauer had expired from a grave illness thought to have been caused by a pie he claimed to have been hit with when leaving the conference, that the conference organizers finally realized the hoax. Nevertheless, other public appearances by fake WTO representatives followed.[9]

Avoiding violent confrontation while making a strong political point

Fooling the business world is one thing; violating its privacy goes a step further. When hackers cracked the computer system of the world leaders' conference in Davos, Switzerland, in February 2001, a line was crossed. As long as privacy is protected hacktivism is tolerated—but exposing the itineraries of VIPs like Bill Clinton, Yasser Arafat and Bill Gates, along with their credit card numbers and expiration dates, is *bad*. When hacktivism is combined with political resistance, the guillotine of political correctness is never far away. The editor of Toronto-based online magazine *The Hacktivist* (pseudonym: metac0m) was willing to draw a line in *Salon*, condemning the theft of personal data, credit card numbers and the like, "for it discredits the legitimacy of hacktivism as a form of protest and civil disobedience."[10]

It's not often mentioned, but although real-life security measures to keep protesters away from big economic summits have become tighter than ever, the virtual dimension of such events is often as full of holes as a Swiss cheese. Stephanie Gruner, a *Wall Street Journal* reporter who was at the WEF's Davos meeting, told me every attendee including press was given a laptop containing all the meeting information and attendees' personal details, plus wireless internet access. Journalists and businesspeople with a technical bent hacked the internal system the first night, she said. It must not have been too hard to tap the wireless connections from outside the building. Swiss radical weekly *Die Wochenzeitung* (www.woz.ch) found out the WEF (SQL) Microsoft server had been suffering from a major protection bug, so hacking it would have been easy for a technically savvy eight-year-old.

In these days of heavy security at street level, it is amazing how simple it is to crash the party on the virtual level. It might be worth devoting more energy to social engineering and technical tricks in order to hack our way in—if only to prove that the powerful of this Earth are not as untouchable as they think they are.

Cross-cultural links provide more options for social struggle

Jesse Hirsch of tao.ca, writing about hacktivism,[11] categorizes its practitioners into three groups—artists, techies, and politicos—"all three of which need to come together in a much more coherent manner (and setting) if Hacktivism is to live up to its potential."[12] The same is true for net.activism. All three groups are active in the field, and they inspire each other's activities, but they are not working together as fruitfully as they might be.

"The Artists (such as the Electronic Disturbance Theatre and RTMark) focus on their artistic attributes and activities, often as an excuse to ignore criticisms from their counterparts, even though they do employ elements of technology for political purposes. The Techies (such as 2600.com) on the other hand, are largely focused on the development of technical tools and platforms, as well as engaging in activities that are centred around said technology (and related issues). While there is certainly an artistic and political element to the activities of the Techies, they at times neglect both the aesthetics and political dynamics of their work, which results in their alienation or distance from other social movements. Similarly the Politicos (such as tao.ca and iww.org) emphasize the political dynamic of their activities, often at the expense of the technical or aesthetic (accessible) elements of their work," Hirsch writes. He concludes that "it has been the Politicos who have done the most so far to bring these three divergent groups together, with hacktivism.tao.ca as one example."[13]

Though the practice of net.activism may still be fragmented, signs that the gaps are closing are appearing from various directions. More hackers and techies are getting involved in street activism. Hackers from 2600.com marched in Philadelphia against the Republican National Convention. And political activists have used hacker techniques, for instance in the Lufthansa netstrike (see Chapter 18, 'Virtual Sabotage').

The hackers' group Electronic Disturbance Theater began advocating political DoS attacks years ago to promote the cause of the Zapatistas in Mexico. In 1998, they organized a number of 'virtual sit-ins' against the websites of financial and government institutions involved in the crackdown against the Zapatistas, one of which was the Pentagon. The group created the hacking tool FloodNet, which was downloaded by thousands of supporters. The program repeatedly asks a targeted page to reload, and when used simultaneously by enough protesters, it overwhelms and 'floods' the site, preventing it from being accessed by others, thus 'denying service'.

Hackers and system administrators have criticized this idea, explaining over and over again that DoS attacks are ineffective. Many such attempts to bring down an enemy server get lost somewhere in the network. They also cause connection problems for innocent Net users. In response to that it now emphasizes the spectacular effects of its actions. The question has lately shifted to the more important one of which models are effective in which situations, taking specific local and cultural circumstances into account.

In the 1990s, the idea of 'tactical media'[14] stressed the importance of strategic collaborations between activists, artists, designers and hackers. It is not just content that counts. Alternative media must constantly debate and strengthen their visual language. After research has been completed, campaigners should have an intense round of consultation about aesthetics and communication strategies. Websites can be much more than just archives for dead information. An open and multidisciplinary approach can help campaigners move beyond outmoded political rituals and the old-fashioned idea of art as illustration. *Adbusters* magazine shows how a critique of mainstream advertisement can be combined with imaginative and subversive 'culture jamming'.[15] And *subsol*, a Web magazine from Zagreb, Croatia, brings together net.art, activist debates, contemporary critical theory and reports from Western and Eastern Europe.[16]

How can the Net take activism further?

Net.activism should be rooted in real-life campaigning, attracting attention in a surprising way, garnering publicity for the cause, and if possible exposing information. It should add a new dimension to the campaign, linking different content and different levels of activism through the innovative use of available technical tools. Additionally, it might cross the borders between the imaginable and the unimaginable, the virtual and the real, the open and the unavailable, the expected and the shocking. Stronger coalitions between techies, activists and artists are crucial in the near future, but it will take a lot of energy to realize them.

When the McSpotlight people tried to plan their Next Big Thing, the only thing they could agreed upon was that they did not feel like repeating themselves, building a similar website about one more Bad Corporation. And they never did. Nor did they ever do anything new and different in that same brilliant combination.

It appears to be impossible to repeat a great project without losing some of its initial power, impossible to develop a concept without getting a bit bored by repetition. Would you get inspired by the tenth redirection of a corporate website to an activist location? The twentieth hack into a corporate system that revealed scandalous deals behind the scenes? Even the Nth gatt.org site could get boring, however original the idea was at its moment of conception. We seem to be children of our time, not so different from the dotcom generation, with its never-ending greed for new experiences ('been there, done that').

The net.activism of the future should break out of the straitjacket of the all-internet experience. Inspiration lies in reaching out, crossing borders, and bringing the internet to those who really need it. Activists could, for example, offer a window on the world to asylum seekers who are restricted from travelling as they wait for a residence permit. Or follow the example of the Australian activists who invited the senior Aboriginal women of the remote Kupa Piti Kungka Tjuta people to present themselves on the internet. Their life stories are inextricably bound up with the poisoning effects of bygone atomic tests; they are now campaigning against new plans to dump radioactive waste from Sydney in the desert.[17]

And that is why the Independent Media Centres (IMCs) are net.activism after all. I did not initially include them in my definition, because I counted them as activists-using-the-Net. But the IMCs have altered the way the Net can be used, if only through the use of the open publishing concept, which allows anyone to easily add news to the site, and the sharing of the software needed to start up a local IMC. Though the IMC started as a badly needed alternative news and background facilitator accompanying the Seattle protests (see Chapter 16, 'Obstructing the Mainstream'), it now has a real-life workspace and facilitates co-operation between groups at the local, national and international levels, in a good example of crossing the border from the virtual to the real and back and helping unconnected groups to do so.[18]

New technologies offer a wide range of opportunities. Net.activism is most powerful when the internet is used in combination with mobile devices, as was seen in the occupation of Shell's London headquarters in 1999. Thanks to webcams, palmtops and cell phones, activists inside the building were able to continue their online reports even after the electricity and phone lines had been cut.[19]

Activists are feeling a need to expand their use of technology. The suggestions for net.activism made in a workshop at make-world, an international media-activist conference held in Munich in October 2001,[20] went in many different directions. The internet in fact plays only a secondary role in the ideas and fantasies of activists.

For example, one-to-many text messaging could be used to keep a crowd informed during a demonstration, which could mean a great tactical advantage. Short-range transmitters carried on the back of a bicycle could disseminate provocative messages on a popular radio station's frequency at rush hour and reach dozens of car radios.

Or the eviction of a squat could be covered and made into a media event online through live-streaming images from wireless cameras placed inside the building and live interviews conducted by mobile phone. Video activists in Korea did something similar when they documented police brutality against striking Daewoo workers and put some of the pictures online, starting a video war. After the police put their own video online in response, the activists published all their material uncut, to prove the police had altered theirs, having conveniently censored their own provocation of violence during the strike.

Where the internet was concerned, the make-world attendees emphasized the importance of the creation of autonomous zones online, the need for independent providers, and the need to fight ISPs as the new moral authorities. They also called attention to the need for practical tools, such as PGP-secure webmail and mailing lists that would enable group communication without eavesdropping. And to involve more of the non-English-speaking world in the movement, a reliable translator network is needed, as well as a database with often-used jargon, such as legal terms, not found in most dictionaries. Professional translators could be invited to volunteer a little of their time, and so could well-paid Web designers—sort of a personal Tobin tax. This could be a way to involve more technically proficient people in activist projects.

Of course, there are many more net.activism ideas still to be worked out, some of them mentioned earlier in this book. The concept of tracking visitors and creating customized pop-ups (see Chapter 12, 'Cyber-surveillance') could be developed. There is also the Korean idea of 'site strikes'—voluntarily redirecting your site to one belonging to a campaign that needs attention at the moment. Or direct mail could be sent to authorities listening in on certain discussions.

And there is still more to learn from the tactics that hired cybersnitches use against campaigners. For instance, would it not be useful to make an inventory of old friends and contacts who now work in useful positions inside companies and have access to information you need, a switch that needs to be pulled, a door (virtual or real) that needs to be opened, a job that needs to be done. A little bit of 'social engineering' can be a great help to the modern activist.

Even commonly used resources, like the popular search engine Google, can do more and more. In November 2001 Google built in a new tool that finds a variety of file types in addition to traditional Web documents. This tool reportedly brings a wide array of files formerly overlooked by basic search engine queries within reach of the average surfer—or the armchair researcher.[21]

On the defence side, a 'flying squad' could be set up to test the safety of activist networks, breaking through firewalls and leaving warning messages to create awareness of what could happen if an intruder had less than good intentions.

Software like Tempest for Eliza could have been a product of such a squad. Tempest is an electromagnetic eavesdropping technique which spies and governments use to remotely monitor computers without having to have access to them. Tempest for Eliza is software that uses the same technology to translate the frequencies disseminated by a monitor into melodies that can be received on AM radio. The software was written as an amusing way to teach people that Tempest really exists, and that their computers can be observed.[22]

We'd better start using technology more creatively. We've got expectations to live up to. Public affairs advisers are writing things like this:

"With each passing month, an advocacy group (usually anti-corporate) comes up with a new way of using information technology to advance its public policy agenda. Companies need to watch what others are doing and think creatively about how to develop innovative ways to connect with supporters."[23]

If we don't do it, somebody else will.

The Pandora Project

Eveline Lubbers

Since beginning work on this book, I have been running the web-based Pandora mailing list, which is meant to help like-minded researchers and campaigners share resources and tactics for obtaining information. People tell me that the list has been a success because it is very focused, has relatively low traffic, and has content that's—almost—always worth reading. The archive is online (see below for the URL), and contains plenty of information on the PR industry and its influence. The list and its archive are called the Pandora Project, after the Greek goddess:

> Pandora, being too curious for her own good, opened a forbidden box, and all the evils of humanity flew out.

Similarly, the Pandora Project intends to crack open the PR industry and spread its noxious secrets to people everywhere.

The making of this book has unearthed a lot of material and sources on corporate counterstrategies, and promising new contacts have grown into inspiring relationships. In order to expand the reach of research about the growing influence of the public relations industry, business intelligence consultants and others involved in developing corporate counterstrategies, several projects are now 'under construction'.

The first idea is to set up a newsletter, comparable with the US quarterly *PR-Watch* produced by John Stauber and Sheldon Rampton, but to have more of a European angle on news and analyses. Editions in other places such as Australia and New Zealand could be considered in due course.

While the Pandora list is primarily focused on PR strategies against campaigning groups and activists (including greenwash, lobbying, the use of front groups, monitoring and surveillance and corporate intelligence), the scope of the newsletter could be broader. It could also contain material on the PR industry and corporate culture more broadly, focusing on PR and privatization, globalization, corporate giving and philanthropy, investor relations, covert and overt PR associations, and the corporate co-option of PR academics. The aim will be to get a good mix of both news and analysis.

The second idea is to have an online database, making information on PR and related topics available in a very accessible way. It will include the research done for this book, and the Pandora material collected so far. However, such a database would have to be more than just a public list archive, both in design, moderation and function.

Compared to a general list archive, the database will have to be easier to browse in order to get an overview. There will be a short summary of every item, and data will be sortable in several ways; the user will be able to choose to view data by company, or by counterstrategy (for instance, greenwash or infiltration).

Material could be posted by subscribers, either via the list or directly via the site. The idea of having a more or less unmoderated online database which grows by means of user contributions would be an experiment in itself. It immediately raises the question of how to deal with 'noise' (useless input), or worse: disinformation. Ideally, both the list and the forthcoming database would be a project run jointly by a core group of people and inspired by a broader network of members.

Both projects are planned, but the database could be free-standing whereas the newsletter would need a website. Together, the newsletter and the database would be intended to provide a permanent forum of experts interested in exchanging information on the PR industry and its involvement in corporate strategies.

The value of sharing resources will have the advantage of combining material and building a common library online. Ideally, these projects will provide resources for anti-corporate campaigners, revelations about corporate front groups and exposures of leaked documents. And, of course, items about research sources and tools, as well as suggested topics for (activist) research.

Once the newsletter is out and the database is up and running, a section for whistleblowers and a how-to guide on common-sense security for activists might be other useful projects to undertake.

To subscribe to the Pandora Project mailing list:
www.oudenaarden.nl/mailman/listinfo/pandora
The Pandora Project Archives: www.oudenaarden.nl/pipermail/pandora/
PR Watch: www.prwatch.org
About the development of the projects mentioned above: www.evel.nl
The US and UK publishers' sites for Battling Big Business:
www.commoncouragepress.com/bbb.html and www.greenbooks.co.uk/bbb.htm

Notes on Contributors

FRANNY ARMSTRONG After eight entertaining years on the outskirts of pop music, Franny hung up her drumsticks. Her first TV documentary, 'McLibel', was censored in the UK, but adored elsewhere. For legal reasons she was definitely not involved in the 'McSpotlight' website, but it was nevertheless described as both the 'deathstar of cyberspace' and 'an image-conscious corporation's worst nightmare'. She is currently three years into a documentary about an Indian family who plan to drown in their homes rather than move out of the way for the Narmada dam. She lives in London and runs Spanner with Will Ross (see below).

THE AUTONOMOUS A.F.R.I.K.A. GROUP is a bunch of part-time desperadoes originating from provincial Germany. In pursuit of a pleasurable way of doing politics, they got into guerrilla communications. They were politically responsible for a *Handbook for the Communication Guerrilla*, published in German, Italian and Spanish; also the collection *Medienrandale* (Media Riots) and some other texts.

SHARON BEDER is an Australian-based academic and writer. Her books include *Global Spin: The Corporate Assault on Environmentalism* (Green Books 1997, revised ed. 2002), *Selling the Work Ethic: From Puritan Pulpit to Corporate PR* (Zed Books 2000), *The New Engineer* (Macmillan 1998), *The Nature of Sustainable Development* (Scribe 1996) and *Toxic Fish and Sewer Surfing* (Allen & Unwin 1989).

ANN DOHERTY is a founder of the Corporate Europe Observatory and co-author of *Europe Inc.: Regional and Global Restructuring and the Rise of Corporate Power*. She works at the international secretariat of Friends of the Earth in Amsterdam.

NICKY HAGER is a researcher and investigative writer living in Wellington, New Zealand. His 1996 book, *Secret Power: New Zealand's Role in the International Spy Network*, documented the previously unknown Western intelligence network Echelon. His 1999 book, *Secrets and Lies: The Anatomy of an Anti-Environmental PR Campaign*, documented an aggressive public relations campaign waged (unsuccessfully) to maintain rainforest logging in his country. He is 43 years old and has one child.

OLIVIER HOEDEMAN has been a researcher and campaigner with the Corporate Europe Observatory since 1996. He is based in Amsterdam. He played an active role in the resistance against the Multilateral Agreement on Investment (MAI) and the proposed new WTO round, in the Netherlands and internationally. He has written many articles on issues including corporate lobbying, economic globalization, the environment and European unification.

KEES HUDIG combines participatory observation of methods of hegemony (sometimes inside police cells) with research and writing about resistance and liberation. Has been writing, under several names, for the alternative press and the commercial media since the early '80s. He is the co-author of books on subjects including the US invasion of Panama, communication guerrilla action and bank robberies. He tries to be a perfect father, cook and lover in between.

GEORGE MONBIOT is the author of *Captive State: the corporate takeover of Britain* and a columnist for *The Guardian*. About 400 of his articles are online at www.monbiot.com.

KATHRYN MULVEY is executive director of Infact. As a grassroots organizer, strategist, researcher, writer and spokesperson, since 1989 she has played a leading role in Infact's effective campaigns targeting transnational corporations such as General Electric, Dow Chemical and Philip Morris.

SHEILA O'DONNELL is a licensed private investigator and partner in Ace Investigations in Pacifica, CA in the western United States. She teaches activists to defend themselves against those who would silence their voices and is the author of *Common Sense Security, a Handbook for Activists*. She works as an adviser on security to numerous non-governmental organizations, news outlets, international unions and other groups. She provides discreet background investigations and also consults with attorneys preparing for trial in both criminal and civil matters in the United States. She consults with organizations not only in the United States, but also in South America, Canada, Europe and Africa.

CLAUDIA PETER is an environmental and consumer health journalist. She is the principal author of the 1995 book *Deckmantel Ökologie: Tarnorganisationen der Industrie missbrauchen das Umweltbewusstsein der Bürger*. She has written numerous articles on corporate and right-wing anti-environmentalism in Germany and the EU, climate change, species protection and other ecological issues. She lives in Germany and Switzerland.

WILL ROSS has been building and running websites for Amnesty International and other human rights and environmental groups for six years or so. His leisure time is spent doing exactly the same thing but for a motley collection of activist sites, including McSpotlight. Next is www.climatechange.tv, a web/tv hybrid which compiles first-hand reports of the impacts of global warming. His background is in philosophy, copywriting and medicine, which hasn't been much help.

ANDY ROWELL is a freelance writer and investigative journalist. He has over a dozen years experience writing on political, environmental and health issues. He is author of *Green Backlash: Global Subversion of the Environmental Movement*, published by Routledge in 1996. Rowell's latest book *Don't Worry—it's Safe to Eat* will be published by Earthscan in 2003.

FLORIAN SCHNEIDER is a filmmaker, writer and activist from Munich. As a consultant to non-profit organizations in internet strategies, he has been involved in numerous online and offline activities around the issues of borders and migration. He is a co-founder of the no-one-is-illegal campaign. As a freelance writer he contributes regularly for various mainstream as well as independent media in Germany. As a filmmaker he is currently working on a 135-minute programme about new global activism for the German-French TV station arte.

JESSICA WILSON is a researcher and writer living in Wellington, New Zealand. Jessica has worked for a range of non-governmental organizations, focusing on environmental issues. Her research work began with a study of corporate influence on New Zealand's key environmental legislation, the Resource Management Act. Prompted by observations made while working within the environmental education sector, she has recently been researching the rise of corporate sponsorship targeted at the youth market.

References and Notes

Introduction

1. See for instance Jem Bendell, contributing ed., *Terms for Endearment: Business, NGOs and Sustainable Development* (Sheffield, UK: Greenleave Publishing, 2000) and Simon Heap, *NGOs Engaging with Business: A World of Difference and a Difference to the World* (Oxford, UK: INTRAC, 2000).
2. Peter Sinton, 'Crisis of Conscience: Corporations Are Finding Social Responsibility Boosts the Planet and the Bottom Line', *San Francisco Chronicle*, Nov. 22, 2001, p. B-1, on the International Communications Consultancy Organization's global summit of public relations advisers in San Francisco in November 2001.
3. For more information about NorWatch, see www.fivh.no/norwatch/english.asp.

Chapter 1: The Spread of Greenwash *Andy Rowell*

1. Jed Greer and Kenny Bruno, *Greenwash: The Reality Behind Corporate Environmentalism* (New York: Third World Network/Apex Press, 1996).
2. Kenny Bruno, *The Greenpeace Book of Greenwash* (London: Greenpeace, 1992), p. 1.
3. Joyce Nelson, *Sultans of Sleaze: Public Relations and the Media* (Toronto: Between the Lines, 1989), pp. 130-1.
4. Frank Graham Jr, *Since Silent Spring* (London: Hamish Hamilton, 1970), p. 48.
5. E. Bruce Harrison, *Going Green: How to Communicate Your Company's Environmental Commitment* (Homewood, IL: Business One Irwin, 1993), p. 4.
6. Advertisement for the Astra ECO4, 'Eco Warrior', *The Guardian*, Jan. 24, 2001.
7. See www.corpwatch.org.
8. Shell ad, *The Financial Times*, Nov. 14, 2000.
9. See www.corpwatch.org: Greenwash Award, Shell, 'Clouding the Issue'.
10. Rowell, *Green Backlash*, p. 86. For an in-depth read on how the oil industry scuppered the climate negotiations, see Jeremy Leggett, *The Carbon War* (Middlesex, England: The Penguin Group, 1999), www.carbonwar.com.
11. Editorial, *World Oil*, May 1992; editorial, *World Oil*, September 1992.
12. Editorial, *The Oil and Gas Journal*, July 29, 1996; William O'Keefe, 'In Defence of Skepticism: Challenging the Political View of Climate Change', remarks to the Economic Club of Detroit, Nov. 18, 1996.
13. John Browne, 'Addressing Global Climate Change', speech at Stanford University, Stanford, California, May 19, 1997.
14. Greenpeace, 'A Decade of Dirty Tricks: ExxonMobil's Attempts to Stop The World Tackling Climate Change', July 2001.
15. See www.wwf.org, especially www.wwfpacific.org.fj/kikori.htm; www.pacificwoods.org; and www.chevron.com.

16. Quoted in Danny Kennedy, 'Papua New Guinea Blues', *Multinational Monitor*, Vol. 17, No. 3, March 1996, www.essential.org/monitor/.

17. WWF, *An Assessment of Kikori Pacific Limited Financial Situation*, internal report, 2000, p. 1; Jamie Resor and Douglas Salloum, *A Treasury of Trees: Business and the Battle for the Forest*, International Finance Corporation, Washington, 1999, www.ifc.org.

18. Danny Kennedy, interviewed by Alexandra de Blas for 'Sustainable Forestry in PNG', on *Earthbeat*, Radio National, Australia, Oct. 4, 1999.

19. See www.wwf.org, especially www.wwfpacific.org.fj/kikori.htm; www.pacificwoods.org; and www.chevron.com.

20. Barbara Wyckoff-Baird, *Report of the Review of the Kikori Integrated Conservation and Development Project*, WWF, Dec. 20, 1997.

21. WWF, *An Assessment of Kikori Pacific Limited Financial Situation*, internal report, 2000, p. 5.

22. Ibid., p. 3; www.macfound.org.

23. Resor and Salloum.

24. See WWF's US website, www.worldwildlife.org, and Resor and Salloum.

25. WWF, *An Assessment of Kikori Pacific Limited Financial Situation*, pp. 1, 5.

26. Ibid., pp. 5, 19.

27. Broadcast on *Channel 4 News,* UK, Feb. 22, 2001.

28. Philip Cornford, 'A Timely Move Upstream, *The Sydney Morning Herald*, March 2, 2001, p. 11.

29. Danny Kennedy, letter to *The Sydney Morning Herald*, March 2001.

Chapter 2: bp: Beyond Petroleum? *Sharon Beder*

1. William Maclean, 'BP Goes Greener with 'Beyond Petroleum' Rebrand', *Planet Ark,* July 25, 2000.

2. Brian Hale, 'BP Goes Green, Solar, Connected', *The Sydney Morning Herald,* July 26, 2000, pp. 25-6.

3. Kruti Trivedi, 'BP Amoco Wants to Sell More Than Gas at Its New Stations', *The New York Times,* July 25, 2000 (www.nytimes.com).

4. Andrew McKenzie and John Macleay, 'Sun Rises on Greener BP', *The Australian,* July 26, 2000, p. 1.

5. Quoted in Philip Rawstorne, 'BP Puts On New 'Public Face' to Meet Challenges of the 1990s', *The Oil Daily,* Feb. 6, 1989, p. 5.

6. Jolyon Jenkins, 'Who's the Greenest?' *New Statesman and Society,* Aug. 17, 1990, pp. 18-20.

7. Julie Gozan, 'BP: A Legacy of Apartheid, Pollution and Exploitation', *Multinational Monitor,* Vol. 13, No. 11, November 1992, pp. 26-30.

8. Ernest A. Lowe and Robert J. Harris, 'Taking Climate Change Seriously: British Petroleum's Business Strategy', *Corporate Environmental Strategy,* Winter 1998 (www.indigodev.com/BPclim.html).

9. 'BP at War: Colombia', *The Economist,* July 19, 1997, pp. 32-4.

10. Bureau of Democracy, Human Rights and Labor, 'Colombia Country Report on Human Rights Practices for 1997', Department of State, 1998; Bureau of Democracy, Human Rights and Labor, 'Colombia Country Report on Human Rights Practices for 1998', Department of State, 1999 (both at www.state.gov/www/global/human_rights).

11. 'Colombia: BP's Secret Soldiers', *World In Action*, ITV, UK, June 30, 1997 (text at www.cdi.org/ArmsTradeDatabase/CONTROL/Small_Arms/Mercenaries/BP's_Secret_Soldiers.txt).

12. Cited in 'Oil Companies Buying Up Colombian Army to Fight Pipeline Violence', *Drillbits & Tailings*, September 1996, p. 2; Human Rights Committee, 'Colombia', Office of the United Nations High Commissioner for Human Rights, 1997 (www.hri.ca/fortherecord1997).

13. 'Colombia: BP's Secret Soldiers.'

14. Michael Sean Gillard and Melissa Jones, 'BP's Secret Soldiers', *Weekly Mail & Guardian*, July 4, 1997 (web.sn.apc.org/wmail).

15. 'Colombia: BP's Secret Soldiers.'

16. 'BP at War: Colombia', pp. 32-34.

17. Quoted in Polly Ghazi and Ian Hargreaves, 'BP's Chief Executive is Making the Running on Green Strategy', *New Statesman*, July 4, 1997, pp. 34-7.

18. 'Colombia: How Green is Your Petrol?'; Athan Manuel, 'Green Words, Dirty Deeds: A PIRG Exposé of BP Amoco's Greenwashing', US Public Interest Research Group (PIRG) Education Fund, 1999; 'Colombian Government Report Accuses BP of Involvement in Environmental and Human Rights Abuses', *Drillbits & Tailings*, Nov. 7, 1996, p. 4.

19. Amnesty International, 'Colombia: British Petroleum Risks Fuelling Human Rights Crisis Through Military Training', Amnesty International, 1997 (www.web.amnesty.org/ai.nsf).

20. 'Colombia: BP's Secret Soldiers.'

21. 'Colombia: The Role of BP', *Blowout Magazine*, January 1998.

22. Human Rights Watch, 'Special Issues and Campaigns: Corporations and Human Rights', 1999 (www.igc.org/hrw/).

23. Ghazi and Hargreaves, pp. 34-7; 'Colombia: BP's Secret Soldiers'; Peter Eisen, 'Group Pressures Oxy, BP on Human Rights', *The Oil Daily*, April 22, 1998.

24. 'BP at War: Colombia', pp. 32-4; Human Rights Committee.

25. 'Colombia: BP's Secret Soldiers.'

26. Quoted in Ghazi and Hargreaves, pp. 34-7.

27. Human Rights Watch.

28. Gozan, pp. 26-30.

29. Peter Sutherland, 'Amnesty International Event', 1997 speech (www.bp.com).

30. Richard Newton, 'Business and Human Rights', 1997 speech (www.bp.com).

31. John Browne, 'The Case for Social Responsibility', 1998 speech (www.bp.com).

32. 'BP's Submission to the UK House of Commons Foreign Affairs Committee', BP, 2000 (www.bp.com).

33. James Bamberg, *The History of the British Petroleum Company, Vol. 2: The Anglo-Iranian Years, 1928-1954* (Cambridge: Cambridge University Press, 1994); James Bamberg, *British Petroleum and Global Oil 1950-1975, Volume 3: The Challenge of Nationalism* (Cambridge: Cambridge University Press, 2000).

34. 'BP to Pay Damages in California Spill', *Oil and Gas Journal*, Feb. 13, 1995, p. 32; Manuel, pp. 11-12; 'Salvage Will Show Toll from Tanker Spill', *Business Insurance*, July 29, 1991, p. 45; Gozan, pp. 26-30; 'European Plants Dwarf US in Toxics', *Chemical Marketing Reporter*, Aug. 3, 1992, p. 5.

35. Gozan, pp. 26-30.

36. Manuel, p. 11.

37. Ibid., p. 7.
38. Russell Mokhiber and Robert Weissman, 'Enemies of the Future: The Ten Worst Corporations of 2000', *Multinational Monitor,* December 2000, p. 12.
39. David Rice, 'Corporate Responsibility in the Marketplace', 1999 speech (www.bp.com).
40. E.J.P. Browne, 'Energy Companies and the Environment Can Coexist', *USA Today,* Vol. 127, No. 2640, Sept. 1, 1998, pp. 54-56.
41. Kenny Bruno, 'Summer Greenwash Award: BP Amoco's 'Plug in the Sun' Program', Corporate Watch, 1999 (www.igc.org/trac).
42. Manuel, p. 8.
43. Quoted in Manuel, p. 11; Danielle Knight, 'USA: Mixed Reaction to Oil Co's Earth Day Award', Corporate Watch (www.igc.org/trac/), 1999.
44. Gozan, pp. 26-30.
45. 'Wash 'n' dough', *SchNews,* Sept. 22, 2000; SANE BP, 'The Resolution', 2000 (www.sanebp.com).
46. Energy Stewardship Alliance, 'Energy Stewardship Alliance Formed; National Support for ANWR Exploration Grows', PR Newswire, March 21, 2000 (biz.yahoo.com/prnews/); Bob Costantini, 'Where The Caribou Roam: The Arctic Oil Debate Heats Up', evote.com, March 2001 (www.evote.com/features); The Center for Responsive Politics, 'Herrera, Roger Charles', 1997 (www.opensecrets.org).
47. Greenpeace, 'We Laughed! We Cried! But Mostly We Cried!' April 22, 1999 (www.greenpeaceusa.org).
48. Natalie Noor-Drugan, 'BP Amoco reverts to bp, launches massive brand campaign', *Chemical Week,* Vol. 162, Aug. 2, 2000, p. 16; 'BP Amoco unveils new global brand to drive growth', BP Press Release, July 24, 2000; *Advertising Age,* Sept. 18, 2000, and *Campaign,* Oct. 13, 2000.

Chapter 3: Dialogue: Divide and Rule *Andy Rowell*

1. E. Bruce Harrison, *Going Green: How to Communicate Your Company's Environmental Commitment* (Homewood, IL: Business One Irwin, 1993), p. 123.
2. 'MDB's Divide-and-Conquer Strategy to Defeat Activists', *PR Watch,* Vol. 1, No. 1, October/December 1993, p. 5.
3. John Elkington, 'The Triple Bottom Line for 21st Century Business', presentation at Greenpeace's 'Brent Spar . . . and After' conference, London, Sept. 25, 1996.
4. Jonathan Bray, lecture at the Institute of Petroleum, London, Sept. 23, 1997.
5. Acción Ecológica, *Oilwatch,* Quito, 1996, p. 17; Rainforest Action Network, *Action Alert,* Jan. 27, 1997.
6. Project Underground and Rainforest Action Network, *Human Rights and Environmental Operations Information on the Royal Dutch/Shell Group of Companies,* independent annual report, April 1997; letter to the Body Shop from M. Jones, Shell Peru's manager for health, safety and environment, Feb. 13, 1997; Shell Prospecting and Development (Peru) (1996), *Camisea Gas: A Background Briefing,* Jan. 30, 1996.
7. Business and Environment Consultancy, *Camisea Dialogue—Stakeholder Workshops,* 1997.
8. Quoted in Wolfgang Mai, *Reflections After the Camisea Project Workshop,* Brot für die Welt, Dec. 22, 1997, p. 1.

9. Mai, *Reflections After the Camisea Project Workshop*, p. 3.

10. Bob Burton, 'Advice on Making Nice', *PR Watch*, First Quarter 1999, p. 6.

11. Shell, 'Shell and Mobil Unable to Proceed with Camisea Project', press release, July 16, 1998.

12. Burton, 'Advice on Making Nice', p. 6.

13. Shell, *Profits and Principles—Does There Have To Be a Choice?* 1998, p. 1.

14. Shell, *Profits and Principles*, p. 16; Michael Birnbaum, *Nigeria: Fundamental Rights Denied: Report of the Trial of Ken Saro-Wiwa and Others*, Article 19 in Association with the Bar Human Rights Committee of England and Wales and the Law Society of England and Wales, June 1995, Appendix 10.

15. Shell, *Profits and Principles*, pp. 16, 34-35.

16. The Shell Transport and Trading Company, *Summary Annual Report 1998*, 1999, p. 27.

17. Browse the 'Listening and Responding' section at www.shell.com.

18. *The Big Issue South West*, Oct. 30-Nov. 5, 2000.

19. Owens Wiwa and Andy Rowell, 'Some Things Never Change', *The Guardian*, Nov. 8, 2000, Society section, pp. 8-9.

20. Andy Rowell, 'Shell Shocked: The True Cost of Petrol', *The Big Issue in Scotland*, Nov. 23-29, 2000, pp. 24-25.

21. The Environment Council, *BNFL National Stakeholder Dialogue, Waste Working Group, Interim Report*, Feb. 28, 2000.

22. Peter Roche, communication with author, December 2000.

23. Sarah Burton, letter to the Environment Council regarding BNFL Stakeholder Dialogue, Nov. 20, 2000.

24. Simon Heap, *Engaging with Business: A World of Difference and a Difference to the World* (Oxford: Intrac, 2000), pp. 27-28.

25. PARTiZANS, *Parting Company: The Newsletter of People Against RTZ*, Autumn 1998, p. 1.

26. Heap, *Engaging with Business*, p. 30.

27. Andy Rowell, 'Greenwash Goes Legit', *The Guardian*, July 21, 1999, p. 5.

28. Andy Rowell, 'GM Food on Trial', *The Big Issue South West*, Nov. 22-28, 1999, pp. 6-7.

29. Ibid.

30. Ibid.

31. Andy Rowell, 'Monsanto Talks in Crisis', *The Big Issue South West*, Jan. 17-23, 2000, pp. 4-5.

32. Ibid.

33. Ibid.

34. Suzannah Lansdell of the Environment Council, in a letter regarding a possible National Agricultural Biotechnology Stakeholder Dialogue, July 14, 2000.

35. Rowell, 'Monsanto Talks in Crisis', pp. 4-5.

36. Clare Devereux, communication with author, December 2000.

37. Martin Livermore, letter to NFWI, April 28, 2000; Andy Rowell, 'Sowing Seeds of Doubt', *The Guardian*, August 2, 2000, Society section, p. 9.

38. Rowell, 'GM Food on Trial', pp. 6-7.

39. Heap, *Engaging with Business*, pp. 15, 23, 260.

40. Greg Muttitt, notes on 'Finding Common Ground' conference, June 30, 2000.

41. Mark Dowie, *Losing Ground: American Environmentalism at the Close of the Twentieth Century* (Cambridge, MA: The MIT Press, 1995), pp. 106-107.

42. Ibid., p. 116.

43. See www.motherjones.com.
44. Ibid.
45. Alex Carey, *Taking the Risk Out of Democracy: Propaganda in the US and Australia* (Sydney: University of New South Wales Press, 1995).

Chapter 4: The Sponsorship Scam *Jessica Wilson*

1. Robin Taylor, letter to the editor, *Sunday Star Times*, Oct. 15, 2000, p. A12.
2. Guyon Espiner, 'WWF and Shell strengthen their relationship', *Sunday Star Times*, Oct. 8, 2000, p. A6.
3. Guyon Espiner, 'WWF has links with oil company', *Sunday Star Times*, Oct. 8, 2000, p. A1.
4. Guyon Espiner, 'WWF endorsed Shell's PR manager: Further links between environmental groups and oil company revealed', *Sunday Star Times*, Oct. 22, 2000, p. A4.
5. Alex Molnar, 'Colonizing Our Future: The Commercial Transformation of America's Schools', article adapted from the John Dewey Memorial Lecture delivered by the author at the Association for Supervision and Curriculum Development Conference in New Orleans, March 25, 2000, at CERU Research & Writing at www.schoolcommercialism.org.
6. Consumers Union, *Captive Kids: A report on commercial pressures on kids at school*, www.consumer.org.
7. John F. Borowski, 'Targeting Children: Industry's Campaign to Redefine Environmental Education', *PR Watch*, Vol. 7, No. 2., Second Quarter 2000, p. 2.
8. Borowski, p. 2.
9. 'Milwaukee Center for the Analysis of Commercialism in Education releases third annual report on schoolhouse commercialism', press release, Sept. 14, 2000.
10. Alex Molnar quoted in Derrick Jensen, 'Invasion of the Classroom: How Corporations Buy Access to Children: An Interview with Alex Molnar', *The Sun*, November 2000, pp. 9-13, (www.thesunmagazine.org).
11. Advertisement in *Starters & Strategies*, No. 45, February 2001, p. 10.
12. See www.minerals.co.nz.
13. Interview with Barry Weeber, Sept. 19, 2000.
14. Schoolresources at Education at www.seafood.co.nz.
15. See 'The Greenshell Mussel Story', www.greenshell.com.
16. See www.bp.co.nz/about/community.html.
17. Agreement between World Wide Fund for Nature-New Zealand and Shell New Zealand Limited dated Jan. 1, 1999.
18. Shell New Zealand, *Year in Review: 1999*, 1999, p. 9.
19. Ibid., p. 4.
20. Interview with Aimee Driscoll, Aug. 23, 2000.
21. Espiner, 'WWF has links with oil company.'
22. Quoted in Espiner, 'WWF has links with oil company.'
23. Espiner, 'WWF endorsed Shell's PR manager', p. A4.
24. Quoted in Espiner, 'WWF and Shell strengthen their relationship', p. A6.
25. Interview on *The Kim Hill Show*, National Radio, New Zealand, Oct. 9, 2000.
26. WWF-NZ, 'The Southern Right Whale Research Expedition: Review of June and November Reports to WWF-NZ', internal paper, November 1998.

27. Bob Burton, 'WWF Signs $1.2M Partnership with Rio Tinto', *Mining Monitor*, March 2000, www.mpi.org.au.
28. Jason Nisse and Louise Jury, 'Greenpeace gets in bed with its foes', *The Independent*, Oct. 15, 2000, www.independent.co.uk.
29. Quoted in Guyon Espiner, 'Fears over business links: Environmentalists concerned about pressure from sponsors', *Sunday Star Times*, Oct. 8, 2000, p. A6.
30. Quoted in Bob Burton, www.mpi.org.au.
31. Quoted in Espiner, 'WWF endorsed Shell's PR manager', p. A4.
32. Interview with Cath Wallace, Nov. 13, 2000.
33. Quoted in Espiner, 'WWF endorsed Shell's PR manager', p. A4.
34. Quoted in Espiner, 'WWF and Shell strengthen their relationship', p. A6.
35. 'Fundraising from Shell for the Suluwesi Sea Ecoregion—URGENT', WWF internal email message, May 3, 2000.

Chapter 6: Krafting a Smokescreen *Kathryn Mulvey*

1. 'Humphrey Achieves Historic $6.1 Billion Settlement of Tobacco Lawsuit with Ironclad Ban Against Marketing to Children', press release from the Office of the Attorney General for the State of Minnesota, May 8, 1998.
2. The Philip Morris Internal Documents can be found at www.pmdocs.com. Searching this site can be difficult: it is slow and crashes often, and the slightest change in search terms can dramatically change the results. For the most reliable results, it is necessary to type in the search terms in capital letters, use quotes on terms that are more than one word long, and be as specific as possible.
3. 'Infact Initial Research', Philip Morris internal document # 2047904454, June 29, 1993.
4. Subrata N. Chakravarty and Neal Santelmann, 'Philip Morris is Still Hungry', *Forbes*, April 2, 1990, p. 96; Nikhil Deogun, Gordon Fairclough and Shelly Branch, 'Philip Morris Agrees to Acquire Nabisco', *The Wall Street Journal*, June 26, 2000. Nabisco was formerly partnered with R.J. Reynolds as RJR Nabisco.
5. Larry White, *Merchants of Death: The American Tobacco Industry* (New York: Beech Tree Books, William Morrow, 1988), p. 208.
6. Philip Morris Companies, Inc. 1999 Annual Report, p. 1; Philip Morris Companies, Inc. 1992 Annual Report, p. 30.
7. Ruth Marcus and Ceci Connolly, 'Tobacco Money Still Filters Into Campaigns', *The Washington Post*, May 8, 1998, p. A1.
8. 'Tobacco Company Strategies to Undermine Tobacco Control Activities at the World Health Organization', Report by the Committee of Experts on Tobacco Industry Documents, July 2000.
9. Geoff Bible, 'Corporate Affairs Conference/Action Plan', Dec. 13, 1988, Philip Morris internal document #2021596422/6432.
10. 'Campaign by Infact Against Tobacco Companies for 1994 Proxy Season', Philip Morris internal document #2023652220, June 15, 1993.
11. 'Infact Update', Philip Morris internal document #2047904452/4453, Aug. 5, 1993.
12. 'Infact Activists', note for Darienne Dennis, Philip Morris internal document #2045994503, March 24, 1994.

13. 'Infact Update', memo from Darienne Dennis, Philip Morris internal document #2023437011, May 10, 1994.
14. 'Infact Activists', Philip Morris internal document #2045994503, March 24, 1994; 'Infact', Philip Morris internal document #2046007907, June 6, 1994.
15. 'Campaign by Infact Against Tobacco Companies for 1994 Proxy Season', Philip Morris internal document #2023652220, June 15, 1993.
16. 'Critic Boycott: History and Strategic Recommendations', Philip Morris internal document #2046019672, Aug. 1, 1994.
17. Produced and directed by AndersonGold Films.
18. 'Infact Initial Research', Philip Morris internal document #2047904454, June 29, 1993; John Stauber and Sheldon Rampton, *Toxic Sludge Is Good For You* (Monroe, ME: Common Courage Press, 1995), p. 208.
19. 'Boycott', memo from Sheila Raviv and Roy Perkins to Barry Holt, Philip Morris internal document #2045994611, April 12, 1994.
20. 'Infact—Issues Analysis', Philip Morris internal document #2047904455, June 1993.
21. 'Infact', memo from Darienne Dennis to Wendy Burrell (Philip Morris International) and Richard Collins (Kraft General Foods International), Philip Morris internal document #2504093016, July 29, 1994.
22. 'Discussion Paper: Critic Boycott: Scenarios and Proactive Program', draft, Philip Morris internal document #2045994659/4671, Nov. 30, 1994.
23. 'Boycott', memo from Sheila Raviv and Roy Perkins to Barry Holt, Philip Morris internal document #2045994611, April 12, 1994.
24. 'Critic Boycott: History and Strategic Recommendations', draft #1, Philip Morris internal document #2046019672, Aug. 1, 1994.
25. 'Critic Boycott: History and Strategic Recommendations', draft #2, Philip Morris internal document #2046019733/9755, August 4, 1994.
26. *The Proxy Resolutions Book*, Interfaith Center on Corporate Responsibility, January 1995, p. 90.
27. Philip Morris memo from Darienne Dennis to Wendy Burrell (Philip Morris International) and Richard Collins (Kraft General Foods International), internal document #2504093016, July 29, 1994; 'Infact Planning Meeting: June 2', Philip Morris internal document #2023437010, May 10, 1994.
28. Amy Vinroot, 'Infact's Tobacco Campaign Targets Philip Morris, RJR Nabisco's Joe Camel', News for Investors, Investor Responsibility Resource Center, July/August 1994.
29. Infact communication with ICCR, autumn/fall 1994, and question by Michael Crosby of ICCR to Philip Morris CEO Geoffrey Bible at Philip Morris annual meeting, April 1995.
30. Reuters (online), June 3, 1997; 'Build A Home America', PR Central/Editorial Media and Marketing International, www.prcentral.com/c98_home_america.htm, 1996.
31. Infact, *1998 People's Annual Report: Global Aggression: The Case for World Standards and Bold US Action Challenging Philip Morris and RJR Nabisco* (New York: The Apex Press, 1998), p. 100.
32. 'Top 100 Megabrands', *Advertising Age*, July 17, 2000, p. s8; 'Top 100 Megabrands', *Advertising Age*, July 16, 2001, p. s6.
33. Judann Pollack, 'Kraft Uses Real-Life Footage for $50 Mil Creative Twist', *Advertising Age*, June 15, 1998; 'Superbrands '98: America's Top 2000 Brands', *Brandweek*, Oct. 20, 1997, pp. 128-132.

34. 'Top 100 Megabrands', *Advertising Age*, July 16, 2001, p. s6.
35. 'Philip Morris Companies: A National Opinion Survey—Topline Results', conducted by the Wirthlin Group, January 1993, Philip Morris internal document #2031599541/9584; 'Reasons Why People Change/Do Not Change Their Ratings of Philip Morris and Kraft After Discovering Their Relationship', the Wirthlin Group, July 1993, Philip Morris internal document #2031599304/9347.
36. 'Survey Rates Companies' Reputations, and Many Are Found Wanting', *The Wall Street Journal*, Feb. 7, 2001, p. 1B.
37. *Harper's*, December 2000, p. 7.
38. Burson-Marsteller, 'Consumer Boycott Participation: Public Attitudes and Contributing Factors', Philip Morris internal document #2045994627, February 1991.
39. 'Philip Morris: What It's Like to Work at America's Most Reviled Company', *Business Week*, Nov. 29, 1999, p. 186; 'Fantasy Jobs: So Where Do You Want to Work?', *Fortune*, April 17, 2000.
40. Philip Morris Proxy Statement, March 10, 2000, pp. 10-11.
41. 'Eckert to Craft Makeover for Troubled Toy Marketer', *Advertising Age*, May 22, 2000, p. 6.
42. 'Mattel Appoints Two New Members of Senior Management Team', PRNewswire (www.prnewswire.com), Nov. 1, 2000; Nicole Maestri, *CBS MarketWatch* (www.cbs.marketwatch.com), Oct. 26, 2000, 'Kellogg adds Keebler to its Pantry'.

Chapter 7: Joining Forces: Big Business Rallies after Seattle
Olivier Hoedeman and Ann Doherty

1. The Multilateral Agreement on Investment (MAI) was a controversial investment treaty negotiated within the Organization for Economic Co-operation and Development (OECD) from 1995 to the end of 1998, when public outrage brought about its demise.
2. 'Katz: Activists use internet to slow trade liberalization. US business leader sees free-trade threat', *Journal of Commerce*, Oct. 12, 1998.
3. WTO critics see the institution as the defender of the kind of globalization one CEO defined as "the freedom for my group of companies to invest where it wants when it wants, to produce what it wants, to buy and sell where it wants, and support the fewest restrictions possible coming from labor laws and social conventions." Percy Barnevik, President of the ABB Industrial Group, quoted in 'The Success of Being Dangerous: Resisting Free Trade & Investment Regimes', Gerard Greenfield, 'Research' section at www.wtoaction.org.
4. 'US Businesses See Ministerial As Setback for Trade Liberalization', *International Trade Reporter*, Dec. 9, 1999.
5. *PR Week*, quoted in 'PR Industry Kicks the WTO When It's Down', *The Boston Phoenix*, Dec. 23-30, 1999.
6. 'Seattle setback not to hit trade liberalization', *Business Line*, Dec. 11, 1999. The ICC is the dominant global business lobby organization, representing hundreds of large corporations, and is one of the fiercest proponents of trade and investment liberalization.
7. 'Seattle Rattles Davos Man', *The Observer*, Feb. 6, 2000.
8. Claus Smadja, 'Time to Learn from Seattle', *Newsweek International*, Jan. 17, 2000.
9. Quoted in 'It's the Society, Stupid', *Time*, Jan. 31, 2000.

10. The theme of the Council on Foreign Relations' Oct. 4, 1999, annual general meeting in Washington, DC, was 'The Backlash Against Globalization.'

11. Its board includes former Secretary of State Lawrence Eagleburger and other right-wing heavyweights from politics, academia and business "unified by their support of free trade, open markets and an integrated world economy"—see 'Trading on a Hot Topic', *The Washington Post*, April 25, 2000. According to Cordell Hull Institute director Hugh Corbet, "the not-so-well-educated don't understand and so this ignorance can be exploited by people who are wanting protection, special treatment, and it's the job of leaders to resist (that) kind of thing." See 'Spinning Free Trade: The Battle for Public Opinion', from the radio programme *Making Contact*, July 5, 2000, transcript at National Radio Project, 'Archive' section at www.radioproject.org.

12. 'WTO Transparency', email from Bruce Silverglade to the TACD Food Working Group, April 5, 2000.

13. This guide, and its cover letter dated Jan. 14, 2000, were leaked to activists and posted on the N30 anti-WTO mailing list.

14. Ibid.

15. From an article by Wes Pedersen, communications director of the Public Affairs Council in the PAC newsletter *Impact*, quoted in *O'Dwyers Inside News of PR*, Feb. 7, 2000.

16. Control Risk warns that "actions can range from nonviolent demonstrations and lobbying campaigns to the more violent attacks against property." 'Security on the Internet', *Oil and Gas Journal*, February 2000.

17. Ibid.

18. 'PR Lessons from the Battle in Seattle: An introduction to how the internet has fundamentally changed PR', *ePublic Relations 101*, Public Relations Management Ltd, December 1999.

19. Ibid.

20. Steve Lombardo, president and CEO of Strategy One, Edelman's research arm, quoted in 'Edelman Worldwide's Survey Reveals the Consumer and Media to Be Key Elements in the War Between NGOs and Big Business', PRNewswire, July 12, 2000.

21. Ibid.

22. While the bill was presented as a necessary part of preparation for China's membership in the WTO, the annual renewal of Normal Trade Relations (NTR) was in fact no obstacle.

23. "'Coming on the heels of the failure at Seattle, it would clearly signal that anti-globalization forces will dominate American foreign economic policy for the foreseeable future," Bergsten stressed. C. Fred Bergsten, 'The Next Trade Policy Battle', *International Economics Policy Brief*, January 2000.

24. 'Spinning Free Trade' —see ref. 11 above.

25. 'Purchasing Power: The Corporate-White House Alliance to Pass the China Trade Bill Over the Will of the American People', Public Citizen's *Global Trade Watch*, October 2000.

26. Ibid., p. 24.

27. Ibid., p. 20.

28. 'Spinning Free Trade' —see ref. 11 above.

29. 73 Democrats and 164 Republicans voted for the bill.

30. www.gotrade.org.

31. www.truthabouttrade.com.

32. www.nomorescares.com.

33. www.earthfiends.org.

34. At the conference 'A Vision for Europe's Trade Policy', Brussels, May 29, 2000; see 'Webnotes for Events' in 'Calendar' section at www.ceps.be.

35. *Financial Times* journalist Guy de Jonquires, 'The International Trade Agenda: Key Issues and Future Prospects for a New Round', Second Annual APCO Europe, Herbert Smith, British Chamber of Commerce Trade Conference, Brussels, Feb. 22, 2000.

36. Plans made included commissioning a research project to provide case studies highlighting the 'benefits' of trade in services liberalization for developing countries. See the GATSwatch briefing paper 'Liberalization of Trade in Services: Corporate Power at Work', October 2001, www.gatswatch.org. As is common in Europe, the government has done most of the dirty work in confronting the coalition of NGOs and grassroot groups that oppose GATS, while the LOTIS Committee has taken a back seat.

37. 'Nichtregierungsorganisationen—Herausforderungen für die Wirtschaftsverbande', BDI Aussenwirtschaftspolitik, Sept. 5, 2000.

38. Among its 200-plus members, the EPC has some 15 NGOs to strengthen its credibility, with WWF the most prominent. A closer look at its membership, funding and political direction reveals the EPC's bias toward corporate interests. The fact that it has a WTO Forum group that runs closed, business-only briefings on how to respond to the backlash against neoliberal globalization speaks for itself. See www.TheEPC.be.

39. Stanley Crossick, EPC chairman, 'Seattle: The Business Fall-Out', www.TheEPC.be, Dec. 23, 1999.

40. Agence Europe, Brussels, Dec. 21, 1999.

41. Michael Edwards, 'Make the protesters accountable', *Financial Times*, June 19, 2000. Edwards, director of the Ford Foundation, authored the report *NGO Rights and Responsibilities: A New Deal for Global Governance*, published by the Foreign Policy Center, www.fpc.org.uk.

42. 'Pressure groups warned on public scrutiny', *Financial Times*, June 19, 2000.

43. www.policynetwork.net.

44. Kendra Okonski, 'Riots Inc.: The Business of Protesting Globalization', *The Wall Street Journal*, Aug. 14, 2001. The IPN report was also covered on Radio Free Europe on Aug. 23, 2001. The IPN has had opinion pieces printed in the *Financial Times*, *The Daily Telegraph* and various other mainstream media outlets.

45. 'Edelman Worldwide's Survey Reveals the Consumer and Media to Be Key Elements in the War Between NGOs and Big Business', PRNewswire, July 12, 2000.

46. *Corporate Europe Observer*, No. 4, July 1999, www.xs4all.nl/~ceo.

47. Andre Driessen, VNO-NCW (Dutch Employers' Federation) senior adviser on international affairs, at the conference 'Finding Common Ground: Industry and NGOs in Dialogue and Partnership', organized by GPC Market Access, Brussels, June 29, 2000.

48. 'Global Guidance', Inspiring the Future Pharaohs, June 2000.

49. 'Tireless evangelist spreads the gospel of globalization', *The Times*, April 21, 2000.

50. See 'The case for globalization' section at www.iccwbo.org. The ICC worried that "special interest groups (were) preparing mass protests and demonstrations to oppose the launch of a new trade round."

51. See 'Campaign for a Corporate-Free UN', *Corporate Europe Observer*, No. 7, www.xs4all.nl/~ceo.

52. 'ICC Steps Up Counter-Campaign Against Critics of Corporate-Led Globalization', *Corporate Europe Observer,* No. 7.
53. *Handelszeitung,* Jan. 5, 2000.
54. C. Fred Bergsten, director of the Institute of International Economics, 'The Backlash Against Globalization.' See www.trilateral.org. Bergsten warned that "all the momentum is with the anti-globalization forces" and predicted that the backlash could become much stronger, "especially when our economies begin to turn down."
55. Maria Livanos Cattaui, 'What business should do to thwart the terrorists', Sept. 18, 2001, 'Archives' section at www.iccwbo.org.
56. 'The Future of the Global Trading System: Where to Form Here?' speech, APEC CEO Summit, Oct. 20, 2001.
57. Dean R. O'Hare, CEO of Chubb Corporation and chairman of the US Coalition of Service Industries (CSI), 'Achieving Services Trade Liberalization', at the European Services Forum conference 'The GATS 2000 Negotiations, New Opportunities for Trade Liberalization', Brussels, Nov. 27, 2000. See www.esf.be.

Chapter 8: Using Libel Laws to Silence Critics
Franny Armstrong and Will Ross

1. Verdict of Justice Rodger Bell in *McDonald's Corporation & another vs. Steel & another,* 1997, see 'Judgement' in 'McLibel' section at www.mcspotlight.org.
2. Verdict, *McDonald's Corporation & another vs. Steel & another.*
3. McDonald's Restaurants Ltd., *Employment Practices Policy Statement,* April 1995, see 'Company' section at www.mcspotlight.org.
4. McDonald's Corp. website, 'Commitment to the Environment', as of May 2001, see www.mcdonalds.com.
5. Extrapolated from 1995 figures as presented by McDonald's to the court during McLibel Trial.
6. George W. Pring and Penelope Canan, *Slapps: Getting Sued for Speaking Out* (Philadelphia: Temple University Press, 1996).
7. Transnationals Information Center, *Working for Big Mac,* London, September 1987, repro-duced in the 'Media' section at www.mcspotlight.org.
8. Barlow, Lyde & Gilbert, *Words Complained Of,* June 24, 1994, a legal document produced by McDonald's solicitors and presented to the court listing organizations that criticized McDonald's and subsequently received letters from the corporation and/or its lawyers.
9. Letter to HRH the Duke of Edinburgh from George A. Cohen, president, McDonald's Restaurants of Canada, June 6, 1983.
10. Letter to George A. Cohen, president, McDonald's Restaurants of Canada, from HRH the Duke of Edinburgh, June 27, 1983.
11. Letter to Robin Hellier of the BBC Natural History Unit from McDonald's solicitors, May 1, 1984, see 'Company' section at www.mcspotlight.org.
12. Handwritten internal memo, McDonald's Restaurants Ltd, 1983 (accidentally given to McLibel defendants by McDonald's solicitors), which contains the following: "In the past 12 months . . . McK's have purchased 4 consignments of meat from Brazil, each of 20 tons." McK's is McKey Food Services, which provides all McDonald's UK burger meat.

13. Apology broadcast on BBC Two, May 17, 1984.

14. Letter to C. Secrett, Friends of the Earth UK, from Annette Allen, public relations manager, McDonald's Hamburgers Ltd, Nov. 20, 1985.

15. David Haith, *Demo beefs over cattle, Bournemouth Advertiser*, Oct. 12, 1989, see 'Company' section at www.mcspotlight.org.

16. Verdict, *McDonald's Corporation & another vs. Steel & another.*

17. Full court transcripts are in the 'McLibel' section at www.mcspotlight.org; for the witness statements see 'Evidence' in the 'McLibel' section at www.mcspotlight.org.

18. McDonald's Corp. invited Helen and Dave to three secret settlement meetings—two in 1994 and one in 1995—at which it offered to give a substantial sum to a charitable organization if Helen and Dave backed down and agreed never to hand out the leaflets again. The defendants demanded that McDonald's agree never to sue anyone again and apologize to everyone it had sued in the past. No settlement was reached. A leaked McDonald's Australia internal memo of 1992 urged staff not to comment on the trial: "We could worsen the controversy by adding our opinion. We want to keep it at arm's length—not become guilty by association."

19. *McLibel: Two Worlds Collide*, 53-minute TV documentary, One-Off Productions, London, 1997, www.mclibel.com.

20. John Vidal, *McLibel: Burger Culture on Trial* (London: Macmillan, 1997).

Chapter 9: McSpying *Eveline Lubbers*

1. Despite its worldwide dominance, McDonald's is extremely sensitive about its reputation. It has fought legal battles across the world to stop people using and abusing its name, symbols and slogans (see Chapter 8, 'Using Libel Laws to Silence Critics'). Yet while McDonald's was busily suing (or threatening to sue) almost everyone who criticized it— from the BBC and *The Guardian* to student unions and green groups—it appeared to ignore the London Greenpeace campaign for some time. Instead, it threatened a Nottingham food co-operative called Veggies which was distributing the same leaflet. McDonald's then made an agreement with Veggies to accept the circulation of the leaflet provided some minor amendments were made to a couple of sections. The company didn't even complain about most of the leaflet. Veggies continued distributing it in bulk.

2. All quotes are taken from the court transcripts in the 'McLibel' section at www.mcspotlight.org.

3. Originally it applied for these four to remain anonymous, but a legal challenge by the McLibel Two forced them into the open.

4. *McLibel: Two Worlds Collide*, 53-minute TV documentary, One-Off Productions, London, 1997; Interview with Frances Tiller in August 1996, at www.mcspotlight.org.

5. Helen Steel, email interview, October 2000.

6. Jonathan Calvert and David Connett, 'Cloaks, daggers and Ms X appeal', *The Observer*, Jan. 26, 1997, reproduced in the 'Media' section at www.mcspotlight.org.

7. The Economic League had 40 current Labour Members of Parliament on file, plus prominent trade unionists, journalists and thousands of shop-floor workers. After the group disbanded in 1994, former Director-General Stan Hardy continued to alert businesses to

individuals and organizations he claimed were opposed to private enterprise through his family firm, Caprim Ltd. See David Hencke, 'Left blacklist man joins euro fight', *The Guardian*, Sept. 9, 2000, at www.guardian.co.uk.

8. McLibel Support Campaign press release, Sept. 17, 1998.

9. Helen Steel, email interview. On the Poll Tax: the British government decided to implement a new Poll Tax on April 1, 1990, replacing a tax on households with one on individuals. It was immediately seen as a tax on the poor and an extension of government powers over the population. More than 250,000 people demonstrated in a call for mass resistance. A carnivalesque gathering turned into an hours-long battle with police that spread through the major commercial streets of central London. About 500 people were arrested, and police raided dozens of activists' homes over the next few weeks. Detective Sergeant Valentine was working on this 'Operation Carnaby' when he agreed to meet with Clare to discuss his knowledge of London Greenpeace members, some of whom were active in the anti-Poll Tax movement.

By 1991, 18 million were refusing to pay the tax. Conservative Prime Minister Margaret Thatcher resigned, largely as a result of the damage to her credibility and strategy. A few days before an anniversary demo in March 1991, new Prime Minister John Major announced that the tax was uncollectable and would be scrapped.

10. McLibel Support Campaign press release, July 5, 2000.

11. Calvert and Connett, 'Cloaks, daggers and Ms X appeal.'

12. British libel procedures are extremely complex and weighted against defendants. By law the party accused of libel must prove from primary sources that what he or she says is not libellous. In most other Western countries, the accusing party has to make clear why it feels libelled.

13. On June 19, 1997, Justice Bell took two hours to read his summary to a packed courtroom. In his view, Steel and Morris had not proved their allegations with respect to rainforest destruction, packaging, food poisoning, starvation in the Third World, heart disease, cancer and bad working conditions. But he ruled the defendants had shown that McDonald's had exploited children with its advertising, falsely advertised its food as nutritious, risked the health of its long-term regular customers, been "culpably responsible" for cruelty to animals reared for its products and "strongly antipathetic" to unions, and paid its workers low wages. In March 1999 the Court of Appeal also found that it was fair comment to say McDonald's employees "do badly in terms of pay and conditions" and true that "if one eats enough McDonald's food, one's diet may well become high in fat etc., with the very real risk of heart disease."

Note that 'not proved' does not mean the allegations against McDonald's were not true, just that in the judge's opinion Steel and Morris did not bring sufficient evidence. This was mostly based on the judge's agreeing with McDonald's interpretations of the exact meanings of the phrases in the leaflet. See 'Judgement' in the 'McLibel' section at www.mcspotlight.org.

Chapter 11: Private Spooks: Wackenhut vs. Whistleblowers
Sheila O'Donnell

1. Michael Sean Gillard, Melissa Jones and Andrew Rowell, 'Oil pipeline disaster "imminent"' and 'Safety versus the bottom line', *The Guardian*, July 12, 1999 (www.guardian.co.uk). A new version of 'Safety versus the bottom line' updated as of June 2000 appeared in *New Solutions: A Journal of Environmental and Occupational Health Policy*, October 2000, Vol. 10 (1-2), pp. 167-183, and also at www.alaskagroupsix.org.
2. John Connolly, 'Inside the Shadow CIA', *Spy*, September 1992.
3. Alyeska Pipeline Service Company Covert Operation, Exhibit 17, *Report of the Committee on Interior and Insular Affairs of the US House of Representatives*, Part II, Appendix— Exhibits 1-83, 102nd Congress, Second Session, July 1992, p. 680.
4. Alyeska Pipeline Service Company Covert Operation, *Draft Report of the Committee on Interior and Insular Affairs of the US House of Representatives*, Part I, 102nd Congress, Second Session, July 1992.
5. *Supplemental Statement of Ricki Sue Jacobson before the US House of Representatives Committee on Interior and Insular Affairs, House of Representatives*, 102nd Congress, November 4, 5, and 6, 1991, serial no. 102-13, p. 307.
6. *Valdez Vanguard*, April 4, 1990.
7. 'Alyeska Pipeline Service Company Covert Operation', *Draft Report of the Committee on Interior and Insular Affairs of the US House of Representatives*, Part I, 102nd Congress, Second Session, July 1992.
8. Ibid.
9. Ibid.
10. Gillard, Jones and Rowell, 'Oil pipeline disaster "imminent"' and 'Safety versus the bottom line.'

Chapter 12: Cyber-surveillance   *Eveline Lubbers*

1. Peter Verhille of Entente International Communication, speech and report at 'Putting the Pressure On' conference, Brussels, July 1998.
2. Simon May, presentation at 'Putting the Pressure On'. May left Shell at the beginning of 2000.
3. Ibid.
4. Ibid.
5. Email interview with Simon May, June 1998.
6. May, presentation at 'Putting the Pressure On.'
7. Email interview with May, June 1998.
8. Figures are from the eWatch Factsheet at www.prnewswire.com, August 2001. Also see www.ewatch.com.
9. Sherri Deatherage Green, 'Internet hoaxes', *Revolution: Business and Marketing in the Digital Economy*, April 1, 2000 (see archives at www.revolution.haynet.com).
10. Marcia Stepanek, 'Now, Companies Can Track Down Their Cyber-Critics', www.business-week.com, July 7, 2000.
11. Personal email from Marcia Stepanek, Nov. 14, 2000.

12. I was the target of a determined attempt at spin, but an unsuccessful one, since I had my facts straight. I knew the site had been up and running while Stepanek was writing her article, since I had written about it myself. Although the link to it had been removed from eWatch's main page on July 18, 2000 (as I easily found by using Netscape's Page Info feature), the Cybersleuth site was still up when I first contacted Aldrich; you just had to know the URL. I told her so, and within a day it vanished. It can now be viewed in the Pandora mailing list archive at www.oudenaarden.nl/lists/pandora/.

13. Email correspondence with Renu Aldrich, Nov. 8-14, 2000.

14. 'Online monitoring goes beyond anonymous postings', press release announcing the agreement between eWatch and ICG, PRNewswire, June 18, 2000.

15. Rebecca Buckman, 'Gumshoe Game on the Internet—Companies Hire Private Eyes To Unmask Online Detractors', *The Wall Street Journal*, July 27, 1999; Borzou Daragahi, 'Private eyes who watch the Web', *Web Watch*, July 11, 2000, at www.money.com. ICG chose not to reply to my repeated questions.

16. Roy Lipski, 'Drowned Out: Rethinking Corporate Reputation Management for the Internet' in *Journal of Communication Management*, December 2000. Also see www.infonic.com, Library section.

17. Email correspondence with Roy Lipski, Nov. 21, 2000.

18. The document, 'NGO Strategy' (a presentation by Andrew Baynes, project manager at Sony International (Europe), July 12, 2000, Brussels), can be found at www.motherjones.com/news_wire/AB_NGO_Strategy_jul00.pdf. For more on the European Information and Communication Technology Industry Association see www.eicta.org. See also 'Industry goes on global offensive against toxics activists: Targeting funding, Internet activities', *Inside EPA Weekly Report*, Vol. 21, No. 37, Sept. 15, 2000, and Danielle Knight, 'Electronics Giant Tracks Environmental Organizations', Inter Press Service (www.ips.org), Sept. 15, 2000.

19. 'NGO Strategy.'

20. Ibid.

21. Email correspondence with Roy Lipski, Feb. 5, 2001; also see Stephanie Gruner, 'He's Not Sam Spade, But Web Detective Digs His Work', *The Wall Street Journal*, Jan. 17, 2001, and Burhan Wazir, 'Eating the greens: Electronics giants such as Sony are using the internet to hit back at troublesome eco-warriors', *The Observer*, Oct. 1, 2000.

22. Private email correspondence with Stephanie Gruner, Jan. 29, 2001.

23. Sony met a delegation from the Clean Computer Campaign in Brussels on Oct. 30, 2000, according to personal email from Iza Kruszewska, Feb. 2, 2001.

24. See www.greenpeace.org/Admin/usage/. Greenpeace does not keep statistics connecting visitors to specific pages.

25. Infonic appeared on the list from Dec. 19, 1999, to July 16, 2000. It was not until early January 2001 that it appeared there again—for three solid months.

26. Knight, 'Electronics Giant Tracks Environmental Organizations.'

27. Northwest employees had accepted pay cuts in 1993 to help keep the airline out of bankruptcy and had been working without a contract since 1997. Flight attendants claimed that their pay therefore lagged dramatically behind the industry standard. Northwest and the flight attendants' union, Teamsters Local 2000, entered contract negotiations in late 1998; they reached a stalemate on Dec. 7, 1998.

28. Background information on the Northwest sickout case was taken from 'Case Study: Northwest Airlines' in the Online Library of Sources at the Digital Discovery Project, Berkman Center, Harvard Law School, cyber.law.harvard.edu/digitaldiscovery/.

29. The website, at www.holisticmed.com/aspartame/, provides detailed scientific and general documentation on the possible toxicity of NutraSweet, Equal, Diet Coke, Diet Pepsi, and other items containing aspartame, including real-life reports of acute and chronic toxicity after long-term ingestion.

30. DeAnne DeWitt, 'Corporate Stalking', *Citizen Engineer*, July 18, 2000 (see column archive at www.chipcenter.com). This column inspired this chapter's conclusions.

Chapter 13: Corporate Intelligence *Eveline Lubbers*

1. Stephen Overell, 'Masters of the great game turn to business', *Financial Times*, March 22, 2000, at stephenstenson.com.

2. Michael Maclay, 'Recruiting Political Scientists', presentation at Academia Meets Business conference, Leiden, the Netherlands, July 2-3, 1999 (www.epsnet.org/news/eurolei.htm).

3. Maurice Chittenden and Nicholas Rufford, 'MI6 'firm' spied on green groups', *The Sunday Times*, June 17, 2001. His hidden agenda may have been to find out who was behind violent attacks on petrol stations following a boycott in Germany. Mike Hogan, Shell UK head of media relations, claimed in a personal phone call in July 2001 that this was what they had hired Hakluyt for. But there are no reports of Schlickenrieder approaching more radical groups, nor hinting at such subjects, from people he did speak to.

4. Otto Diederichs and Holger Stark, 'Greenpeace, Das Auge der Multis', *Die Tageszeitung*, Dec. 10, 2000.

5. See 'About Us' section at www.riotinto.com.

6. Evidence that Schlickenrieder researched Rio Tinto is unpublished and is in the hands of members of Revolutionaire Aufbau, which exposed him.

7. Thomas Scheuer, 'Enttarnung im Internet', *Focus*, Feb. 12, 2001 (www.afbau.org), and personal conversation with Otto Diederichs.

8. Chittenden and Rufford, 'MI6 'firm' spied on green groups'.

9. 'Business Intelligence Notes: UK', *Intelligence Newsletter*, No. 364, Aug. 26, 1999, p. 3.

10. Nicholas Rufford, 'Cloak and Dagger Ltd: Former spies of the Cold War era engage in industrial espionage', *Management Today*, Feb. 1, 1999, p. 9.

11. Chittenden and Rufford, 'MI6 'firm' spied on green groups', and www.shell.com

12. The Canadian Security Intelligence Service, 'Anti-Globalization—A Spreading Phenomenon', report #2000/08, Aug. 22, 2000; see 'Other Documents' section at www.csis.gc.ca.

13. Naomi Klein, 'Will Cops Ruin the Next Anti-Globalization Protests in Quebec?' Aug. 30, 2000, *Globe and Mail*, Sept. 5, 2000, at www.alternet.org.

14. *Intelligence Newsletter* also pointed to the latest focus of the Regional Information Sharing System, originally set up to counter organized crime, drugs and terrorism: "The RISS also act against any political activist group deemed to be a threat and over the last year has found itself focusing on anti-globalization groups." One of the six RISS centres, the Mid-Atlantic Network, whose region includes New York and Washington, is supposedly particularly efficient at spying on activists. Unfortunately there are no other sources to confirm these activities by RISS.

15. Abby Scher, 'The Crackdown on Dissent', *The Nation*, Jan. 30, 2001. I relied on this article for the summarized information on CoIntelPro. In Dutch, also see Eveline Lubbers, 'CoIntelPro: Inbraken, dreigbrieven en brandstichting', *Konfrontatie*, July 1992.

16. Examples of such collections are Jim Redden, 'Police State targets the Left', April 17, 2000, widely published on the internet, and Paul Rosenberg, 'The Empire Strikes Back', www.indymedia.org or la.indymedia.org/images/empire_strikes.pdf.

17. Ross Gelbspan, *Break-ins, Death Threats and the FBI: The Covert War Against the Central America Movement* (Boston: South End Press, 1991); also see Brian Glick, *War at Home: Covert Action Against US Activists and What We Can Do About It* (Boston: South End Press, 1989). For documentation on COINTELPRO released in September 2001 under the Freedom of Information Act, see 'News Briefs' section at www.house.gov/mckinney and 'Cointelpro' section at www.icdc.com/~paulwolf.

18. Louis J. Freeh (director of the FBI), *Congressional Statement on the Threat of Terrorism to the United States before the United States Senate Committees on Appropriations, Armed Services and Select Committee on Intelligence*, May 10, 2001, full text at www.fbi.gov/congress/congress01/freeh051001.htm; PB Floyd Slingshot, 'Is Dancing Terrorism?' *Urban75 Action News*, July 1, 2001, www.urban75.com.

19. 'Manipulating Anti-Globalization NGOs', *Intelligence Newsletter*, Dec. 21, 2000; Roy Godson, *Dirty Tricks or Trump Cards: US Covert Action and Counterintelligence*, Transaction Publishers, Somerset, 2000 (updated version).

20. Strategic Forecasting, 'WTO: Splinter Groups Breed as Activists Fracture', Nov. 8, 2001; abbreviated version in the archive at www.stratfor.com (easiest to find in a Google search); full text widely published on the internet.

Chapter 14: Investigating and Exposing *Nicky Hager*

1. Nicky Hager and Bob Burton, *Secrets and Lies: The Anatomy of an Anti-Environmental PR Campaign* (Monroe, ME: Common Courage Press, 1999).

Chapter 15: Digging up Astroturf *Claudia Peter*

1. See www.astroturf.com.
2. The Center for Media and Democracy, at www.prwatch.org.
3. Interview with Mark Green of the New York Consumer Affairs Commission, *Advertising Age*, June 29, 1992, p. 8.
4. Telephone interview with Manfred Geisler-Hansson, Feb. 2, 1993.
5. Waste Watchers, 'Abfallpolitik des BUND—Anspruch und Wirklichkeit', June 1994.
6. 'Waste Watchers Warn of BUND Environmental Policy', press release, June 15, 1994.
7. Waste Watchers advertisement in BUND newsletter, April 1994.
8. Waste Watchers newsletter, October 1992.
9. Signatures in 'Satzung der Waste Watchers', 1992, p. 14.
10. Claudia Peter/Hans-Joachim Kursawa-Stucke, *Deckmantel Ökologie. Tarnorganisationen der Industrie missbrauchen das Umweltbewusstsein der Bürger*, (Munich: Droemer-Knaur, 1995).
11. 'Glaubt den Narren nicht. Deutsche Industrie unterwandert Umweltbewegung', *Der Spiegel*, Vol. 1995, No. 35, pp. 82-84.

12. Articles in *Ebersberger Neueste Nachrichten* and personal communications with Mayor Peter Dingler.
13. Michael Franken, 'Windpark—Gefahr für Leib und Seele?', *Die Tageszeitung*, July 2, 1998, p. 18.
14. Michael Franken et al., *Rauher Wind. Der organisierte Widerstand gegen die Windkraft* (Aachen, Germany: Alano-Herodot-Verlag, 1998), p. 137.
15. Franken et al., *Rauher Wind*, p. 42.
16. Today both companies have been subsumed into EON, whose core business is still energy, both conventional and nuclear.
17. Interview with Franken.
18. Michael Franken, 'Fast erstunken und erlogen', www.wendlandnet.de/wendland-wind.
19. www.windkraftgegner.de
20. Email from Greenpeace spokesperson Almut Ibler, Nov. 5, 2000.
21. Interview with Franken.
22. Ibid.

Chapter 16: Obstructing the Mainstream: Lessons from Seattle *Kees Hudig*

1. Seattle (WTO, November 1999), Washington (IMF/World Bank, April 2000), Prague (IMF/World Bank, September 2000), Melbourne (WEF, September 2000), Nice (EU, December 2000) or Davos (WEF, January 2001).
2. In Washington, it was called the Coalition for Global Justice (www.a16.org). One background site is www.50years.org.
3. For a list of indymedia centres see www.indymedia.org.
4. www.ruckus.org; www.directactionnetwork.org.
5. See, for example, the list of Britain's WDM, which summarizes 50 anti-IMF actions of 1999 and 2000, at www.oneworld.org/wdm.

Chapter 17: Communication Guerrillas: Using the Language of Power *autonome a.f.r.i.k.a. gruppe*

1. autonome a.f.r.i.k.a. gruppe, Luther Blissett and Sonja Brünzels, *Handbuch der Kommunikations Guerrilla* (Hamburg, Göttingen and Berlin: VLA/Schwarze Risse/Rote Strasse, 1998). See www.contrast.org/KG.
2. Gareth Branwyn, *Jamming the Media: A Citizen's Guide* (San Francisco: Chronicle Books, 1997); Mark Dery, *Culture Jamming: Hacking, Slashing, and Sniping in the Empire of Signs* (Westfield, New Jersey: Open Magazine Pamphlet Series, 1993).
3. Slavoj Zizek, *The Sublime Object of Ideology* (London: Verso, 1989).
4. See www.deportation-alliance.com, and for the flyer see www.deportation-alliance.com/class/.
5. Theatre performed in public, without making clear to the audience that what it is watching is theatre.

6. Rhea Wessel, 'Lufthansa Agrees to Change Policy On Deportees After Tragic Death', *The Wall Street Journal*, Jan. 29, 2001.

7. Guy Debord, 'The Situationists and the New Forms of Action in Politics and Art', *Internationale Situationniste*, No. 8, 1963 (English translation at www.situationist.cjb.net).

8. Michel de Certeau, *The Practice of Everyday Life* (Berkeley: University of California Press, 1992).

9. The production of an urban architecture designed to exhibit, sell and produce cultural symbols to attract investors, merging the spheres of consumption and entertainment. See Klaus Ronneberger, 'Symbolische Ökonomie und Raumprofite: Der Umbau der Städte zu Konsumfestungen', in Hedwig Saxenhuber and Georg Schöllhammer, eds., *Ortsbezug: Konstruktion oder Prozess? Materialien, Recherchen und Projekte im Problemfeld 'Öffentliche Kunst'* (Vienna: edition selene, 1998), p. 11.

10. See Hakim Bey, *T.A.Z.: The Temporary Autonomous Zone, Ontological Anarchy, Poetic Terrorism* (New York: Autonomedia, 1991). See also 'Hakim Bey' at www.hermetic.com.

11. 'Blagging' is a British slang term that means something like 'scamming', or getting something for nothing.

12. The events of Sept. 11, 2001 had not yet taken place when this chapter was being written.

Chapter 19: Net.activism   *Eveline Lubbers*

1. Edited part of a winter 2001 email exchange between Chris Carter, Ricardo Dominguez, Geert Lovink, Margaret Quan and Bruce Simon.

2. See 'op Internet' section at www.evel.nl.

3. Erik Wesselius, 'Liberalization of Trade in Services: Corporate Power at Work', GATSwatch research paper, October 2001, at www.gatswatch.org/LOTIS. The minutes are also available on this site.

4. 'Troubled Water', www.xs4all.nl/~ceo/mai/.

5. Held in Melbourne Sept. 11-13, 2000, just days before the Olympics.

6. See www.insanex.dk and 'Insanex vs. Europabio', *Corporate Europe Observer*, No. 8, April 2001, www.xs4all.nl/~ceo.

7. Days before the start of its November 2001 trade rounds in Qatar, the WTO tried to shut down the gatt.org domain for copyright violations. To counter the attack, the Yes Men released a piece of open source 'parodyware' which their spokesperson Elaine Peabody says will "forever make this kind of censorship obsolete". The software, called "Yes I Will!" automatically duplicates websites as needed, changing words and images as the user desires, with results that can be telling. For instance, the WTO site can be made to speak of "consumers" and "companies" rather than "citizens" and "countries". Unleashed on the CNN.com website, the software can simplify the reporting even further by referring to Bush as "Leader" and the war in Afghanistan as one between "Good" and "Evil". The parody site updates itself automatically as the target website changes. "The idea is to insure that even if they shut down our website, hundreds of others will continue our work of translation," said Peabody. "The more they try to fight it, the funnier they're going to look."

8. Barnaby J. Feder, 'The Long and Winding Cyberhoax: Political Theater on the Web', *The New York Times*, Jan. 7, 2001.

9. www.theyesmen.org/wto/ and Feder, 'The Long and Winding Cyberhoax'.

10. 'Anti-WTO activists turn to hacktivism', *Salon* (www.salon.com), Feb. 9. 2001.

11. Net.activism should not be confused with hacktivism or media activism: though these concepts all deal with similar activities, they differ slightly. Hirsch defines hacktivism as "social activism augmented by an advanced literacy of communication environments".

12. Jesse Hirsch, 'Thoughts on Hacktivism: Post-Y2K', Jan 5, 2000, www.tao.ca.

13. Hirsch, 'Thoughts on Hacktivism: Post-Y2K'.

14. See www.n5m.org.

15. See www.adbusters.org.

16. See subsol.c3.hu.

17. See www.iratiwanti.org.

18. Of course one can have doubts about the effectiveness of the consensus decisionmaking model within the IMC structure, which has been delaying the growth of the network for some time. Or one might point out the unmoderated and rather one-sided news diarrhoea that the IMC network generates as fast as its counterpart CNN. But these might be just the growing pains of something truly beautiful.

19. For pictures see 'Actions' section at www.kemptown.org/shell/.

20. make-world, Munich, October 2001, www.make-world.org.

21. Paul Festa, 'Google, Others Dig Deep—Maybe Too Deep', Nov. 26, 2001, CNET News, news.cnet.com. Google can find files including Adobe PostScript; Lotus 1-2-3 and WordPro; MacWrite; Microsoft Excel, PowerPoint, Word, Works and Write; and the RichText Format.

22. Tempest for Eliza can be found at www.erikyyy.de/tempest; there is discussion about it on slashdot.org. For more on Tempest see www.tscm.com/TSCM101tempest.html or (in Dutch) www.burojansen.nl/afluisteren.

23. Lincoln Hoewing, 'Using the Internet in a Corporate Public Affairs Office', Public Affairs Council Report, Washington DC, 2000, p. 15.

Index